ZUBIN MEHTA

ZUBIN MEHTA

Martin Bookspan

Ross Yockey

ROBERT HALE · LONDON

Copyright © 1978 by Martin Bookspan and Ross Yockey
First published in Great Britain 1980

ISBN 0 7091 7862 X

Robert Hale Limited
Clerkenwell House
Clerkenwell Green
London, EC1

Printed in Great Britain by
Lowe & Brydone Printers Limited, Thetford, Norfolk

Contents

Acknowledgments

We wish to express our gratitude first of all to Joann Yockey, without whose devoted assistance and encouragement the task might have been too great.

It was a particular pleasure to have the cooperation of the entire Mehta family—Zubin, Nancy, Tehmina, Mehli, Zarina, Merwan, Zarin, and Carmen; we thank them all.

For sharing their memories of and insights into Zubin's life and career, we are grateful to Daniel Barenboim, Olive Behrendt, Pierre Beique, Martin Bernheimer, Leonard Bernstein, Pierre Boulez, Dorothy Buffum Chandler, Abe Cohen, John Connell, Placido Domingo, Jacqueline du Pré, Joseph Fishman, Ernest Fleischmann, Lukas Foss, David Frisina, Joan Bonime Glotzer, Eugene Husaruk, Seymour Lipkin, Fredric R. Mann, Sherrill Milnes, Nathan Milstein, Carlos Moseley, Uri Pianka, Itzhak Perlman, John Pritchard, Artur Rubenstein, Isaac Stern, Albert K. Webster, Catherine Wilkinson, and Pinchas Zukerman.

We are particularly indebted to Russ Mack and Joe Vergara of Harper & Row for their professional knowledge and expertise, and to Dick Boehm, who always provided welcome counsel and intelligent direction. A special note of thanks also to the Research Division of the New York Library of the Performing Arts at Lincoln Center and to Charles Croce of the New York Philharmonic.

Finally, to Janet Bookspan go our loving thanks for "being there," for her enthusiastic support and her wisdom provided in abundance.

Illustrations

To what land shall I go
to flee? Whither to flee?
From nobles and my peers
they sever me, nor are
the people pleased with
me, nor the liar rulers
of the land. How am I
to please thee, Ahura Mazda?

Gatha Ustavaiti,
Yasna 46

1

✣

To What Land?...

How perverse, how unreasonable the music must have seemed to those who heard it.

To the vendors extolling in their hundred tongues the virtues of toasted cashews, of oranges and mangos sweeter than sugar cane; to the craftsmen and weavers thrusting their belts, saris, and sandals into the windows of the British cars that struggled through a glut of oxcarts and cows; to the begging children running behind the cars for coins and behind the cows to gather up the dung, to be dried on the walls of their *chawls* and then burned for fuel; to the Sikhs, with their blue turbans and short trousers, beards rolled under their chins, who aim their taxis like warhorses; to the lovely young girls from the seacoast carrying their wares on their heads, their bank accounts around their necks; to the orthodox Muslim beggar women, forbidden to ask aloud for alms, who hide like beekeepers in their burkas, holding out scraps of paper with written pleas; to the Hindu swamis in saffron robes; to any of them could this agitated tinkling and reverberating in the air be understood as music?

A Western ear would certainly have recognized the sound. A cultured European might even have hummed along, might, out of homesick curiosity, have followed the Beethoven tune through the alien Bombay streets to its source, expecting to find some displaced countrymen.

It was a live performance of Beethoven's *Archduke* Trio that came over All India Radio that day in 1935. And in all likelihood the only Indian listeners were members of Bombay's small Parsee community, as was the energetic twenty-seven-year-old violinist, Mehli Mehta, who sawed away so naturally at this alien music.

There were only about a hundred thousand Parsees in all of India, most of those in Bombay. Businessmen, traders, and brokers, they constituted a sort of upper-middle class outside the caste system that still prevailed. Parsee women had servants to do their housework. Parsee men conducted their affairs in Western-style offices or else, as members of the cotton exchange, they clung to straps in the gallery, screaming their bids and gesturing like the carved monkeys on the Vishnu temples.

In many ways the Parsees identified more naturally with the ruling Westerners than with their Hindu and Muslim countrymen. Their ancestors, followers of the prophet Zoroaster, had been driven by proselytizing Arab invaders from the Persian homeland. Though the date of their exodus is lost to history—it may have been as early as the seventh century or as late as the eleventh—the Parsees settled in India, where they had preserved their identity and their faith in the One God, Ahura Mazda, Lord of Light. Almost as foreign to the Parsees as the proliferating thousands of Hindu gods and goddesses was Hindu music, that serpentine *om* music meant to lead the listener toward *samadhi*, the merging of the self with the totality of the One. Although they accepted many aspects of the Hindu and Muslim cultures, the Parsees eagerly embraced Western music and the other forms of art brought to India by the British.

When an Englishman traveled or lived abroad, it was not his intention to adopt the ways of the native; he would carry as much of England with him as he could. In Bombay, that most British of Indian cities, it was impossible to walk anywhere without seeing the British hand, warm and well intentioned, lying very heavily over everything. The large new buildings, pompous and dignified, their domes and minarets adorned with Victoriana, had about them the solidity of a colonialism that meant to endure and endure. At teatime in British hotels, on wind-up phonographs in British homes, and over the wireless came the music of Beethoven, Schubert, and Mendelssohn. Growing up in the Bombay of the 1920s and 1930s, it seemed natural to a Parsee boy named Mehli Mehta to teach himself how to play this music.

Mehli's father, manager of the New Islam Cotton Mills, had been pleased at his son's interest in the violin, and at age seventeen he was allowed to study with the Italian Oddonne Savini, leader of a salon orchestra that played in the British hotels and Bombay's only violin teacher. Yet no one ever thought of music as a profession for Mehli. In keeping with a tradition in his family—whose very name, Mehta, signified accountant or bookkeeper—he was educated as an accountant, receiving his Bachelor of Commerce degree. His job as a tax collector for the government promised a secure future.

But to Mehli there was nothing auspicious in the daily rounds of examining account books and collecting taxes. He did not look forward to a career in the mills or in the world of trading, to long hours under the *tambura*-like drone of ceiling fans, to huddling under umbrellas at Bhuleshwar Corner, haggling over mundane business propositions. As his father's associates, the pink-turbaned, money-lending Marwaris, would say, Mehli's stars were not propitious for commerce.

At the simple Parsee fire temple, Mehli prayed and tried to resolve the conflict within him. As he placed sticks of dried sandalwood on the fragrant sacred fire—the fire the ancients were said to have carried from Persia—he felt one with the soul of Arta Viraf, standing on the Kinvad Bridge. He could almost see Humat, the place of good thoughts, on one side and Dush-humat, the place of evil thoughts, on the other. The Parsees knew well that pursuit of a wrong idea in this life could condemn one's soul in the next.

He offered prayers, but no Srosh the Pious came to him, no Angel Ataro led the way, as they had for Viraf in the holy books. Only the voice within him replied, with the answer he already knew, that he must devote his life to music.

Had Mehli been a Hindu or a Muslim, the whole idea of a career of music would have been unthinkable. In the first half of the twentieth century, India had begun to shake off the fetters of the caste system; but, while castes were now more like professional guilds, membership in which was passed down from father to son, the caste of musician was one of the lowliest, not so many rungs away from the untouchable cesspool of Pariahs at the bottom.

The occasion was graven in Mehli's memory when, having been invited with his family to dine at the home of a wealthy Brahmin on Malabar Hill, he watched and listened as a beautiful Hindu woman entered with her *tabla* player and sang for them in a deeply sensuous voice. When the songs were finished, the singer bowed stiffly to the host and hostess, leaving without a word. When Mehli asked why the singer did not stay so they might converse about her voice and her art, the hostess replied, "One must never speak with a musician on equal terms. They may entertain at our tables but never sit down at them." The singer, he later learned, was one of the most famous musicians in all of India.

The lack of professional Western-style musicians in Bombay created a problem in 1935, when the international ballet company formed by Anna Pavlova arrived to perform for the British. The company had brought along a Russian conductor, expecting to put together an orchestra in the city, but finding no official organization of musicians they were forced to seek help from the preeminent Parsee amateur, Mehli Mehta.

Mehli's experience up to then had been in living rooms, playing solos and chamber music with his friends, along with an occasional radio appearance. The idea of putting together an entire orchestra had never occurred to him. It seemed as though Ahura Mazda had sent this ballet company in answer to his prayers.

"It happened just one week before I was supposed to get married. I had a good post and a good salary, so I could be sure my wife was going to be well taken care of. But this was the chance of a lifetime, and Tehmina, my bride-to-be, encouraged me to take it." Mehli quit his job as a tax collector, appointing himself concertmaster of Bombay's first ballet orchestra.

"We did *Giselle,* we did *Raymonda,* we did all sorts of things and I played every one of the violin solos. It was three weeks of ballet. And that was the first time anyone ever paid me for making music."

The wedding was on March 6, and afterward, according to Parsee custom, there was an evening reception to which more than a thousand people were invited. Unfortunately, Mehli was scheduled to play in the ballet orchestra at the same time. He told a disappointed Tehmina she would have to greet the reception guests without him.

"The head of All India Radio was very sympathetic to me," Tehmina says with a smile. "He told Mehli if he left the reception he'd never play on the radio again. It would be breaking tradition for the groom to leave, and to us Parsees tradition is very important."

Mehli agreed to remain at the reception. Since he was the only man in Bombay who could play the violin solos, those parts in the ballets had to be canceled for that evening's performance.

"After three weeks," says Mehli, "the dance company went away, and I said to myself. What am I going to do now? Then I realized, here are all these musicians—why don't we make a symphony orchestra? And so the Bombay Symphony was born."

Supported by the British and his proud Parsee community, Mehli kept the orchestra together and began taking his string sextet to the "Indian Gothic" hotels, where they played dinner and dance music under the potted palms. Quickly he became the center of Western musical life in Bombay. His Bombay Symphony was made up of other young Indians, a number of Jewish refugees who had seen the handwriting on the walls of central Europe, and members of the British Navy Band who agreed to spend their free time with Schubert and Mozart instead of with the *devadasis* of the red-light district. The conductor was a displaced Belgian named Jules Crain. Mehli, of course, was concertmaster and principal soloist.

A year after the birth of the orchestra, at 2:50 A.M. on April 29, 1936, a son was born to Tehmina and Mehli. They gave him the ancient Persian name of Zubin, "the Powerful Sword."

At first the name seemed less than appropriate to his father. "I thought, That can't be my son. He looks like a wrinkled old man. He was just six and a half pounds, a little monkey. I decided he must be a wise old soul."

The Parsees were great believers in reincarnation as well as in astrology. They were convinced that the course of a man's life could be charted by the configuration of the stars and planets at the moment of his birth. So when Zubin was six days old, as custom dictated, Tehmina sought out a Hindu astrologer, a *jotisi,* to have her newborn son's preliminary horoscope cast. It was to be the first hint of what life held in store for this tiny, wrinkled "powerful sword."

"I see this child as leader of a group of people," said the *jotisi*. "But I cannot tell you what kind of group it will be."

And at the bottom of the chart the astrologer wrote in English: "The child born on this day will be changeable, overconfident, and much too sure of himself. He will desire to lead but requires training in judgment and moderation."

Zubin learned to sing as he learned to speak. Music was integral to the air he breathed, to the space through which he crawled. Musical instruments were his toys, and when he was only one year old his parents bought him a wind-up Gramophone. He learned to know his father's records by the colors of their labels and to point to the one he wanted to hear. The *ayah* who looked after him would place the records on the turntable and he would listen for hours.

At the age of two Zubin received a pair of drumsticks, and they became his most prized possessions. Nothing in the house—pots, tabletops, chairs, or vases—was safe from the drummer boy's assault. When the sticks were taken away as punishment for some particularly inappropriate banging, he would sneak into the kitchen for two of his mother's spoons and the racket would start again. He even slept with the drumsticks under his pillow.

His father's rehearsal studio was the family living room. There, every evening, the members of Mehli's chamber ensemble would gather to go over their programs, with little Zubin hanging on every note. He got to know many of the pieces by heart and would walk around the house humming melodies by the great composers, to the constant amazement of the Mehta family and their friends. Even today there is wonder in Mehli's voice as he describes an incident that occurred when Zubin was five.

"We were going to play a program of Schubert in a radio broadcast that lasted an hour and a half. It was to be *Death and the Maiden* and the *Trout* Quintet, but when we timed it out in rehearsal at the studio the engineer told us it was about a minute too long. I suggested that we cut the little variation in the slow movement of the *Trout* that goes *ya-da-da-da-da-da-daa*. It takes about a minute and a half, and we all agreed that nobody would miss it.

"Of course, Zubin had to come along to the radio station that night for the performance. It was at ten o'clock, and his little brother Zarin was fast asleep at home, but he wouldn't hear of missing it. So we played the two pieces and they went very well and everybody in the studio applauded. But as soon as the red light went out and we were off the air, that little monkey broke away from his mother and came running up to me, shouting, 'But Daddy, why didn't you play that part that goes *ya-da-da-da-da-da-daa?*'"

To Zubin music was like a game, to be taken no more seriously than the game of cricket he was learning to play quite well. Just as his own friends got together every day for their games, his father's friends convened with their instruments.

There were several new members of the orchestra now, German and Italian nationals discovered by Mehli in the British internment camps outside the city. These were supposed to be enemies of the Empire, though in fact some were Jewish refugees. At any rate, the war seemed to be passing Bombay by, and Mehli had little difficulty getting British officials to look the other way where musicians were concerned.

Zubin watched in fascination as the Bombay Symphony Orchestra grew in quality as well as quantity. There were Indian Christians and Parsees, mostly Mehli's pupils, in the strings, along with a Prussian violinist and a Czech cellist; there was a flutist from Italy, an Albanian bass player, and a Greek who offered to play oboe and bassoon, but since neither was available settled on the clarinet; there were wind players and percussionists wearing the uniform of the British Navy Band. It was a wartime League of Nations, convened by his father and, the boy thought, a mighty achievement for this small, wonderful man.

One evening in the summer of 1944, Mehli and Tehmina returned from a concert to find Zubin in bed with a high temperature. At first they thought it was nothing more than some usual childhood fever, but the second day he felt nauseous and continued to vomit throughout the night. And a few days later the doctors diagnosed Zubin's disease as spinal meningitis.

"It was just at the time the sulfa drugs were coming out," Tehmina remembers. "The doctor said if we are lucky and those drugs suit him then we have hope. Zubin had an enormous strength to bear pain. They put huge needles into his spine and drew out the fluid. For ten days we did not know if he would live or die. It was the worst time of our lives.

"But the drugs must have worked. He started to get better, and within a week he was sitting up in bed reciting poems and wanting his Gramophone records and eating chocolate pudding."

The prescribed therapy called for a month at a Himalayan sanitarium at Simla, where the temperature was much cooler than in the crowded city. For nearly a whole year Zubin had to be kept out of school and away from his playmates while he recovered his strength. It seemed the only thing he was permitted to enjoy was his father's music.

The leaders of the Parsee community were also taking an increased interest in Mehli's music making. When the war in Europe ended and sea travel became possible again, they decided to send him to America to study. The wealthy and prominent Tata family, for whom Tehmina's father had built a cotton mill, provided a grant for Mehli to live in New York and study with the famous violin teacher Ivan Galamian.

It was another of those chances Tehmina realized her husband could ill afford to miss. When asked by a friend how Mehli could leave her and his two sons for four years, she answered, "How can he *not* go?"

Mehli arrived in New York in the summer of 1945 and immediately bought a newspaper to see what concerts he could hear. He settled on an economic choice, an outdoor concert at Lewisohn Stadium, with Alexander Smallens conducting the New York Philharmonic in a performance of Puccini's *La Bohème*, with Grace Moore and Jan Peerce. It was his first night in New York, his first chance to hear an orchestra other than his own, his first opera.

The letters Mehli wrote from his tiny apartment on Fifty-seventh Street and Lexington Avenue told of the excitement of New York, of learning violin all over again on open strings, and, most of all, of the concerts he attended. Every month he would send programs from recitals, from concerts of Rodzinski, Mitropoulos, and Walter conducting the Philharmonic. And finally from performances of the violinist Jascha Heifetz, to whom Mehli referred as "god."

One of the letters that impressed Zubin most came after Mehli heard an orchestral concert conducted by Leopold Stokowski.

"I felt," wrote his father, "as though I were hearing an orchestra for the first time. This man Stokowski is sixty-five and I thank God I was privileged to hear him before he retires from the podium. His strings are silken perfection. They play with such precision, such clarity, and yet with such emotion that one is constantly amazed. I am going to bring back some Stokowski recordings with the Philadelphia Orchestra so you can hear for yourselves."

The mention of recorded music stuck in Zubin's mind. He began haunting the bazaars, looking for 78-rpm recordings of classical music, which he would buy with money begged from his mother and grandparents. With one of his father's broken batons he would conduct the records, putting himself in the place of Arturo Toscanini, Felix Weingartner, or Wilhelm Furtwängler.

Ancient Hindu law decreed that, when a husband went on a journey, the wife should be as a widow in mourning. "She shall not hear music, nor shall she behold anything choice and rare." Fortunately, Tehmina was not bound by such a law, for her elder son filled the house with music, making it seem almost as though Mehli had never left. And the boy himself, she observed proudly, grew every day more "choice and rare."

Zubin was quick to lose the angular awkwardness of a boy. Even at ten, there was passion lurking in those deep, laughing eyes. His nose was not thin and hooked like those of many Indians, but was the forceful, spear-like nose of a Persian, with eyebrows arching up from the bridge in a way that made his face half a question and half a command. His unusually fair skin, inherited from his mother, was set off by thick and wavy hair, blue black, as one found occasionally in Muslim men. His personality was forceful, with a calm assurance that was disarming. Yet those who remember him as a boy speak of him also as a dreamer, as one who seemed somehow unrelated to the world about him.

Often during Mehli's absence, Tehmina would take her two sons to the beach, just a few miles from the center of town, where Zubin would imagine his father just beyond the horizon of the Arabian Sea, as immense to him as any Pacific could have appeared to Balboa. Looking out to the West, he wondered not how soon his father would return, but how long it would be before he could see the wonderful places Mehli was seeing now.

"The further from the center of things, the more one daydreams, and it was not possible to be further away from the center of Western music than I was in Bombay. My father's letters were filled with descriptions of America and that seemed like Utopia to me. I dreamed of going there someday as a musician."

For India, this was a period of great uncertainty. The British governors agreed to a separate homeland for Muslims, to be called Pakistan, and the last Viceroy, Lord Mountbatten, departed Bombay with a great deal of ceremony. Zubin was next to his mother in the parade stand as Mountbatten shook hands with Pandit Nehru and pronounced India a free, self-governing nation.

Independence brought disruption as the hideous two-way migration began, with caravans crawling through floods and famine, carrying Muslims to Pakistan and Hindus to India. Mahatma Gandhi was murdered and the nation plunged into mourning. Mohammed Ali Jinnah ruled but a few months in the Pakistan he had "chalked out" before he, too, was dead.

From China came more bad news. Mehli's brother, who managed a silk mill in Shanghai, wrote that a takeover by the Communists appeared imminent. He was getting his family out quickly.

That family included Zubin's cousin Dady, the only Mehta besides Zubin and Mehli to be seriously interested in Western music. Dady's piano study took a great leap forward when his studies moved from Shanghai to Paris. Occasionally Dady would write of his exciting discoveries—musical and otherwise. Zubin would lie awake long into the night, rereading those letters and dreaming of what life must be like outside India.

At last in 1949 Mehli returned from his four years of study in America.

As a violinist he had matured rapidly under Ivan Galamian; as a musician he had discovered what an orchestra was supposed to sound like. He knew now what could be achieved in music and how impossible it would be to reach that level of achievement in Bombay. Nevertheless he was determined to try.

He found his orchestra disbanded, stranded without a conductor when Maestro Crain, the Belgian, ran afoul of local authorities. Now Mehli would have to lead as well as play. But first there was the matter of reforming the orchestra, which began to take shape rapidly in the Mehta home.

The Viceroy had left India, taking the British Navy Band with him. Their places in the brass and percussion sections were filled with members of the local regimental band of the Indian Army. The war had sent even more homeless Jewish musicians to India, and Mehli found them eager to be recruited. And with so many musicians coming and going, the Bombay Symphony suddenly needed an assistant manager and a music librarian.

Zubin was appointed to fill both positions. He helped his father arrange the chairs and the music stands and, when a saxophonist was recruited though a third horn player was needed, Zubin could write out the B-flat horn part in the key of E-flat so the Bengali with the saxophone could play it.

Noting his son's increasing interest in music, Mehli started him on violin, continued his piano instruction, and sent him to his old professor,

Oddonne Savini, to learn music theory. Once a week Zubin would take the hundred-mile train ride to Poona where Savini had moved.

Despite his obvious involvement with the orchestra, Zubin had to, be prodded to practice his violin and piano. "Instead of practicing after school," Mehli recalls, smiling, "he would sneak out and play cricket. The whole crux of the matter was that my son had no intention of becoming an instrumentalist."

No one ever thought seriously that Zubin would follow in his father's footsteps as a professional musician. There seemed to be no point in it. Mehli's audience in Bombay was always sparse, comprised exclusively of Europeans, Anglo-Indians, and Parsees. The Hindus and Muslims who made up the great bulk of the city's population and who had music of their own, almost never attended. To Tehmina, Mehli seemed to be "beating his head against a wall."

"I watched my husband slave to make people understand and want to go to concerts, but it was a thankless task. I can't tell you how much of our own money we lost in making music. I didn't want that to happen to Zubin. Of course, it never occurred to me that he might not live in India all his life. Always I thought that even if we sent him abroad to study, eventually he would come back and put his knowledge to work in India."

So Tehmina and Mehli began to prepare Zubin for a career in medicine, just as they were preparing his younger brother Zarin for accounting. Health and finance—there were two fields of endeavor in which serious young men could be useful to themselves, their family, and their country. Tehmina was overjoyed when Zubin was admitted to the scientific curriculum of St. Xavier's College to begin his premedical training.

He got along well with the Jesuits who ran St. Xavier's, particularly with Father Ramón de Rafael, the Spanish priest who headed the physics department. Indeed, Zubin took an instant liking to Father Rafael when the entire first week of classes was given over to discussions of the Pythagorean theorem and of the *Sangita-Ratnakara,* in which the Hindu Sarngadeva, like his Greek counterpart, had demonstrated that the pitch of a note varies inversely as the length of the string between the point of attachment and point of touch.

It was not long before Zubin was asking more questions in class about music than about physics, and Father Rafael sat him down for a talk after school. Zubin was astonished to learn that before he took his vows his physics professor had been a music student in Barcelona, working under the famous composer Enrique Granados. That very afternoon, Zubin had a lesson in music theory from the priest, and from then on his after-school hours were spent in the college residence hall, studying theory, especially counterpoint, with Father Rafael. The family's design for a medical education began to look like a self-defeating proposition.

In April of 1952 Zubin was surprised to receive a letter from his cousin, postmarked not Paris but Vienna. Dady's piano teacher in Paris had died and he was living in Vienna by himself. He had been accepted as a student by Bruno Seidlhofer at the Vienna Music Academy.

Dady wrote Zubin that Vienna was a good place to be, with marvelous opportunities for making music, where the Viennese classics are played like nowhere else. As an added incentive, he noted that living in Vienna was quite cheap and it cost hardly anything to enjoy the music.

Dady's letters from Vienna rekindled the fire that had been sparked by Mehli's letters from New York. Zubin felt there must be room for him in the world of music beyond Bombay.

At home, in the meantime, even as his interest in a musical career was discouraged, Zubin's duties with the Bombay Symphony increased. Sometimes he was required to sit in on rehearsals. If the strings were going over the Mendelssohn Octet and the second cellist was missing, Zubin had to be there to sing the part. If a certain section of a symphony could not be played without an English horn, let Zubin transpose it for one of the violas.

That same year, 1952, India was struck by famine. When news photographs of starving farmers and villagers went out to the world, they struck a sympathetic chord in the hearts of many Westerners. Among those prompted to respond was the violinist Yehudi Menuhin. In a letter to Prime Minister Nehru, Menuhin volunteered to come to India and perform a series of recitals to raise money for the victims. Just as in 1935, when Mehli was asked to produce an orchestra for the Pavlova company, he was approached to arrange the tour for Menuhin.

"Of course I agreed. It was a wonderful experience for me. We traveled all over India, Menuhin, his very accomplished pianist, and myself. Along the way I asked them if it might also be possible to play some benefit concerts with my orchestra in Bombay, and they said of course."

Mehli put together two programs for Menuhin and his accompanist. They included the Mendelssohn E-Minor Violin Concerto, Lalo's *Symphonie Espagnole,* and the Bach E-Major Violin Concerto, as well as piano concertos by Schumann and Brahms.

To cut down on rehearsal time for the visiting musicians, Mehli decided to play the violin solos at rehearsals himself. Seeing the orchestra struggle without a leader, Zubin stepped up to the podium, picked up his father's baton, and began to conduct. It was the beginning of the end of his medical career.

From that day on he found it increasingly difficult to memorize the names of bones in the human body, increasingly dissatisfying to study chemical reactions in the laboratory. As he sat in anatomy class one day, looking at a dogfish he was supposed to dissect, he heard the Mendelssohn concerto he had conducted running through his head. He remembered the glorious feeling of standing among the musicians, coaxing chords from the orchestra, almost as though the music were streaming from the tips of his fingers.

"Why haven't you started cutting up that fish?" It was the voice of his anatomy professor.

Zubin picked up the lifeless dogfish, studied it for a moment, then on sudden impulse threw it across the room. "Cut it up yourself," he shouted and stalked out of the room.

"I was in my bedroom that afternoon," Mehli remembers. "We would say our prayers every day, and normally we wouldn't disturb each other. It is a very private time. But suddenly I felt there was somebody behind me. I looked back and there was Zubin, standing very quietly.

"I went back to my prayers, thinking he had come into the room to get a book or a piece of music or something. But after a few minutes he was still standing there, so I said, 'Yes, darling?' He said, 'I need to talk to you.' I said, 'Of course, but not now because I'm praying.' And Zubin said, 'Well how long will you take?'

"He had never asked me anything like that and I knew it must be important for him to interrupt me, so I closed my book and told him to go ahead. He came up to me and put his hand on my shoulder and said, 'Daddy, I can't go on with the medicine. I must quit because I'm a musician. I must go to Vienna and take up music.'

"Now I knew that was a moment of truth, and it touched me very, very deeply. I felt that God's hand was in it. My wife and I agreed we must let him go."

In October of 1954, when the monsoon rains had gone and the Bombay air was dry and still, Zubin embarked by ship for Italy, where he would board a train to Vienna. It had been arranged for him to enter the Academy of Music and to live with his cousin Dady in a small apartment in the Vienna Woods. His expenses would be met by a trust fund from Tehmina's father.

The day after Zubin left, Tehmina took his horoscope to an astrologer, not the Hindu who had drawn it up but a Parsee *jotisi* who had been highly recommended to her. The old man sat cross-legged on the floor and unrolled the horoscope scroll to its full length of nearly five feet. With his long, curved fingernails he traced the mysterious patterns of stars and planets drawn in blood-red ink on the yellow paper. Tehmina had looked at it many times and had never been able to make sense of the intricate symbols and curling script. At last the *jotisi* looked up from the scroll, and there was a broad smile on his face as he spoke.

"I don't know what you are worried about. We astrologers get a horo-scope like this once in a lifetime, if we are lucky. You have nothing to worry about with this child."

A week later, the *jotisi* handed Tehmina a sheet of paper containing the whole of his reading. Tehmina's hands trembled, and she could scarcely force her eyes to follow the words in order without jumping ahead.

> Jupiter is the ruler of the Tenth House, which signifies that he will rise high in life by dint of his own hard work and perseverance, thus acquiring great honor, respect, and a leading position in his profession. Jupiter, being in the Tenth House, also signifies that he is bound to follow the same profession as that of his father.
>
> Again, this Jupiter, occupying a high place in the Tenth House, is looking with great favor at Venus, in the Second House of Wealth, Beauty, and Art. This combination signifies great fame and fortune in the Arts, in addition to great personal charm. This combination only occurs in the rebirth of a highly evolved soul.
>
> Two important factors are evident in this horoscope. First, very strong inner inspiration. Secondly, an everlasting name, particularly in the Western world, which clearly proves that this child is definitely the reincarnation of a great Western artist's soul.
>
> Taurus the Bull, complemented in his stride by Uranus, Mars, Mercury, and the Sun, assures him of clear inner vision as well as clear outer vision and comprehension, great courage, independence, strong mental powers, and a noble nature. Neptune and Saturn in the Seventh House influence him most powerfully with an uncanny and deep inspiration.
>
> Due to certain influences of this planetary combination, his marriage be-fore the age of twenty-five will come to an unhappy end. But from this tragedy he will experience a highly spiritual and artistic growth. After age twenty-five, under the strong influence of a long period of Mercury, he will not only find his Soul Mate, but also achieve greater glory, success, and honor everywhere.
>
> Due to several weaker planetary influences he will be susceptible to colds, coughs, rheumatic or arthritic conditions in the joints, about which he will have to be very careful.
>
> He will always live in his own world of Art and will follow, even obstinately, only the dictates of his own heart and mind.

Tehmina looked up from the paper and saw the *jotisi* smiling, his eyes closed. Somehow, he sensed that she had read and understood.

"You see, there is nothing to fear in connection with this child. You must encourage him, for he will win every competition. There can be no doubt from this horoscope that your son is the reincarnation of a great Western artist's soul and that his fame will spread far and wide all over the world."

2

⤲⤳

Uncanny and
Deep Inspiration

To leave one's home and family at age eighteen is seldom easy. It means taking a headlong plunge into the dark unknown, hoping one's private star will still be shining in the future firmament.

In America and Europe, our usual justification for such rash behavior is the inner conviction that we are Doing the Right Thing, a conviction bolstered by the great Western tradition of heroes forged in the furnace of independence, pounded by the hammer of self-assertion on the anvil of solitude. Should our break with the past be painful, we are reassured by a revered analgesic bromide: Only by breaking with the past can one truly stride toward the future.

In the culture of India, that bromide does not exist. Leaving the place of one's birth runs contrary to the Indian concept of heroism. In India, the truly great man is solicitous to his parents, available to anyone with the slightest claim of kinship.

Despite his Parsee upbringing, Zubin had read the *Ramayana*. He knew of Lakshmana, who leaves hearth and home only for the sake of helping his exiled brother Rama make his "darksome way" through the forests. Then, as soon as his exile ends, Rama forsakes what has become an idyllic life to rejoin his clan at the palace. There another brother

14

gladly hands over the throne to Rama, purely out of fraternal loyalty.

When these Indian heroes suffer, it is not with the angst of alienation and anomie but with the heavy burdens of tradition and duty. An Indian hero can smother in his own enormous security blanket.

There was, then, no tradition to absolve Zubin from breaking with tradition. His self-imposed exile could be justified only by his own certainty that this was the only road for him to travel. Any doubts had to be yanked out by the roots and quickly gotten rid of, for there was only faith in himself to keep him from turning back.

His first impressions of Vienna were not those of *The Great Waltz*. The Vienna of October 1954 was a scarred and pockmarked city only beginning to recover from the battles and bombings of World War II. The Südbahnhof, the railroad station in the south of the city at which Zubin arrived, was nothing more than twisted, blackened girders and beams. As he stepped off the train, he realized for the first time how protected he had been in Bombay. There the worst effects of the war had been a general uneasiness, an occasional flyover by a squadron of Japanese fighter planes, and rationed rice. He saw immediately that life in Vienna had been something else entirely.

War had drawn Viennese belts and pursestrings even tighter than their inbred frugality demanded, and, for a boy who had never been taught to turn off the lights when he left a room, there was a great lesson to be learned. In Vienna, one not only extinguished lights but heat as well; the apartment house in the Vienna Woods was never cozily warm.

Zubin could not repress a shiver as he undressed for bed his first night in Vienna. His apartment had only a tiny electric radiator, pitifully inadequate against the autumn chill. What would it be like in January, he wondered. Thinking of his warm bed in Bombay did not help, because these Vienna bedclothes were sheets of ice. How would he ever get to sleep with his knees knocking and his teeth rattling?

Suddenly he had what he deemed a brilliant idea. Stretching the electric cord to its full length, he set the little radiator in his bed and covered it with the goose-down quilt. That should warm things up. Impressed with his own inventiveness, he went down the hall to brush his teeth.

He returned to his room to find the bed quite warm. In fact, merrily ablaze.

"Somehow I managed to put out the fire," Zubin says, laughing. "And I did it without waking anybody else in the house. I went to sleep that night on this charred, black mattress. Of course, I was still cold. You don't know what kind of hell I caught the next morning from my landlady! Thank God I didn't understand the language yet."

The business of taking a shower provided another lesson in frugality.

Cold water, only a few degrees above freezing, could be had in quantity; it came with the apartment. For hot water, however, Zubin had to pay the landlady two schillings. This got him the promise of five minutes' worth of warm shower. But five minutes on the landlady's inner clock turned out to be of capriciously variable duration.

"I never did figure out how much time I really had," Zubin recalls with a shudder. "I was always overstepping my mark, and she must have been standing in the kitchen with her hand on the *Geiser*. Without any warning I would be showering in icy mountain water. *Ach!*"

The Viennese reluctance to part with money had rubbed off on his cousin Dady after a year, and his first advice to Zubin was to ride a bicycle to the Music Academy rather than shell out the fare for the ten-mile tram ride each day.

"What he forgot to tell me was that most of those ten miles were over cobbled streets. On a bicycle? By the time I got to the Music Academy I had a natural tremolo. Parkinson's disease at age eighteen! After that first one-way trip, I left the bicycle there and never rode it back."

Though his music education had yet to begin, Zubin wondered whether he'd really been right in abandoning the security of home, family, and country for this cold, inhospitable place.

Then, on the third day after his arrival, Zubin awoke and stepped out on the balcony to see a marvelous sight. The rolling, wooded hills, the city in the distance, everything was covered with a fresh blanket of snow, the first snow he'd ever seen.

He rode the tram into town and, for the first time, felt the magic of Vienna. The scars were gone, the rubble-filled lots invisible; he saw only the elegance of the city that had been, rising softly from the snow. On the Ringstrasse, the great horseshoe boulevard that encircles the inner city, Vienna's ensemble harmony became clear in the collection of architectural styles made into a marvelous symphony of stucco and stone by rows of snow-boughed trees. This was the Vienna that had blended the baroque with classicism and romanticism to create a new musical universe.

The principle industry of Vienna has always been the industry of taste. And while such delights as embroidery, tapestry, and porcelain, merely niceties in other cities, are vital necessities in Vienna, it is music that is the chief product of this industry: the city is crowded with music makers of every sort. Today you can pick up a telephone, dial 1509, and receive an A at the proper 440 Hz pitch to tune your oboe or violin. There are as many as fifteen hundred musical performances a year in Vienna, organized in a *kaiserlich-königlich* bureaucracy. The musical state-within-a-state has its own chancellors, ministers, secretaries, and ambassadors. By most accounts, the city's chief cultural export firm is the Wiener Philharmoniker.

Since its beginnings as the Court Orchestra of Emperor Leopold I, the Vienna Philharmonic has endured many changes, has gone through bad years as well as good. The period of 1954 to 1958, the years of Zubin's first stay in Vienna, would have to be classed among the orchestra's better times.

The Philharmonic was then and is today an orchestra dedicated to beauty. That dedication is handed down from one generation of musicians to the next, from professors to pupils. For the most part, those pupils came from the school where Zubin was enrolled, the Akademie für Musik und Darstellende Kunst.

In his first year at the Academy he would study form, analysis, harmony, and counterpoint, along with whatever electives he chose. Only after two semesters of elementary music studies would he be allowed into the conducting school, providing he passed the entrance examination.

At first, though he was struggling to learn the language and familiarize himself with his new surroundings, Zubin could permit himself a certain superiority. He could write his family that he was "a step ahead of my class," being familiar with a far wider range of music than were any of his classmates. And what he knew, he knew with assurance that came from studying entire orchestra scores, not simply instrument parts. But it was not long before Zubin discovered he had at least one weakness: harmony.

His rude awakening came when he started theory class under Karl Schiske, a composer who had been taught by the great Hindemith. Schiske was dismayed that his Indian pupil, adept at so many things, had real problems with harmony.

Recalling Schiske today, Zubin says, "That man was unbelievable. You could give him any theme and he could play it in the style of Bach. He could make a fugue on it immediately, or a canon. He could play it in the Brahmsian manner, with threes against twos, or like Chopin. I had never heard anything like it."

Along with Zubin's musical discoveries came a growing awareness of Western civilization, as reflected in the city that had once been its center. Vienna cast its spell over him.

Zubin felt the spell as he searched through the Altstadt, the old town, a winding tangle of cobbled *Gassen,* more alleys than streets. On Bäckerstrasse, hidden within the heavy aroma of baking breads, he could detect the scents of spices the Viennese imported for their famous tortes and soufflés. Cardamom, nutmeg, coriander, and cloves—they reminded him a little of home. If only one had the peppers, he reflected, one might compose a passable curry.

He was amused to hear the other foreign students complain about the Viennese diet. Too heavy, they said. But to an Indian, no deep-fried schnitzel could stand up beside the *chapati* and *pilaws* his mother used to cook. In a few weeks he lost fifteen pounds. The only things that saved him from wasting away were the desserts. Especially the chocolate—there was something the Viennese could brag about. He developed a craving for chocolate that would serve as a lifelong souvenir of his early student years.

Zubin followed streets like Sommerheidenweg and Haubenbiglstrasse, streets whose names he couldn't pronounce, into suburbs that dissolved into meadows, vineyards, and woods, and he began to understand the *Stimmung* of Vienna, the atmosphere that had inspired such dissimilar musical personalities as Brahms and Bruckner to create their masterworks.

There was no place like Vienna for musicians. At one period, almost simultaneously, it had been the home of Gluck, Haydn, Mozart, Beethoven, and Schubert. Again, toward the end of the nineteenth century, the Viennese could hear Richard and Johann Strauss, Mahler, and Hugo Wolf—all at the peak of their creative powers—and, if they listened at the windows of the Academy some years later, they might have perceived the beginnings of an entirely new kind of music in the persons of three young men named Schönberg, Berg, and Webern.

Everyone seemed to be a performer or artist of some sort in this city of *Musenkinder.* One could see the carefully cultivated mannerisms, full of charm and smiles; the degree of sincerity mattered little. This was the *Lebenkunst,* the "life art" of Vienna's glittering stage. If a foreigner placed himself on that stage, he had better perform well.

From all indications, Zubin was performing well. His professors seemed to take to the Indian student with a mixture of curiosity and affection, just as the Viennese had accepted coffee from the Turks in the seventeenth century. Around the Academy he became know as *der Inder,* thus receiving the all-important "title" without which no one could truly be at home in the city. But the true sense of belonging came only when one of his professors presented him with his first ticket to a concert of the Philharmonic.

The concert was sold out that afternoon, as the Philharmonic concerts generally were, and Zubin's ticket was for a seat on the stage, practically within the ranks of the orchestra. He sat there, feeling rather conspicuous as he listened to the musicians warm up, and he gazed out at the red-and-gold resplendence of the Musikverein. He was surely a long way from Bombay.

The featured work on the program was the Brahms First Symphony, to be conducted by Karl Böhm. Zubin anticipated the beginning of the work as one awaits the arrival of an old friend. He'd studied the score with records at home and had even played a four-hand reduction on the piano. He knew the dark C-minor symphony from its swirling, nebulous introduction to its triumphant conclusion. It was one of the works he knew best—or thought he did, until the Vienna Philharmonic began to play.

"You must try to imagine the feeling," he says. "Me, completely without knowledge of the sound of a live orchestra, a real one in a real auditorium.

"I knew that symphony backwards and forwards, yet—" and his voice falls to a barely audible whisper—"when I heard it played that afternoon I just couldn't believe it. I was hearing the Brahms First for the first time. I was hearing *music* for the first time! Suddenly I realized I had not simply come from a small town where I heard only a small orchestra. I had heard *no* orchestra. And now, here I was, a boy from India sitting in the best concert hall in the world, hearing one of the greatest orchestras in the world under a great conductor. It suddenly came to me what I was trying to do."

It was as though his life had at last taken form, just as the First Symphony unexpectedly solidifies in the theme of the fourth movement. Zubin was gripped by the strings in their first statement of the simple theme, reminiscent of Beethoven's Ninth Symphony. He was swept up by the full orchestra and carried along in the arms of the legendary Austrian conductor.

Zubin needed every ounce of control to keep from bursting into applause before the final beat of the concluding chord. At last he jumped up from his chair, cheering Karl Böhm, cheering the musicians who somehow breathed life into this magic thing called music, bravoing Brahms, and applauding Vienna for bringing them all together.

Perhaps Zubin's greatest discovery that day was the importance of the bass line in music. Like most people, he had always listened first to the melody, the part that had its own movement in time; the bass line he had thought of as the underpinning, the almost static support on which the moving melody rested. Perhaps he had simply never paid such close attention to the basses as he did that night, his stage seat having made him practically a member of their section. Whatever the reasons for his weakness, Zubin determined to convert it to a strength.

"It was simply incredible," he recalls, "to hear the basses in that hall. I never understood how important the bass line could be. In Brahms, if you have the melody and the bass, you needn't play the inner voices, because everything is said right there, everything. And on the stage of the Musikverein . . . well, I had never heard a sound like that before. So I just knew I had to learn that instrument."

Behind Zubin's decision to take up the bass was his dissatisfaction with Vienna's approach to the violin. Despite the overall lushness of the string sections, he could see that the violinists were not playing the way he'd been taught, and he had no desire to change his whole approach, as Mehli had done under Ivan Galamian. The double bass offered an opportunity to start fresh on a new string instrument, the concepts of which he understood from studying the violin. Furthermore, he knew the Vienna Academy was world renowned for its bass instruction.

If there was anything deeper behind Zubin's switch from violin to bass, it may have lain in the nature of the instruments. The violin is highly personal; it can yield up its music with the gentlest caress. A violin can be enjoyed in privacy or in the select company of a closed piano.

The double bass, on the other hand, is an extrovert, bombastic instrument that loves company, at its best in a crowd, at home in a *tutti*. Barring the odd vacancy in a string ensemble, any classical musician who commits himself to a bass commits himself also to an orchestra. It was the entire orchestra that Zubin wanted.

"I knew I was going to be a conductor, but I never intended to go right from the classroom to the podium. I wanted to spend a few years playing in the orchestra first. I wanted to know the psychological relationship between a musician and a conductor and I wanted the experience of feeling what a man feels on the other side of that fence."

Zubin was sustaining himself in Vienna on the princely sum of seventy-five dollars a month, from the trust of eight thousand dollars shared equally with his younger brother Zarin, who was now in London as an apprentice accountant. If he was careful, Zubin could stretch out his share of the trust for four years.

Staying away from the better Viennese restaurants helped ease the financial burden, and, since alcohol had never been a part of his family's life in India, he had no trouble with beer and wine, those traditional strains on a student's purse. Nor did coffee, even the Viennese coffee *mit Schlag,* tempt him. Instead, he restricted his drinking to water, which was served grudgingly but gratis at the *Kaffeehäuser.*

The coffeehouses, so different from the teahouses of Bombay, were the students' taverns and reading rooms, fraternity houses and sorority houses. Before, after, and between classes at the Academy they would gravitate to the nearby Liesingerkeller or Gösserkeller, foreign students at one table, Viennese at the next, there to debate current events of life and music.

Prominent in such discussions was the Philharmonic. They lamented the uneven soloists among the orchestra's woodwinds and its tired brass section. They made jokes about the stodgy Sunday audiences, stiff men in morning coats and wives in wrinkled furs, all bowing and embracing and kissing hands, bumping into one another at intermissions, feeling happy and sad to be among their own vanishing aristocracy, remembering the glorious old days before the two wars.

Zubin heard the Viennese students' witty remarks about the *herr Barons* of the Gesellschaft der Musikfreunde, the conservative organization that virtually ruled Vienna's musical life. Idiots, someone proclaimed, to have blackballed Schönberg! Not to mention Mahler, said someone else. An American at Zubin's table expressed surprise that Mahler could be snubbed and Bruckner lionized . . . weren't they just two of a kind? That brought a good laugh from the Viennese. Everyone knew Mahler was a musical thief!

So it went at the coffeehouses. Important discussions on the great issues of the day, by the musicians of tomorrow. It was a time for enjoying life, not for worrying. No one reflected that one day some of them would be tired old horn players themselves, remembering their own good old days as they bowed and scraped to the Gesellschaft der Musikfreunde, happy to blackball the difficult music of Schönberg and sneer at the complexities of Mahler, knowing that before long they would be replaced by their own students as members of the Wiener Philharmoniker.

Zubin made few close friends among the Viennese students, most of whom lived with their families and took their meals at home. On the other hand, nearly all the foreign students lived in one-room apartments with shared bathrooms and no kitchen privileges. They were treated to coffee and bread in the morning, but all other meals had to be taken out, usually at Barry's Restaurant, the "fast-food" place near the Academy that catered to students. Students who spoke the same language banded together to share their poverty and their meals, becoming one another's substitute families. Zubin's crowd all spoke English.

The group included Englishmen, Americans, Dady and Zubin—the only Asians at the Academy—Canadians, and an Egyptian Jew.

When summer brought the end of the school year, all his friends went home or to summer master classes in France and Italy. Zubin stayed behind to prepare himself for the Fall entrance examination for the conducting school. Travel, on his budget, was impossible.

Even the tram fare from the Thirteenth District Wienerwald apartment was becoming a strain, so Zubin moved into a less expensive room in the Third District, nearer the Music Academy. The building was owned by a large and friendly woman named Frau Mumb, who raised chows in the cellar. Learning to memorize scores to the yelping of hungry puppies was not easy, but Zubin put his mind to it and discovered he could block out any sound by "hearing" the music in his mind.

"But those chow chows never learned to recognize me in the eight months I lived there," Zubin remembers, laughing. "Every night I would come home and one would start barking, then all ten would bark at once. And they had blue tongues!"

During the summer break, Zubin joined the Singverein, the official chorus of the Musikverein, in order to "involve myself in music as soon as I could, not being good enough yet to play the bass in an orchestra."

The highlight of the summer came when he sang in the bass section in Beethoven's Ninth Symphony under Herbert von Karajan. In those years Karajan was director of the Vienna Symphony, the city's second orchestra, but he was making his first recordings of the complete Beethoven Symphonies with London's Philharmonia Orchestra, and he brought the whole orchestra to Vienna in order to use the Singverein as his chorus for the Ninth. Thus Zubin made his first recording, not as a conductor or even as an instrumentalist, but as a singer.

"It was a great experience to be suddenly part of the international music world. I remember that for some reason I was particularly broke that week. For the recording I got fifty schillings, which was about two dollars, so I went to a good restaurant and treated myself to a real veal schnitzel, not the cheap kind made of pork."

After singing in the chorus all day and standing at concerts in the evening, Zubin would long to discuss the music he'd heard with his friends at the coffeehouse. Instead he returned to his room and stayed awake long into the night, sitting cross-legged on the bed and filling his head with scores, trying to understand what messages lay hidden between the notes and bar lines. He became very close friends with Mozart, Beethoven, Schumann, Tchaikovsky, and Webern during those three months, because he simply could not bear to be alone.

More than ever, he cherished letters from home. His favorite letters came from Tehmina, who at last disclosed what the Parsee astrologer had seen in Zubin's future.

"I had him read your chart," she wrote, "and he told me I had nothing to worry about as far as your future is concerned. He says you're going to be famous. But he says also that under no circumstances should you get married before your twenty-fifth birthday."

Zubin had a good laugh as he read that. He wrote back, "You know, Mommy, I wish I had as much confidence in that astrology business as you do. At least we can be certain of one thing—I did not come to Vienna to get married."

One of the Canadians in Zubin's *Bund* was a violin student named Terry Gabora. When he went home in the summer of 1955, Terry looked up some of his old friends from high school, to regale them with tales of his grand times in Vienna, of the cheap and easy living, of the endless round of concerts and musical events, of the teachers, so enormously superior to anyone they had in Canada. To a twenty-one-year-old singer-pianist named Carmen Lasky, it all sounded very inviting.

After two years at the local conservatory in Saskatoon, Carmen had become a teacher, taking her music to the Indians and poor white families who lived in outlying villages. A pity, some of her own teachers said, that a beautiful girl like Carmen, with such a lovely voice and a passion for music, was not having a career on the concert or operatic stage. But Carmen really had no ambition to perform. She was quite content as a teacher, revealing to others the joy she'd discovered in music.

What impressed her about Gabora's stories was that in Vienna there was much more to be learned about music than she'd ever dreamed. If she could go there now, while she was still young and things were still inexpensive, perhaps she could achieve far greater results with her own pupils in Canada. She was engaged to be married, but it wouldn't hurt her fiancé to wait a bit longer.

So it was that in September 1955, just as the foreign students were returning from their summer vacations, Carmen Lasky and two other Canadian girls arrived in Vienna, and Terry Gabora took them to a party to meet some of his friends.

About twenty of them were crowded into the one-room apartment of an American bassoonist, each trying to remember the others' names, when suddenly the door flew open and a rather slight, dark-eyed boy with black hair strode into the room.

"I have great news and I must tell you all right now," Zubin shouted above the din. "I just found out I passed my entrance examination. They're letting me into the conducting school!"

It was an evening Carmen Lasky never forgot.

"He was so elated. I don't think I'd ever seen anybody that enthusiastic over anything. He bounced around the room, asking about everyone's summer. He had been there practically all by himself and he seemed to me very lonely, but exuberant at the same time.

"When he found out that we were newcomers, he said not to worry, he would take care of us. I had turned twenty-two that week and I suppose I felt very mature; but here was this young boy acting so exuberant, it just carried me off.

"I don't mean to say that I was swept off my feet by him as a man, because he was very much a child really, only nineteen."

Only nineteen, perhaps. But in one year Zubin had so inundated himself with Viennese music that he astonished the soprano from the backwoods of Canada.

"He rather took over, I suppose. All of us were taken with his knowledge of music and of what was going on in Vienna. You must remember that we were from very small towns, finding ourselves all of a sudden at the center of the world. The other two girls and I were naturally quite willing to be shown around by someone who knew the ropes. So he sold us on Vienna. In the process, I suppose he sold us on Zubin."

For the Academy students, the day began and ended with music. When they weren't at class or practicing their instruments, they were standing in the backs of theaters, hearing the elite and the would-be elite of the music world in performances of opera, symphonies, chamber music, and solo recitals. Not a day went by that they did not hear at least one live performance. As to *what* they heard, that was left to *der Inder*.

"Zubin was very much the leader of our group," Carmen says. "There were nineteen or twenty of us, I being the only singer, and everyone seemed to fall in line behind Zubin.

"He was always the one who knew what was going on, which concerts were not to be missed. At the end of the evening, as we left the theater or sat in the Liesingerkeller, Zubin would say, 'Now, here's what we're going to do tomorrow.' Then the next day he would go and pick up the tickets and we'd all meet at the concert hall."

For most concerts, standing room tickets could be purchased the day of the performance at about twenty cents each, affordable even on Zubin's seventy-five dollars a month. Sometimes with the tickets he was like a child in a candy store, unable to decide on one choice and grabbing as many as he could clutch. So the students would find themselves leaving one theater at intermission and rushing to a different hall in time to catch the second half of another performance.

More important musical events created the inconvenience of having to wait until one hour before performance time to buy standing room tickets. So as soon as classes were finished, the students would rush to the theater and stand outside, often in the snow. For several hours they would wait in line, just for the privilege of standing several hours more in the rear of an auditorium, sardined among as many as a hundred fifty fellow standees, all sweltering in heavy coats and sweaters. Small wonder that Carmen found herself feeling woozy one night during the fourth hour of *Die Frau ohne Schatten* at the Vienna Opera. When she fainted there was luckily no place to fall but against Zubin, who quickly got her out into the vestibule and onto a chair.

"Are you all right?" he asked. "Can I get you something, some water . . ."

"No, no," she said, managing a smile. "I'm all right now."

"You're sure?" Then, apparently satisfied she was not suffering from some terminal illness, he said, "You stay here and I'll go hear the end of the opera."

The day after the concert or opera, Zubin was always eager to get to the coffeehouse to see what the important critics had said in the newspapers. He could tell which critics knew what they were talking about, and those he took very seriously.

Foremost among these was Josef Marx, himself one of the last great composers of the lied. When Marx was present to review a concert, the students could always spot him by the white mane flowing above most other heads in the audience. A gruff, stiff-spined old man over six feet tall, Marx seemed to Zubin "the embodiment of all musical knowledge." His special field of expertise was the music with which Zubin was growing more and more sympathetic, the late romantic.

"Whether it was a quartet, an oratorio, an opera, or a symphony, we would always read his reviews and discuss what he had written. What Josef Marx said, one simply had to take seriously. He was the finest critic I have ever read. He was a prominent composer himself, you see, an accomplished musician. So that he was writing about the interpretation of a *colleague's* work, with deepest knowledge of the score, and not just comparing a performance to a hi-fi recording he had at home."

In November of 1955, Zubin's circle of followers grew by three when Mehli, Tehmina, and Zarin came to visit.

For the better part of a year now, Zubin in Vienna and Zarin in London had been urging their father to leave the unhealthy musical climate of Bombay and emigrate someplace where his work would be more appreciated. Prodded by his sons, Mehli found an agent to book him a recital tour in the north of Italy. Meanwhile, Zubin used his rapidly expanding influence to get a date for Mehli at the Brahmssaal in the Musikverein.

Mehli's violin recital was a minor event in Viennese musical circles, but an event nonetheless. It was the first time an Indian had ever performed there, and at that time Asians were still a rarity in central Europe. The theater manager noted in the program that Mehli's elder son was enrolled as a conductor in the Music Academy.

The recital was a perfect excuse for a reunion. The family's closeness had not been altered by time or distance, and, even in the cramped quarters of Zubin's apartment, they delighted in each other's company. To the parents, their son was still "darling," and he still called them "Mommy" and "Daddy," a display of affection that has continued unashamedly to the present, even in the face of Western reticence.

Using his accumulated three weeks of vacation time, Zarin joined the family reunion by boat and train from London, where he was taking giant steps up the accounting ladder. The firm to which he was articled was quite pleased with his progress, both in the evening courses and on the job, and the senior partners had given him several accounts of his own to handle. Zarin had, of course, tasted the cultural life of London, but he was flabbergasted at Vienna's musical wealth.

"I remember Zubin taking me to my first concert at the Musikverein. It was Hans Knappertsbusch conducting the Bruckner Eighth Symphony. Zubin had a standing room ticket, but he bribed one of the ushers—he knew all of them, I think—to let me have a seat. He couldn't stay because he had a class that evening. What a performance that was!"

The autumn of 1955 was a special time in Vienna, because the State Opera was opening for the first time since it had been bombed and almost totally destroyed in the Second World War. For ten years the important opera performances had been held at the little Theater an der Wien, but now the entire city was buzzing about the gala reopening of the Staatsoper.

Since top price for an opening night ticket for *Fidelio* was $200, the nearest standing room Zubin could get for his family and friends was across the Ringstrasse, near the Bristol Hotel, where they watched the limousines drive up to deposit the wealthy ticket holders.

Three nights later, they were all outside the opera house again, this time waiting in line to buy their standing room tickets for the same production of Beethoven's *Fidelio*, conducted by Karl Böhm.

"None of us had any money in those three weeks," Zarin reminisces with a laugh, "but my God, what we heard! Böhm conducting George London and Sena Jurinac in *Don Giovanni*, a *Meistersinger* with Fritz Reiner, *Rosenkavalier*, *Wozzeck*. And one Sunday I'll never forget—we heard Mozart's Requiem in the morning, Verdi's Requiem in the evening. I had been to operas in London, but this was before Rafael Kubelik took over; London opera was not so good. I thought, My brother sure knew what he was doing when he came to Vienna."

Zubin was fascinated by the hugeness of opera, the world that seemed so larger-than-life. The opera house itself was a home for gods, with its grand staircase that rose, soaring, in crimson splendor from a blue-and-ivory vestibule all burnished with gold leaf; and above, the nine Muses looked down in marble from their loggia on Mount Olympus.

The performance that particularly moved him in those early weeks of opera was Wagner's *Die Walküre*. The night he heard it, he was standing with Carmen up near the ceiling, and he nearly fell over when he heard the opera's first bars. When the eight double basses in the pit thrummed that thundering opening, he thought the Staatsoper would tremble and collapse. He could hardly wait until intermission to find his father and tell him, "You hear those basses? One day I'm going to have a bass section that plays like that!"

As his first evening at the Musikverein had been, this first brush with Wagner was a night of discovery for Zubin. Most opera lovers, particularly those in the United States, find their way to Wagner only after gradual exposure to Verdi and Puccini; for Zubin in Vienna, it was a headlong plunge into the *Ring*.

"My affinity for Wagner stems, I suppose, from the early romantic chamber music I grew up with in Bombay, the late Beethoven quartets, the Schubert quartets. Wagner seemed like the ultimate outgrowth of these, and I never found his music heavy going. The contrapuntal elements were so accessible I didn't have any trouble unraveling voices. I was never awed by the complexities or the incredible umbrella of sound. I found this door and I sort of walked through it."

After listening to Wagner's music, Zubin began to read everything he could get his hands on about the composer. He discovered that the man had been as interesting and controversial as his operas. It was only natural that this supreme romantic would appeal to a young man caught up in discovering his own remarkable potential.

"Wagner was a revolutionary in his politics as well as in his music. Let's face it—if he were alive today he'd be one of those Maoists. But somehow, like Mozart, his personal life didn't really influence his music. This whole idea and world of Wagner is what I entered into.

"Along with this went my slow mastering of the German language. I found that all of Wagner's tempos come out of the language. I heard the tempos fluctuate from one singer to another, depending on how the singer could express himself. Because, you see, he is really *speaking*. It just happens to be that there is a melody coming out as well.

"In subsequent years I heard *Tristan,* and Karajan did the whole *Ring.* I felt completely immersed in Wagner. And side by side, at the same time, I discovered Bruckner, the great symphonic by-product of Wagner."

From that first *Walküre,* Zubin promised himself that he would someday devote himself to the study and interpretation of Wagner. But not now. Unlike so many young people, who find themselves equal to any task that presents itself, Zubin realized there was a lot he had to learn before he could conduct opera, let alone one of Wagner's operas.

To Mehli it seemed that there must be a great deal for his son to learn before he was ready to conduct anything. What chance could there be among these sophisticated Europeans for a boy from Bombay whose only example had been the struggling efforts of his virtually self-taught father? As the three weeks of musical family reunion drew to a close, Mehli went to the conducting teacher, Hans Swarowsky, for an appraisal of Zubin's progress after one year in Vienna and just a few weeks in conducting class. Swarowsky's assessment, in broken English, nearly bowled him over.

"Your son is a born conductor. There is simply not much I can teach him. He knows everything already. But I will try to do whatever I can."

Mehli could not be certain whether the professor was simply condescending to a doting father from the benighted East, so he kept the curious praise to himself. Still, he could not help feeling pleasurably confident as he said good-by to his son and, with Zarin, boarded the train for Calais.

From there, Mehli intended to look for work in England. He had given up hope of creating a taste in Bombay for the music he loved; the Bombay Symphony Orchestra was again disbanded. Tehmina would stay for a while with Zubin in Vienna, joining Mehli when and if he found employment as a musician. If the effort proved unsuccessful, the two of them would return to Bombay and Mehli would go back to his job as a tax collector.

Four weeks later, as Tehmina's patience with the world of professional musicians was wearing thin, word came from Mehli. He had been hired as a first violinist by the Scottish National Orchestra and would have found a place for them to live by the time Tehmina arrived in Glasgow.

With his family gone, Zubin could concentrate on his classes, which were now in full swing at the Academy. He was especially delighted with his bass professor, Otto Rühm, and with Swarowsky, his conducting teacher.

Zubin remembers Otto Rühm fondly as "the one who made me conscious of what beautiful sound was. It is the sort of thing one cannot learn in books, but only from someone like him, who has had that sound in his ears for many, many years.

"I realized that in Vienna one could not separate beauty from music, that the Viennese could not help playing beautifully, just as one cannot help speaking with one's accent. Otto Rühm helped me understand that."

His conducting professor, on the other hand, had no time for such ephemeral concerns. Hans Swarowsky, a pupil and disciple of Richard Strauss, was a strict constructionist of the musical constitution. His tyranny was legendary at the Music Academy.

The first week of conducting class was a dreaded experience for the would-be Furtwänglers and Toscaninis of Vienna. One by one, like condemned prisoners on their way to the gallows, they mounted the podium to lead an orchestra of students in the first movement of Beethoven's Fifth Symphony. The sound of the ax falling was the inevitable *Da-da-da-daaa* from the orchestra and the equally inevitable *"Nein!"* from Professor Swarowsky.

Incredibly, Zubin lasted a full ten measures before he received his first reprimand from the master. The other students looked at each other in amazement. One of them, Ukrainian-born Eugene Husaruk, dividing his time between violin and conducting, recalls the day with a still-evident sense of awe.

"It was a revelation. The gestures were so natural. Everything was full of energy, tremendous energy. The students all thought that he was a great talent, and we wanted to know what the hell he was doing here studying with the rest of us. The only thing he seemed to be doing wrong was that he gave the orchestra too much. He was baby-feeding them, thinking they needed to be told everything.

"But it was exciting to watch his hands. Some people express themselves well with their hands and others don't. We had all seen conductors, like Otto Klemperer and Furtwängler, who always looked clumsy; even though they made great music, there was never anything clear about their gestures. But in conducting they say a clear gesture is worth a thousand words, and that's how Zubin's gestures were."

If Zubin's fault was "overconducting," then Professor Swarowsky had the sure cure.

"He came up behind me while I was conducting, threw his arms around me, and stuck his fingers in my coat sleeves and pulled downward, leaving only my wrists free. 'Now you conduct,' he told me." Zubin saw instantly what Swarowsky was after. If one could master complete freedom of the wrists, so many flailing arm gestures would be unnecessary.

"He told me I was a wild man, and one day he made me conduct the entire *Don Juan* of Strauss like that, with his fingers pulling down on my sleeves."

Besides Richard Strauss, Professor Swarowsky's musical heritage flowed from Webern, Schönberg, and Clemens Krauss. His personal heritage was somewhat more difficult to trace.

Though adopted by his wealthy Jewish stepfather, a prominent Viennese banker, Swarowsky kept his mother's name, and in later life he took to wearing a signet ring of the Hapsburg dynasty, with a bar sinister to indicate illegitimacy. According to the story he told Zubin, Swarowsky was the product of his mother's liaison with one of the Hapsburg Archdukes.

Apparently satisfied by his claims to non-Jewishness, the Nazis put Swarowsky to work in Goebbels' Ministry of Propaganda. He was later reputed to have sent secret messages to the Allies by means of musical notations. Along the way he established himself as a translator of operas, and many of the much-maligned German versions of French and Italian operas still sung today are credited to Hans Swarowsky.

Swarowsky had a love of painting, inherited possibly from the cultured Hapsburgs, certainly from his art-collecting stepfather. Consequently, his analyses of music scores contained many references to similar ideas expressed in painting, thus giving his students a grasp of interrelationships within the arts. As though that were not enough, Swarowsky had spent a number of years as a pupil-patient of Sigmund

Freud, gaining insight into why composers created their music just so and how it could be expected to affect a listener.

"Swarowsky was unlike most of the Viennese I met in that he was generous," recalls Zubin. "He would give me the shirt off his back. But in Swarowsky's case the shirt was his knowledge, his incredible musical knowledge. I learned from him how to look at a score and analyze what he called the 'handwriting' of a composer, the thing that made one master's music different from every other's."

If one knew how to read that handwriting, Swarowsky maintained, everything that could be said about or by a piece of music could be found right in the score.

"This," he shouted, lifting a score from the podium, "this is your Bible . . . or"—half smiling for an instant in Zubin's direction—"your Koran or whatever it is they have where you come from. You will adhere to this absolutely. In here you will find everything there is to know about style, about form, about architecture, about rhythm. When you make a rubato, when you take a liberty of any kind, you had better find something in here that told you to do that. Because if you do something that is not written in this book, then you have broken all ten commandments at once."

Considering Swarowsky's absolutism on the matter of the score, Zubin decided that the only way one could confront an orchestra was with every bit of that score's information lodged firmly in one's memory. From that day on he determined that he would try never to conduct a piece of music until he had first memorized it. Since he did not have a "photographic" memory, as Dimitri Mitropoulos and some other conductors were said to have, he could only accomplish this by going over and over the music until he completely understood it, until he knew how and why one note, one chord, one measure, one phrase led inevitably to the next, how each sprang necessarily from what came before. To his friends, it seemed that one part of Zubin's mind was constantly reviewing a score.

"Some of the other student conductors would see Zubin and ask, 'How long did you study today?'" Carmen recalls, "as though you could reduce everything to hours and minutes.

"I thought, That's funny, I never hear Zubin say that. I began to realize that he must be studying all the time, even when he was talking to me, from morning till night. It was never, 'I studied *five hours* yesterday.' Study was very much a part of his everyday life, and he never mentioned it to anyone. Even today I think he studies all day long. Not that he has no other interests, but to a good musician work is life and life is work."

Today Zubin laughs when he recalls how total was his Viennese immersion in music. "I remember once a friend of ours was singing Gilda in a performance of *Rigoletto*, so of course we wanted to attend. But the next day I was supposed to conduct Strauss's *Don Juan* in class, so I had that on my mind.

"During one of those scenes when Gilda wasn't singing I excused myself and left my seat. I went into the men's room, sat down, and went through the entire *Don Juan* in my head. Then I went back and heard the rest of *Rigoletto*."

If Zubin had any advantage over his fellow students, other than his remarkable powers of concentration, it was his olive skin—light for an Indian, but distinctive in Austria. That, along with his Bombay accent, made him an oddity in the Viennese music world. People listened to what he said and did with keener interest than they showed the typical Music Academy student. As Carmen says, "The Viennese were very interested in anything faintly Oriental, and Zubin was made much of."

Der Inder had a built-in notoriety that he could parlay into fame, providing he played his cards right.

"He began to meet people," recalls Eugene Husaruk. "He would meet Mr. A. and Mr. A. knew Mr. B., who would talk about Zubin to Mr. C., who was very important. That's the way it began to snowball. And he made a positive impression on everybody he met, something so many artists think is unimportant. As a person he made a very positive impression on other people. He was gregarious, too, and charming, and in addition he always did his work very well.

"You know, when you have talent you become everyone's star pupil, and when you are the star you have the best chance to get ahead; you are chosen to conduct the right concerts and be heard by the right people."

If his Oriental heritage made life in Vienna easier for Zubin, it was having just the opposite effect on his parents. In Scotland, Mehli and Tehmina were having trouble finding a decent place to live. "There is," Mehli wrote to Zubin, "a very strong anti-Indian feeling here." Moreover, the standard starting salary was low, even for a back-chair first violinist, about the equivalent of fifty dollars a week.

After a few months with the Scottish National Orchestra Mehli got an audition with Sir John Barbirolli through one of Zarin's accounting clients, who was on the board of the Hallé Orchestra of Manchester. Barbirolli took him on, and before long Mehli was promoted to assistant concertmaster at a salary of twenty pounds a week—about eighty American dollars. It was still not much money, but Zubin noticed an immediate change in his parents' letters.

There was a renewed sense of pride and commitment on his father's part, which buoyed Zubin's own spirits even as they made him homesick—not for Bombay, but for his family in England. To fight the longing to be with them, Zubin buried himself in his work and his friends' company, refusing to be alone.

"During the whole time we were in Vienna together," says Eugene Husaruk, "I don't think he had a meal by himself once. He had to go out in a big gang always, always."

Gregariousness, leadership, and a disarming directness are the qualities his friends in Vienna remember about Zubin. These, combined with his charm and good looks, were the key elements in the Mehta approach to winning friends and influencing young ladies.

"There are some people," Husaruk observes, "who become so sophisticated they get all tied up in knots. Not Zubin. It was not a sophisticated approach," he says, laughing, "and it still isn't. The way he deals with musicians professionally, that's the way he deals with people privately. There's nothing complicated about it. And if you ask what made him so appealing to women, this is the key. There's nothing else to it."

There are those who will tell you that Vienna is the most romantic city in the world, that no matter how far north it may seem on a map, it's a southern city by temperament. They say the springtime scent of the linden trees along the Ringstrasse may drive a girl *deppert,* that a young man may lose his heart as he rides the Riesenrad, the ancient and enormous ferris wheel from which one sees the city as in a dream. For Carmen Lasky and Zubin, it didn't happen like that at all. It just happened.

"I can't tell you how we got together," Carmen says. "I was even engaged at the time. The first thing I knew, we were together more than everybody else. It doesn't sound very romantic, I'm afraid."

After a pause, she continues in her soft, western Canadian accent with its faint Highland lilt. "As I said, he was the leader. In the summer he led us all to Siena. Zubin just said, 'Let's go to Siena,' so we went."

3

⧜

"He Will Win
Every Competition"

Summer in Siena, the picturesque town in the Tuscan hills of Italy, meant studying at the famed Accademia Chigiana. There were classes by such instrumental masters as Andrés Segovia and instruction in conducting by Carlo Zecchi, with whom Zubin was eager to study.

"In 1955, a lot of the foreign students took off for Siena and I was left alone in Vienna, so I said this year I must go there too. I sent a letter to Carlo Zecchi telling him what little bit I had done and he accepted me."

Taking Carmen, Gene Husaruk, and a few others along, Zubin went by train to Tuscany and quickly made himself a prominent figure. Husaruk, who shared a room with Zubin near the palatial Accademia, recalls that "Zubin spent a lot of time in the room going over new scores, but as soon as he was finished he immediately went out to see who was there that he could meet, and there were a lot of important artists in Siena that summer."

At an *al fresco* café, Zubin introduced himself to a young guitarist named John Williams. The two struck up a friendship, and soon Williams got Zubin admitted to the very select master class of Segovia. Though it was extremely unlikely Zubin would ever encounter a need for the fine points of guitar playing, his appetite for musical knowledge on any level was insatiable. He also found time, as well as permission, to join André Navarra's cello class as an auditor.

He auditioned for Carlo Zecchi's conducting class and was accepted without the slightest hesitation. Feeling very good about himself, he dropped by the theater the following morning to listen in on some of the other students' auditions.

As he entered the beautifully decorated Renaissance theater, he heard the music of Schumann's Fourth Symphony. The pacing was impeccable, and the orchestra sounded particularly good. It was quite apparent that he was going to have some stiff competition here in Siena.

Opening the door of the auditorium, he blinked his eyes, thinking they must not be adjusted to the darkness. For a moment it seemed that the orchestra was playing without a conductor. Then he saw, on the podium, a tiny figure, barely able to reach above the heads of the front-row musicians. A dwarf!

Then he realized the truth. It was a very young boy. He had read about Mozart, but this was Zubin's first encounter with a living child prodigy. He determined to get to know this little fellow, whose name was Daniel Barenboim.

Danny was thirteen but looked much younger, certainly no more than eleven. Born in Argentina, he had moved with his family several years earlier to Israel. His parents, Enrique and Aida Barenboim, had brought him to Siena hoping to improve his skills as a conductor, which were already not so far behind the boy's amazing command of the piano keyboard.

Zubin became like a big brother to Danny and took to carrying him around Siena on his broad shoulders. He also became fast friends with the boy who was clearly the top conducting prospect among the Italian students. This young man, three years Zubin's senior, was named Claudio Abbado.

From Danny and Claudio, Zubin learned about Israel and about the great opera houses of Italy. In turn, he introduced them to his friends and filled their ears with stories of life in Bombay and music in Vienna. Claudio seemed particularly interested in the Vienna Music Academy, for he felt he had already plumbed the depths of the Milan Conservatory.

There was no professional jealousy, none of the backbiting that one frequently finds in professional students. Instead, the young conductors—Abbado, Barenboim, and Mehta—shared a camaraderie born of mutual love for their work. This is not to say that Zubin was reluctant to take advantage of another conductor's misfortunes. On the contrary, the Accademia Chigiana afforded his first opportunity to fill in for an "indisposed" colleague, something that was to figure prominently in his budding career.

Plans had been made for a gala concert in the main piazza, but Zubin was not on the program. The day before the concert, the student who was scheduled to conduct the first movement of Tchaikovsky's Fifth Symphony did not show up for class. Word was sent that he was too ill to conduct.

"Well," said Professor Zecchi, "the orchestra is ready to play this piece and it seems a shame to cancel it. Is anyone else familiar enough with it to conduct?"

Zubin's hand shot up. "I studied the piece last term in Vienna."

"Do you think you could manage it tomorrow night, then?"

"Certainly, Maestro," Zubin replied.

"Very well. Here's a score. You'd better spend some time this evening with it to refresh your memory."

Refreshing his memory was not the problem. Zubin had never even looked at the Fifth Symphony before. But as he says, "You must be ready to take a chance when it is presented to you. And when you get those chances, you had better do well or you may not get any others."

All afternoon and evening he sat in his room with the score spread out on the bed, trying to get the notes on the pages to make music in his head.

"He told me he was going to have it memorized," Husaruk recalls. "I told him that was impossible, especially while I was standing there in the room practicing my fiddle. I said, 'You want me to stop scratching around and leave you alone?' He said, 'No, no. It doesn't bother me at all.' What marvelous powers of concentration that man had! There he was studying that complicated score while I was standing practically in his ear playing my scales."

And at the concert the next evening, "Zubin was a tremendous success. He knew every little note in the score."

Besides learning new music, Zubin played tennis and Ping-Pong, thus filling a void created by the Viennese ignorance of the cricket he had loved in India. He also picked up a new language, Italian, with the ease born of switching from dialect to dialect in the streets and on the playgrounds of Bombay. The months in Siena passed infinitely more quickly than had his previous summer alone, and almost before he knew it he was back in Vienna.

In October the Viennese press seemed on the point of bursting with news of anti-Soviet activities in Poland and Hungary. There was still a great sentiment in Austria against the Russians on account of the Red Army's barbarous treatment of that country after the Second World

War. The Soviets had ensured a long life for this bitterness first by erecting, in Vienna, a huge statue of a Russian soldier and then guaranteeing its protection as an article of the peace treaty. The statue was named "The Unknown Soldier," but to the Viennese it was "The Unknown Rapist."

When Hungarian students chased that same Red Army from the streets of Budapest, the Viennese cheered. Hungarian refugees began streaming across the border into Austria, to be given food, shelter, and asylum, chiefly by units of the American and British armed forces, who still shared powers of occupation with the Soviets.

A British Army officer hit upon the idea of improving the spirits of the refugees by means of a concert, to which end he approached the directors of the Music Academy. An orchestra of volunteers was put together, with Zubin as conductor. The students were asked to assemble that same evening, to be taken by bus to the refugee camp, about fifty miles away in the province of Burgenland.

Zubin was delighted that at last he would lead an orchestra by himself, not as one of a group of fledgling conductors. His first public concert. To his dismay, he opened his closet and found that both his pairs of shoes had holes in them. And it was snowing outside. He thought of wearing his boots, but they simply would not do for a young man stepping off on his career. Then he noticed that, of his four dress shoes, one right shoe and one left shoe had soles that were not quite worn through. They were not a pair, but at least they were both black. Better, he decided, than rubber boots.

The musicians and their instruments were crowded aboard the bus supplied by the British, and they rattled through driving snow to a place near the Hungarian border. There they were led into a long mess hall, already filled with six hundred or so refugees, smiling and chattering among themselves in Hungarian. A British officer explained that the people were so looking forward to the concert that they had forgone their evening meal in order to attend.

There was no stage, so the students set up their music stands on the floor at one end of the hall. Zubin had no need of a podium, since he had chosen pieces he knew from memory: the Overture from *Die Fledermaus;* a Mozart violin concerto, with Terry Gabora as soloist; the first movement of Schubert's *Unfinished* Symphony; and finally the Liszt Hungarian Rhapsody no. 2.

The applause for each piece was warm and enthusiastic, but at the conclusion of the Hungarian Rhapsody Zubin turned to see the people out of their seats, some cheering, others hugging one another and crying. A bearded priest made his way through the crowd to Zubin and threw his arms around him, kissing him on both cheeks and speaking words the young conductor could not understand. The old man faced the audience and said something that made them burst into cheers all over again; then, as the crowd fell silent, he made the sign of the cross over the orchestra, giving them his blessing. Suddenly Zubin felt outside of himself, looking on the scene with a strange mixture of involvement and detachment.

"I couldn't understand his words, yet I felt what he was saying. I was very touched by his blessing. It seemed as though music had an important place in the flow of history, along with politics and war and economics. I knew that my life in music was somehow beginning, there, in that cold, crowded mess hall, and that I would never again cut myself off from the world and its problems."

Now even more than before, Zubin threw himself into the mainstream of Vienna's musical life. His growing proficiency on the double bass made him sought after as a substitute bass player in the secondary orchestras of Vienna. The money he earned provided occasional relief from the austere budget he was forced to live on, and the experience of watching other conductors at work was perhaps even more valuable.

There was additional experience to be gained as a member of the Singverein. Zubin, who had been delighted when Claudio Abbado appeared to enroll in Swarowsky's conducting class, talked his friend into joining the chorus as well. They soon made a pact to attend only rehearsals of important conductors, not the routine practice sessions held by chorusmaster Reinholdt Schmidt. They delighted in singing under Josef Krips in Haydn's *Creation,* Erich Kleiber in Verdi's Requiem, and Bruno Walter in the Mozart Requiem. Fritz Reiner, Herbert von Karajan—they all conducted the Singverein that season. Then, rather abruptly, the halcyon days were over.

"One day we were on stage with the Vienna Symphony, waiting for Karajan to start rehearsal. There was some delay, then Karajan walked on, with chorusmaster Schmidt right behind him. The chorusmaster pointed to the bass section and said, 'Abbado, Mehta, out! You don't come to *my* rehearsals, you don't get the sugar either.' Were were thrown out right there, in front of Karajan, the chorus, the orchestra, and everybody."

Zubin was also being threatened with eviction from his apartment. Frau Mumb, whose rules about visitors were strict, caught Zubin bringing Carmen into the building one afternoon and launched into a tirade against the loose morals of foreigners and the younger generation that would have put a Victorian Englishman to shame. Since Zubin was a good deal fonder of Carmen than he was of the Mumbs, he decided it was time to move on, and soon he was settled in the home of an old Russian lady who said she was a countess and who had no objection to visitors.

Zubin and Carmen never even discussed living together, as several foreign "couples" among the music students were doing, but as the winter wore on toward 1957 they found themselves growing closer. With Carmen, more than with any other of his friends, Zubin shared his musical thoughts, shared the ideas about music that were taking root and shooting up in his mind. He also shared with her an increasing fondness for Vienna.

At Christmas the city became a fairyland. Mariahilferstrasse, the big shopping street, glittered with lights of every color. The windows of Demel's came alive with marzipan trains, nougat castles, and sugar waterfalls.

On Christmas Eve the shops were dark, the streets deserted. Even the Staatsoper closed down—its only other dark night from the start of September till the end of June being Good Friday. Carmen, who was Catholic, took Zubin to midnight Mass at St. Stephen's and they joined in the singing of carols. Standing amid the forest of pillars, gazing at the Romanesque tapestry in stone, hearing German carols in the soft, lilting accent of Vienna, Zubin might have been on another planet from the one where he had grown up, where worship meant a few well-remembered prayers and a stick of sandalwood for the temple fire.

On New Year's Eve the ritual was just as strict, and just as foreign to Zubin. At the Opera there was *Die Fledermaus,* in which the only change from year to year was the topical jokes of Frosch the Jailer, certain to bring down the house and embarrass the city fathers.

Meanwhile, across the Ringstrasse, the Philharmonic played more Strauss—waltzes, polkas, and overtures—in its annual *Neujahrskonzert,* predictable as the evening's program at the Opera. From their standing room positions, Zubin and Carmen could hear some of the comments from the old women who sat toward the back of the house. As concertmaster Willi Boskovsky strode to the podium, one of them sighed, "Just like *der Strauss* himself." "Dear Willi!" exclaimed another, "this is always his moment."

Boskovsky had conducted the *Neujahrskonzert* ever since the death of Clemens Krauss. Wearing a turn-of-the-century morning coat with patterned waistcoat and striped pants, he conducted with his bow, as Mehli had done in Bombay, occasionally lifting the violin to his chin to play some lilting solo melody. Zubin watched Boskovsky, swaying in three-quarter time, his eyes closed, and knew that this *must* be the way to conduct Johann Strauss. Whether or not it was great music was academic. This was great Strauss.

The concert ended with several encores, followed by the ultimate encore, the "Blue Danube." Zubin watched the audience cheering, crying, jumping from their seats, and he felt certain that the Philharmonic would never invite anyone but a born-and-bred Viennese to conduct its New Year's Eve concert. That, at least, would be one goal he did not have to add to the goals he was rapidly accumulating for his still unborn career.

As for Carmen's goals, they were no clearer in 1957 than they had been when she left Saskatoon a year and a half earlier. Nearly twenty-four now, she was content to let her voice guide her career as she let Zubin guide her life.

"I'm not a person who has a great deal of projected ambition," she admits. "I studied music because I liked it. I kept on studying music because I liked it. My teachers in the opera and lieder classes were very encouraging, but I was very much caught up in just going ahead and letting the voice take me where it would. I actually never even thought of myself on the stage performing, I just kept on studying and absorbing."

Zubin, whose "projected ambition" was very strong, but still largely unfocused, kept on studying and absorbing as well. His repertoire was growing by leaps and bounds, already including many works by the great German and Austrian composers, from Bach to Berg, along with a number of pieces from the French and Russian schools.

His reputation as a voracious learner had spread beyond the Academy, and now *der Inder* was a familiar sight at rehearsals of the Vienna Philharmonic as well as the Vienna Symphony, no mean accomplishment in the regulation-ridden atmosphere of musical Vienna.

"I was always at rehearsals," he says, "be it Karajan, Böhm, whoever was conducting. My bass professor was first bass, my chamber music professor one of the first violins. When the final tuning up began, it was always, 'Everybody out of the hall.' They had restrictions, but not for me. 'The Indian can stay.' So I stayed and I learned. I can't tell you how much I learned at those rehearsals."

From Swarowsky Zubin had learned the theory of conducting, but, watching the great conductors at close quarters, he began to cross the bridge from theory to practice. Training an orchestra, he quickly learned, was one of the essentials of a conductor's trade. This he observed in Josef Krips's rehearsals.

"Krips knew about training an orchestra. Swarowsky knew the music backward and forward, but he couldn't control the orchestra and cajole them into playing it that way. Krips seemed to breathe with the musicians, and his performances came out polished and sparkling."

From Herbert von Karajan he learned about conducting style, another thing not taught in Swarowsky's class.

"To Swarowsky, there was only the beat—pure, simple, and clear. He could not be concerned with atmosphere or emotion. Let the music say what it would say. But in Karajan's conducting was an added dimension. There was tension in his whole body, and he made conducting into a very sinuous and sensual art. His movements made him *part* of the music, not merely the leader of musicians."

Zubin got to know the classical and romantic repertoire the way the Viennese played it, with their sensitivity to tone especially throughout the rich, mellow string sections. He listened and he listened to that sound till it became the only sound he wanted to hear.

There was no question in Zubin's mind that the playing of the Vienna Philharmonic was the ultimate in orchestral excellence, certainly in the range of his experience to date. Yet in listening to that playing he came to accept the occasional blemishes that appeared during any given performance. If a solo horn cracked a crucial note in a Brahms symphony, for instance, there was no complaining that the orchestra had an off night.

Indeed, the Vienna Philharmonic set its own standards of perfection. If the music was beautiful, the audience was happy. And the Philharmonic only played beautiful music. At any rate, could perfection ever be possible in anything so diverse and multiple as an orchestra? Zubin doubted that the ideal could be attained—until he heard an orchestra from Cleveland, Ohio.

"It was the first time I had heard an American orchestra in Vienna. Or anywhere else, for that matter, except on recordings. But when George Szell came with the Cleveland Orchestra, I was amazed. They simply did not make mistakes. I assumed that mistakes were just part of any live concert. But these people from Cleveland came to Vienna and refused to make a mistake. I was impressed."

The next American orchestra he heard was one of the best in the world, and that performance, too, was clean and successful, until the closing piece of the concert, Johann Strauss's "Tales from the Vienna Woods."

"It was terribly un-Viennese, and everybody in the audience knew it. It was clear to me then that one of a conductor's most important jobs is to learn his own limitations, to learn the limitations of his orchestra."

Zubin was discovering what any young artist must discover: that the very concept of "taste" implied limitations. If one's life was to be devoted to the creation and interpretation of beauty, then one would have to see things in terms of being *more* beautiful or *less* beautiful. Sometimes it seemed to him that, in Vienna at least, the relative merits of a piece of music might just as soon be determined by its relative German-ness, with Brahms somewhere near the top of the scale and, say, Debussy somewhere very close to the bottom.

Since the years in Vienna were the formative years for Zubin's musical taste, it would be strange had he not been influenced by the preponderance of German works among the city's annual output of music. There are probably some music lovers who would consider this growing bias for the German repertory an unfortunate shortcoming. Zubin was aware of the bias, but he never saw it as anything but an advantage for himself as a young conductor.

"German music was definitely my repertoire," he says. "But when you think about it, it's everybody's repertoire. The German always makes up at least sixty percent of any conductor's programs over the years. The other stuff is peripheral, no matter how much you may love it."

Yet he was not about to let the Viennese lead him by the nose in this matter of musical taste. Having learned to love French impressionists, he understood that the chief reason the Viennese audiences did not appreciate French music was that Vienna's favorite conductors had never really learned to do justice to it.

"My father was always a great Debussy and Ravel man, and he taught me to love French music. But in Vienna I heard it played very badly. *Very* badly. I went to rehearsals and I saw André Cluytens going out of his mind trying to conduct the Philharmonic in the French repertoire. It simply did not seem to be in their ears as it was in his."

Spring of 1957 brought the end of Zubin's second year as a conducting student and the end of his matriculation at the Music Academy. He, Claudio, and four other students were to conduct the professional Tonkünstler Orchestra in a public concert at the Musikverein as their final examination, Zubin's piece to be Tchaikovsky's *Romeo and Juliet*, while Claudio was to conduct the Concertino for Piano and Chamber Orchestra by Leoš Janáček.

As the week of the concert drew near, Carmen reminded Zubin that he did not have a full-dress suit. In a panic, he went around to tailors and haberdashers, only to discover that he could not afford the price of a set of tails and trousers. Then he happened to see a group of waiters reporting to work one morning at the fashionable restaurant, Urbani Keller. They were resplendent in their white ties and tails, as though they were on their way to a wedding.

Zubin ran up to the waiters and explained his situation, asking whether they knew of a place where he might buy tails at a bargain price. The waiters wrote down the name of a *Volksladen*, which outfitted him with a coat and trousers that fit perfectly, all for only about twenty-five dollars. Only when he arrived for the concert and compared himself to the other young conductors did he realize the reason for his good bargain. Someone had forgotten to stitch a pocket into his coat.

The concert went well, the young conductors cheered on by friends and fellow students. Zubin and Claudio were only disappointed the next morning to find that no newspaper had sent a critic to review their debut performances.

Three days later, however, one of their friends spotted their names in a column by Gerhard Bronner, a noted political satirist and cabaret performer. Unable to get tickets for the opera, Bronner had "stuck my head into the Musikverein to see what was going on." He continued at length about the young conductors and the high quality of musical training available in Vienna. Then, toward the end, Bronner mentioned that two of the young conductors, Claudio Abbado and Zubin Mehta, had given especially praiseworthy performances. The music circles of Vienna would do well to take notice of this young foreign talent, he wrote, for before very long the world would be hearing from them.

It seemed as though everything was going well for Zubin and Claudio, almost too well. They returned to Siena that summer, expecting to take the town by storm.

"I was slowly beginning to feel invincible," Zubin recalls with a laugh. "I just knew I was going to knock everybody dead in Siena. Then I found out that the conducting professor was not Carlo Zecchi again, but Alceo Galliera. He got my feet back on the ground, and fast."

Galliera was an excellent conductor, but his teaching technique was a far cry from the gentle coaxing of Maestro Zecchi. Soon the morale and confidence of the young conductor were at an all-time low.

"He just *kvetched* us to death. He played everything on the piano along with the orchestra while you conducted. I didn't think I could do a thing right. Finally it came to the point where I felt as though I had two left hands. I couldn't breathe, phrase, give an upbeat. Nothing. I was feeling very put down."

Carmen was not at the Accademia Chigiana to cheer Zubin's faltering spirits. She had chosen this time to visit her parents in Saskatoon, parting company from Zubin for the first time since they'd met. Fortunately, his brother Zarin arrived to illuminate the gloom.

Zarin, doing quite well as an apprentice accountant, had earned a holiday and was spending it hitchhiking through southern Europe. He brought Zubin word that their grandfather, Nowrowji Mehta, had made the decision to leave Bombay and join Mehli and Tehmina in Manchester.

Zubin was deeply attached to his grandfather, who at the age of ninety-two was still riding the crowded double-decker buses to and from work each day, still pursuing his hobby as a journalist and columnist for the Bombay newspapers. He had even written a pamphlet on how to live to be a hundred. Now he was going to leave his beloved India, where he had been left all alone, to be with his son in England. Zubin's only concern was that the old man, who thrived on work and sunshine, might succumb to boredom and the cold climate of Manchester.

He told Zarin he was glad his grandfather would be able to meet Carmen. She had arranged to make her return trip through England to spend a few days with Mehli and Tehmina in Manchester. Zubin felt it was time they got to know each other, since she would likely be joining the family before long.

Zarin did not pursue the matter of Zubin's affair of the heart. The two brothers were very close, but they had never discussed such personal matters. They talked rather of the things they could share—music, sports, and having a good time. And, oh yes, Zarin remembered something he had in his knapsack for Zubin.

It was an article he'd clipped from one of the British weeklies regarding a new competition for conductors in Liverpool, to be held the following May. Sponsored by the Royal Liverpool Philharmonic, it was open to any conductor below the age of thirty, with a minimum of professional experience. Principal judge would be William Steinberg, and top prize was a season as assistant conductor at a salary of eight hundred pounds.

"If you're accepted in the competition," Zarin pointed out, "at least you'll have an excuse to visit Manchester. It's only forty miles from Liverpool, you know."

Zubin mailed in the application, thinking no more about Liverpool. With the end of the summer season, he bade farewell to the Accademia Chigiana, to Maestro Galliera, and to his friend Claudio. Back in Vienna, he joined up as a bass player with the orchestra of the Jeunesses Musicales, which was leaving for Paris.

The Jeunesses Musicales, destined to play a large part in Zubin's first years as a struggling conductor, was an organization begun in Belgium and dedicated to fostering and encouraging a love of serious music in young people. By the mid-fifties, the Jeunesses had taken hold in practically every nation of Europe, and it was firmly established in the Viennese musical hierarchy. Zubin had been introduced to the organization's directors by Hans Swarowsky, who "just brought me over there one day and said, 'Here, take this guy. He's a conductor.'"

The Jeunesses Musicales was planning a program for conductors, but their immediate interest in Zubin was as a bass player. He agreed to join the orchestra for its trip to Paris, where they played at the Sorbonne. Then he left the group and traveled to Manchester, where he met Carmen, saw his parents and his grandfather—and feasted on Indian food for the first time in nearly three years.

Back in Vienna, Zubin was delighted to receive word that he'd been accepted in the Liverpool conducting competition. Each contestant was required to know all the compositions on a long list provided by the orchestra. Most of the works were standard and already in Zubin's repertoire, but one stood out from the others as unfamiliar and intriguing, Igor Stravinsky's score for the ballet *Petrushka*.

The 1910 composition makes a great many demands upon a large orchestra, complete with a bold array of percussion instruments and a pianoforte. Zubin had no idea how the Royal Liverpool Philharmonic might play it, but he felt that a young conductor might score a few points with the judges if he could demonstrate his control over so rich and complex a work.

In the course of his preparation of *Petrushka*, Zubin read whatever he could get his hands on about the piece, its composer, the historical backgound—anything that might help him to a clearer understanding of the music and its proper interpretation. This was the way he studied any piece of music.

The more he learned about the tragicomic character of Petrushka, the marionette with human feelings, the more he became fascinated with it as a subject for music. Petrushka was only one of his names, the Russian version; in French he was called Pierrot. It was only a matter of time before Zubin began investigating another musical treatment of the subject, this one by one of Hans Swarowsky's former mentors, Arnold Schönberg.

Zubin found himself discussing Schönberg's *Pierrot Lunaire* with Erwin Ratz, the president of the Mahlergesellschaft, the Mahler Society, in Vienna. Together they evolved a plan for Zubin to conduct a concert of the work, to be sponsored by the Mahler Society. Zubin threw himself into the task, his first job being to recruit the necessary musicians. He required a female voice and five instrumentalists playing eight instruments: one for flute and piccolo, another for clarinet and bass clarinet, another for violin and viola, a cellist, and a pianist.

Pierrot Lunaire is a transitional piece, one of the composer's important atonal works; besides demanding a great deal of the singer and players, it requires enormous concentration on the part of the conductor. The highly expressionistic music is built around twenty-one rather decadent surrealist French poems in German translation. Each song is accompanied by a different instrumental combination, determined by what Schönberg found most appropriate to express the central idea of each poem.

Zubin would work with the violinist for several hours, going over his part measure by measure. Then he would go over the same section with the cellist, then both together, then he would add another instrument. He practiced each part so thoroughly with each group that when they put it all together it worked perfectly.

Carmen remembers watching him rehearse the Swiss contralto who was performing the *Sprechstimme* vocal solo. She was having a difficult time with the intricate canons of the seventeenth and eighteenth songs and was making no secret of her problems.

"She kept saying, 'I'll never do it, I'll never do it.' But Zubin told her, 'When you're nervous or scared, you must never admit that. Never even to yourself, let alone to anyone else.'"

The Mahlergesellschaft hired the Brahmssaal, the small auditorium in the Musikverein where Mehli had given his recital in 1955. They voted also to pay each of the musicians a small fee for the performance, but Zubin did not expect to be paid.

"Come, come," said Erwin Ratz, "you must take a fee. You are a professional conductor now. What shall we pay you?"

Zubin thought for a moment, and then he recalled Ratz speaking of a facsimile of Mahler's original score for *Kindertotenlieder*. Ratz had it under the bed in his tiny apartment, where he kept all the materials and records of the struggling Mahler Society.

"If you can make me a copy of the *Kindertotenlieder*," he said, "I will take that as my fee."

Ratz agreed, and that became Zubin's first earnings as a conductor.

Word of the *Pierrot Lunaire* performance began circulating. The newspapers picked it up, and before long someone realized this would be the first performance of any of Schönberg's music in Vienna since the performances he himself had conducted before the First World War.

Suddenly Zubin and his ad hoc chamber ensemble were celebrities. The concert was a sellout and a critical success. Even the Austrian government took an interest. Zubin's group was asked to make a musical goodwill tour to Italy, in exchange for which the Italian government would send a similar chamber ensemble from Milan to Austria. Conducting the Milanese orchestra would be none other than Claudio Abbado.

So Zubin embarked on his first tour, to Milan and Rome, with a twentieth-century program of Schönberg, Webern, and Stravinsky. Claudio's ensemble tempered Hindemith with the Bach Brandenburg Concerto no. 3.

Never one to shun companionship, Zubin brought Carmen along and encouraged several of the instrumentalists to invite their girlfriends as well. Since the Austrian government was in part sponsoring the tour, these travel arrangements were bound to raise a few eyebrows.

"I'll never forget the look on the face of the head of the Austrian Cultural Institute in Rome as he met us at the railroad station. His name was Egon Hilbert. He looked us over and then, in his stiff Austrian-German, said, 'There will be a reception following the concert. It is taken for granted that the ladies are *not* invited.' Then he went and put us in one of the cheapest, most awful hotels in Rome."

It was fortunate for Zubin that his reputation rested chiefly on his conducting rather than on his flouting of public morals. The concerts in Milan and Rome were applauded as a credit to Austria and to the Academy, as well as to Herr Hilbert's Cultural Institute. This was especially fortunate in that Hilbert was destined soon to become director of the Vienna Music Festival and, later, of the Staatsoper.

Zubin's new facsimile score of *Kindertotenlieder* was soon put to good use when the Jeunesses Musicales invited him to conduct that, along with Beethoven's Symphony no. 5, at the Musikverein. Again, the orchestra would be the Tonkünstler, which, after the Philharmonic and the Vienna Symphony, was the city's third-ranking orchestra.

The audience, mostly young people, was enthusiastic, but the concert turned into the occasion of Zubin's first bad review. At any rate, he considers it bad. The negative comments had to do with the young conductor's too-obvious homage to Herbert von Karajan.

"Mr. Mehta suffers from Karajanitis," the critic wrote.

"That upset me," says Zubin. "Of course, when you observe another human being so closely and you respect him, some of his conducting style is bound to rub off. Just like when you're a kid and you worship your father, so you make your signature like his. I suppose he was right in that criticism. But the man never said anything about the tempi or my handling of the great transition from the third movement to the finale of the Beethoven Fifth."

It may have been a blessing that Hans Swarowsky was no longer in Vienna to see his star pupil falling under the spell of a "showman" conductor like Karajan. Swarowsky had resigned his teaching post to take over music directorship of the Scottish National Orchestra, with which Mehli had spent a few unpleasant months the year before.

It had been Swarowsky's intention, once he was established, to hire Zubin as a bass player and assistant conductor. Meanwhile, he left Zubin in charge of a group he had founded called the Haydn Orchestra.

This organization was to serve two purposes. First, it would keep Swarowsky's foot in Vienna's musical door. Second, it would serve as his entrée into the recording business, since he was in the process of promoting the recording of a complete set of all 104 Haydn symphonies. Zubin was to rehearse the orchestra and to conduct its first public concert in March.

There are conductors who can thrive on a diet of Haydn, but Zubin was not among them. He soon had the orchestra rehearsing pieces from the romantic and post-romantic literature, the music with which he felt most at home.

As March drew near, Swarowsky wrote requesting the program Zubin had chosen for the first concert. The reply came back: Debussy's *Prelude à l'après-midi d'un faune*, a Haydn aria for soprano, a piece for chamber orchestra by Darius Milhaud, and, as the *pièce de résistance*, Brahms's Variations on a Theme by Haydn. It was a nice try.

Swarowsky fired off an angry reply. Zubin could almost hear Swarowsky's voice bellowing with rage as he read, "Not what this orchestra is meant for. Get back to Haydn or else."

Zubin reluctantly changed the program, keeping only the aria from the first foolhardy attempt. He tempered the Haydn-only decree by opening with a Mozart overture and violin concerto. The concluding work was Haydn's *London* Symphony.

The performance at the Konzerthaus went quite well, with excellent notices, redeeming the pupil in the eyes of his master. In those days, unfortunately, Swarowsky could not do as well for Zubin in Glasgow as Zubin had done for him in Vienna.

"When I proposed your name as assistant conductor," Zubin recalls Swarowsky writing him, "the board resisted strongly." The implication was that Zubin was too little experienced and someone with much experience was needed. Zubin speaks of that incident with bitterness today because he is convinced that the main reason for his rejection was his father's olive-coloured skin.

Racial and religious discrimination was becoming a matter of some concern to Zubin. He had seen it affect others, but now it was hitting home. Close on the heels of the snub from Scotland, he was approached by his landlady on the subject of his friend Amnon Zalmonovitz.

"This tall fellow you bring over here sometimes," said the smiling woman, "what's his name?"

"You mean Amnon?"

"Amnon. Yes, that's it." Something was eating away at her façade of pleasantries and conviviality. "Where is this one from?"

"He's from Israel," answered Zubin innocently.

The woman's crinkled smile twisted into a hateful grimace. "A Jew! I thought so."

Zubin was astonished to see her rise from her parlor chair, no longer the accommodating, gentle person he had known.

"I will have no Jews in my house, you understand? No Jews!"

Zubin backed away from her, still too stunned to speak. The next day he found another apartment, even though he would be moving again in only a few weeks, moving in with Carmen at last.

Their summertime separation, their few days together with his family in Manchester, the unsettling encounters with landladies—all this reinforced a longing that was growing steadily in Zubin. He yearned for a woman to come home to, for the life of a family man. He was nearly twenty-two years old. If he waited much longer he was bound to miss out on much of the happiness he saw in his father's life. He could have that sort of life with Carmen, and there would be little argument from her.

"It more or less *happened,* I suppose," says Carmen now. "Zubin decided we'd get married sometime in the spring and I said all right."

Getting the bride to say yes turned out to be the only easy part of the wedding arrangements. Had Zubin trusted his mother's faith in astrology, he might have seen the ensuing complications as portents of the problems that would lie ahead. As it was, he attacked and unraveled Viennese red tape with the determination he applied to a Schönberg score.

To begin with, Austrian law required a civil wedding and Carmen's conviction required a church wedding, so there would have to be two ceremonies. This gave Zubin the opportunity to name two best men, violist Eddie Kudlak and Amnon Zalmonovitz, the Israeli singer.

Setting a date was complicated by the resistance of the Dominican fathers of the Dominicanerkirche, the parish to which Carmen belonged. In the first place, they were not at all certain that "Parsee" was a religion, and, in the second place, canon law in 1958 would permit the couple to be married at the altar only if Zubin converted. Since he had no desire to become a Catholic, Carmen would have to settle for a brief ceremony in the sacristy—provided Zubin would promise to raise any children as Catholics. Zubin agreed, but reserved the right to give them Parsee names.

When the church finally gave them a date in March, the state seemed bent on obstruction. Twenty years later, Carmen could afford to look back in laughter, but it didn't seem so funny at the time.

"After we got the permission from the church, we went to an office to arrange for the civil marriage. Oh, that would be very difficult, the clerk said. It would take him a good three weeks just to arrange the papers. It was obvious that this man was going to make things very difficult. Zubin went back and forth with him. The man said, 'You don't understand,' and he took all his papers and showed them to us, one by one.

"Finally Zubin said, 'Now listen, *Herr Direktor,* we've been here an hour and a half and you've done nothing but show me these papers that are going to take you three weeks. Now let me tell you something. I think that in the time we've been sitting here I could have filled out all these papers myself.'

"For some reason the clerk thought that was very funny. He laughed and laughed. I suppose no one had ever spoken so bluntly before to such a distinguished officer of the government. He decided he would do it. Zubin could always convince people to do things they didn't want to do."

Eventually, the day of the wedding arrived. First there was the civil ceremony, with the six-foot, five-inch Amnon Zalmonovitz towering a foot over his Indian friend as Zubin and Carmen said their *jawohls*. In the confusion Zubin had forgotten the ring and had to borrow a friend's.

Then it was off through a driving snowstorm to the Dominicana-kirche, where about thirty of their friends and professors were squeezed into the sacristy. This time the best man, Eddie Kudlak, was only six feet, three inches tall. After the second ceremony, they all walked to Carmen's one-room apartment, which the newlyweds planned to make their home. There were no gifts to open, since all their friends were just as poor as they were.

"We had sandwiches and cake. That was it. Zubin insisted on having chocolate cake—forget about tradition. He likes chocolate, so we must have chocolate cake. And on the top were these ridiculous little bride and groom figures.

"Zubin had been running around for weeks trying to buy a groom with a black face. That's how he saw himself, you see. But he never could find one. Then out comes the chocolate cake with its little white bride and a groom with his face colored in black shoe polish. It looked like the Moor of Vienna."

The matter of marriage seemed like a lark to Zubin. If he had any notion of the responsibilities it would bring, he managed to keep it to himself. With the hundred-dollar check Carmen's parents sent, he purchased that most basic of newlywed needs, a phonograph.

The few dollars left over were just enough for a one-night honeymoon in the old Imperial Hotel, just recently "liberated" from the Russian sector of the city by the deoccupation treaty. Carmen was afraid the management would suspect them of using the grand old hotel as a trysting place, so she insisted they put on a show of respectability.

Obligingly, Zubin hauled out a suitcase huge enough to hold nearly all his belongings. Into that Carmen placed a neatly folded nightgown, Zubin's pajamas, toothbrushes, and a change of underwear for the morning. The bellboy's astonishment at the feathery weight of this leaden-looking luggage was exceeded only by his disappointment at the tip he received for lugging it to their room.

After that briefest of honeymoons, Zubin looked forward to May, when he would take his beautiful blond bride to England and new fields of conquest. Soon after what he hoped would be a victory in Liverpool, Zubin would be traveling to the United States, for both he and Claudio had been accepted as conducting students in the Berkshire Music Center at Tanglewood, in Massachusetts.

Just when it seemed that everything was going perfectly, a letter arrived from Tehmina with painful news. Zubin's grandfather, to whom he felt so close, had passed away, unable to last even one Manchester winter. The ceremonial *pilaw* Tehmina had prepared, celebrating Zubin's wedding, was the last food to pass the old man's lips. Two days later he was gone.

The family's sorrow was increased by the knowledge that this man who had lived his religion for nearly a hundred years would not receive a Parsee funeral, would not be laid to rest on the *dakhma,* the "tower of silence."

The Parsees believed that neither air, water, earth, nor fire should be contaminated by mortal remains, so they carried the bodies of their dead to the tower, marked on every map of Bombay, just up the shore from where Zubin had swum as a child.

There were always birds there, gulls and kites, like a screaming cloud that hovered above the wooden platforms, where fragments of ancient fabric stuck and blew in the wind. Zubin knew that his grandfather would have wished to be left there to the beaks and talons of the birds, until there was no flesh to contaminate the earth, until his bones could be swept off the platform and finally, crushed by the weight of bone falling upon bone, become no more than dust, his soul free to cross the Kinvad Bridge into eternity.

It was of little comfort to Zubin that his grandfather was not buried in the earth. Mehli and Tehmina had decided to follow Hindu custom since, there being no *dakhmas* in England, there were at least crematoria.

Perhaps it was only fitting, in angst-ridden Vienna, that this time of joy should be so tainted with sorrow. It was no more than another premonition of the difficulties that lay ahead, though neither one was thinking very far into the future, least of all Carmen. How would they live? What if a baby came? The questions never occurred. They were as far from her thoughts as the notion of her husband ever becoming a famous conductor.

"I remember that right after we got married I was talking to a friend of mine, a Norwegian voice student, and she said to me, '*Mein Gott, Carmen, du hast eine gute Gescäft gemacht.*' I'd made a good business deal! As though I had sold a diamond or something.

"I said, 'What do you mean?' And she was really surprised. 'Don't you realize he's going to be a great conductor?' I hadn't thought of it, not at all."

Zubin found Liverpool pretty much as he'd imagined it, a drab, factory-filled place. Yet in the springtime it had a certain British charm about it: the row houses all with their own row gardens, tulips and daffodils opening everywhere, laburnum draped in golden splendor from the welcoming arms of elm trees. It didn't seem like such a bad place to spend a year—providing he won the competition, of course.

His confidence on that score soared when the judges picked *Petrushka* as his first-round selection. More than any other work he'd prepared for this competition, *Petrushka* was the one he'd developed an affinity for. He felt the gods, perhaps even the judges, must be on his side. Not wanting to seem overconfident, however, he conducted the Stravinsky from the score.

"Right from the first I spotted him as the winner," proclaimed the man who was then music director of the Royal Liverpool Philharmonic and director of the competition. "It was perfectly clear to me," says John Pritchard, "that this boy had something special. But when he conducted the Schubert Fifth in the semifinals, my heart sank."

The Englishman was standing in the rear of the orchestra as Zubin strode out to conduct his semifinal test, the third movement of Schubert's Fifth Symphony. This time, confidence soaring, he came out without a score. Things might have gone easier had he brought it along: just placing it unopened on the podium might have refreshed his memory as to the composer's name at least.

John Pritchard knew something was amiss, though he had no idea what. "Zubin started that movement at a very lethargic pace. The musical pulse was lacking and I thought, Well, he's in a mood or in a state or overly nervous."

Zubin's problem was actually quite different from what Pritchard had imagined. He was, in fact, conducting at just the right tempo. But he was conducting the wrong symphony—for the first measure, at any rate.

Schubert's Symphony no. 5 in B-flat was composed according to classical symphony tradition, which stated that the third movement should be a *menuetto,* or minuet, followed by a trio. The tempo of the minuet being left to the composer, Schubert had marked his *allegro molto,* which is a lively pace.

But when Zubin faced the orchestra and raised his arms, he was thinking of another classical symphony, Mozart's Symphony no. 40 in G-minor, which was also on the long list of compositions the Liverpool contestants were supposed to have prepared.

Like the Schubert Fifth, the Mozart no. 40 has a minuet third movement. In fact, the two movements begin in almost identical fashion, with an upbeat to a downbeat, and with the same interval between the two opening notes. A young conductor in his first competition might be forgiven if he confused the two.

Unfortunately, whereas Schubert's tempo is *allegro molto,* Mozart's minuet is marked a significantly slower *allegretto.* Zubin heard Schubert's music at Mozart's tempo and, "I said to myself, 'My God, what am I doing?' It was coming out all wrong."

As soon as he reached the second beat of the first measure, Zubin realized his mistake. But once launched on the "lethargic pace" he had no choice but to continue that way until one of the judges might suggest he begin again. He saw the pained expression on the face of John Pritchard, knew that William Steinberg and the other judges must be having a good laugh out in the hall at his expense. But no one said a word. They let him go on until finally he reached the end of the movement. He walked offstage, agonizing over what he would tell his father, who had put up the hard-earned money for him to come all this way and conduct the wrong piece of music.

He felt John Pritchard's hand on his shoulder and heard the Englishman's voice ask, "Why on earth did you *do* that?"

On the verge of tears, Zubin moved away, saying brokenly, "Why on earth didn't you stop me?"

Perhaps there is something to be said for taking the minuet of Schubert's Fifth at a snail's pace. After all, coaches and commentators use slow-motion videotape to analyze a football player's technique and execution, so why not the same approach for judges of conducting competitions? At any rate, the judges were not moved to ridicule. In fact, when the names of the three finalists were read out, Zubin Mehta's was among them.

There was a packed house for the final, public concert. Mehli could not be there—he was off on the Hallé's first tour to eastern Europe—but Tehmina and Carmen had seats in the rear of the hall. There was a third seat saved for Zarin, but, this being the day of his intermediate accounting exam in London, there was little hope of his catching the last possible train to Liverpool. Then, just as Zubin made his entrance, his brother eased into the seat, out of breath from running.

Zarin squeezed his sister-in-law's hand for encouragement, but she only smiled nervously as Zubin bowed and stepped to the podium, again without a score. Why, Carmen wondered, had they given him something as worn and weatherbeaten as Beethoven's Fifth to conduct? What could he do with it that anyone with a record player and a baton couldn't manage almost as well? It was as though the judges had already made up their minds that one of the others would get the prize. Carmen was almost shocked to hear Steinberg announce her husband as the winner.

In the ensuing two decades, Zubin has had a lot of time to go over that symphony and to think about the way he conducted it in Liverpool that night. He never has to go much beyond the opening measures to decide what made him win.

"There are two kinds of human beings in this world," he says, with

Zubin's first portrait, as a child of three in Bombay.

With his "little brother," child prodigy Daniel Barenboim, thirteen, in Siena, Italy, 1956.

Hans Swarowsky's conducting class at the Vienna Academy, 1956. Directly behind Zubin, at his left shoulder, is Claudio Abbado; in front is Maestro Swarowsky.

Zubin's first rehearsal with the New York Philharmonic at Lewisohn Stadium, 1960.

The Montreal Symphony's first tour under its new music director, Leningrad, 1962.

An elated Daniel Barenboim embraces Zubin after the Six-Day War Victory Concert in Jerusalem, 1967.

An unorthodox *chupah*-bearer, "Moshe Cohen," in the wedding of Jacqueline du Pré and Daniel Barenboim, 1967.

An historic performance in Manger Square, Bethlehem, in 1968. Verdi's Requiem, with (*left to right*) Martina Arroyo, Shirley Verrett, Richard Tucker, and Bonaldo Giaiotti.

Artur Rubinstein's conducting "debut" under the watchful eye of the Israel Philharmonic's other conductor, Tel Aviv, 1969.

Music for peace, a volunteer concert on the U.C.L.A. campus, 1970.

The Israel Philharmonic under its first music director, in Mann Auditorium, Tel Aviv, 1972.

Worshipping at the Parsee fire temple on his first return to Bombay, 1967.

Photograph by Eugene Cook

Staging rehearsal at the old Met.

Photograph by Eugene Cook

After his Metropolitan Opera debut, Zubin is congratulated by Mr. and Mrs. Artur Rubinstein and Madame Pandit, the Indian ambassador to the United States, as Franco Corelli (as Radames) looks on.

creases at the corners of his eyes to let you know a joke is coming. "There are those who make breaks after the fermatas in Beethoven's Fifth and those who do not. I am one of the latter."

Anyone who has had musical training will know that a fermata is the symbol that indicates a note, chord, or rest is to be held longer than its assigned value. In the opening *da-da-da-daaa*s of Beethoven's Fifth Symphony, there is a fermata over each of the *daaa*s, filling up a measure of two-four time. The next measure, in each case, begins with an eighth rest, followed by the eighth-note triplet that constitutes the *da-da-da* part of the all-too-familiar phrase. The question is whether or not to stop between the fermata and the eighth rest. Simplified, it comes down to how long a conductor waits between one *daaa* and the next *da*.

No doubt all this seems like the tiniest teacup that ever held a tempest, but it is on just such minutiae that the careers of conductors are made and broken. For that reason, if for no other, Zubin's own explanation is worth listening to.

"Practically the entire first movement of the Fifth Symphony is made of four-bar periods, with each bar consisting of one beat. Now, if you break off after one of those fermatas, you're adding a beat—in effect inserting an extra bar of music. That is, in my mind, a mistake.

"In fact, when I rehearse the Beethoven Fifth first movement with an orchestra for the first time, I don't start at the beginning. To make the players feel the four-bar period, I start toward the end of the exposition, then go back. And it comes naturally to them.

"Now, in the romantic times, toward the turn of the century, they took these fermatas ad libitum. But there are no ad libitum fermatas in classical music. There are a lot of people who understand that, who hold the fermata for the metrical time, but then they go and cut it off before they go on to the next beat, and *that's* what I learned not to do in Vienna, from Swarowsky. And Steinberg must have agreed and said, 'Ah! First prize.'"

Whether or not all those things occurred to Zubin when he heard his name called out is doubtful. As for Carmen, "My only thought was, Thank God." Tehmina rushed out to send a cable to her husband.

The telegram was waiting at the desk for Mehli when the Hallé Orchestra players arrived at their hotel in Prague. His hands were shaking as he tore open the envelope.

"Zubin wins competition!" he read, his high-pitched voice sounding almost girlish in his excitement.

Sir John Barbirolli, swaddled in layers of sweaters and scarves, pulled the telegram from Mehli's hands and began showing it around to the orchestra. "Look here!" he shouted, "Mehli's son is after my job."

Mehli dashed to a telephone and called home to receive confirmation from Tehmina, who put Zubin on the line. It was as good a moment as there would ever be, Zubin decided, to break the other news. After all, now he had a job and a steady income to count on.

"Yes, Daddy, they gave me the first prize. We'll be moving right near to you and Mommy now."

"That's wonderful news, darling. I'm very proud of you."

"And, guess what else, Daddy."

"What? Tell me."

"Carmen is pregnant."

Tehmina's jaw in Manchester and Mehli's jaw in Prague dropped as one. Though they had grown to love Carmen as their own daughter, and had even convinced themselves that the astrologer must have been wrong about this marriage not lasting, they had prayed that Carmen and Zubin would wait to start a family.

Their greatest concern for their son in those days was that he would have no means of earning a living. Had he pursued a career as a violinist, there would always be an opening for him in some orchestra somewhere. He often joked about joining a bass section—in fact, this had once been his plan—but Mehli and Tehmina could see that he no longer thought of himself as anything but a conductor.

To conduct, one required an entire orchestra, and what Western city would be inclined to trust its orchestra to a young unknown from Bombay? The Liverpool assistantship was a good beginning, but what about when the year was over? What sort of security could Zubin offer a wife, let alone a wife and child?

Zubin did little to set his parents' minds at ease when, after getting Carmen registered in the National Health Service in Manchester, he borrowed the money she'd saved and bought an airplane ticket for the United States. Expectant father or no, Zubin had to open a door when opportunity knocked. And he thought he heard opportunity knocking at Tanglewood.

Mehli Mehta's introduction to the United States in 1945 had been a sort of culture shock, as a man whose entire life had been spent in India was suddenly swept up in the unsympathetic currents of New York City. For Zubin, thirteen years later, the first meeting was almost too good to be true. He had not imagined that an American music festival and summer academy could be held in surroundings as idyllic as those at Tanglewood.

The Berkshire Festival, as it is formally called, was launched in 1934—and not, as most people today suppose, by Bostonians, but by New Yorkers. Its first orchestra was not the Boston Symphony Orchestra but the New York Philharmonic under Henry Hadley, rushed to the

Berkshire retreat after its concerts at Lewisohn Stadium. Even today, though the festival is considered an outgrowth of Boston's musical life, it is New York that supplies the largest part of its crowds each year. Yet Tanglewood is physically and spiritually a New England experience.

Zubin and Claudio Abbado found themselves in a setting that nature seemed to have intended for the making of music. From rolling lawns they looked out over tranquil Lake Mahkeenac, like liquid crystal gathered in the bottom of a mountain bowl. At one end of the 210-acre estate was the Music Shed, where the Boston Symphony performed, at the other end the Theater, where they would rehearse and conduct the student orchestra.

The student musicians, nearly four hundred strong, were gathered through auditions held by the Boston Symphony in cities all across the country; others, like Zubin, came from abroad on the recommendation of recognized authorities in the international music world.

Zubin was immediately impressed by these so-called students; the Berkshire Music Center Orchestra was as good as or better than many of the professional orchestras he had heard in Europe. Coupled with the expertise the young musicians had gained in the best conservatories and music schools was a vitality, an enthusiam for music that was undimmed by the disenchantments of the professional musician's life. "It was," he says, "an exhilarating experience for me."

There were eight young conductors, studying primarily under Eleazar de Carvalho of Brazil (later of the St. Louis Symphony). Ostensibly, they were also under the guidance of the Boston Symphony's music director and ex officio chief of the Berkshire Music Center, Charles Munch. However, Munch cared little for the administrative workings of the school and concentrated instead on the performances of his own orchestra, as well as on his golf game at the Stockbridge Country Club.

"I had really hoped to get to know Munch. The Boston Symphony sounded glorious under him and also under Pierre Monteux, who was there as guest conductor. But it seemed as though Munch was impossible to meet. He just never paid much attention to the students.

"He would sometimes come to rehearsals and just sit there, and every now and then he would scream at us or at the members of the orchestra. Claudio he ignored completely, but he did say something to me once. He yelled at me, 'Put your feet together!' That was the only instruction he ever gave me."

Much later, Zubin discovered that Charles Munch had indeed been paying very close attention to the young man from India who stood with his feet apart, but at Tanglewood Zubin's compliments came only from less influential sources.

In fact, the Tanglewood crowd of 1958 was buzzing with gossip about the amazing crop of young conductors. Not the visitors, of course, who came with their picnic suppers to commune with nature and to hear the Boston Symphony under the stars. But the students, at the beach and in the dormitories, discussed the prodigious talent evident in Zubin Mehta, Claudio Abbado, and David Zinman (who would go on to conduct the Netherlands Chamber Orchestra and the Rochester Philharmonic). The orchestra members were particularly impressed with Zubin's handling of Richard Strauss's *Don Juan* and Schönberg's Chamber Symphony.

At least two members of the faculty were also impressed. One of them was conductor-pianist Seymour Lipkin, who remembers, "It was obvious that there was really somebody there, a big, big talent. And I, well, I just filed it away." The other faculty member was Lukas Foss, of the composition department at the Music Center.

Under Serge Koussevitzky, Foss had been a member of another distinguished Tanglewood conducting class, that of 1940, which included Thor Johnson, Richard Bales, and Leonard Bernstein. Foss had been seventeen then; now he was thirty-five, a familiar face at Tanglewood and an accomplished musician who had learned to recognize talent when he saw it.

"I have my own definition of a conductor's job," says Foss. "First, he must be a detective, finding the trouble spots at rehearsals; then he must be a doctor, diagnosing the trouble and finally curing it. That makes a good conductor. It usually takes many years to learn, but Zubin had that from the start, which seemed incredible to me.

"On top of that he had charisma, the commanding personality it takes to work with others and get them to do their jobs. He got results. He had enthusiasm, which of course many young people have, but in him it was coupled with a natural talent and technical skill. That was rare."

Zubin spent six weeks in the Berkshires, totally immersed in music. He worked with students and professionals in interpretation, technique, and theory. He worked in studios in the gabled Main House, in the East and West Barns, in unfinished sheds scattered about the grounds, in the rehearsal hall, which consisted of a stage and no space for an audience.

One of the great lessons of Tanglewood for Zubin was the value of ensemble playing in an orchestra. The string students were together virtually every moment of the day, as were the winds, the brass, and the percussionists. Communication, awareness of the other members, "team spirit"—these things came about of themselves and produced an ensemble sound that could not help but be appreciated by the audience. On the bulletin board backstage at the Theater, someone had posted a sign that read, "Remember, the Orchestra That Plays Together Stays Together." The sign was still there in 1976.

At the end of the second week in August, the festival was over and prizes were awarded. In the conducting class, the first-place Koussevitzky Prize went to Claudio Abbado, while Zubin won the runner-up Gertrude Robinson Smith Prize.

After the awards presentation, Zubin found himself sitting in the cafeteria with Lukas Foss, who complimented him highly on his work with the student orchestra. Zubin thanked the older man, but there was a sadness in his dark eyes. He had hoped that, somehow, something would come of his Tanglewood experience, that Tanglewood would lead to something greater, as the Liverpool competition had. Now that he appreciated the potential of American orchestras—as demonstrated by the Berkshire students—Zubin hated to leave the United States without establishing some more permanent connection.

Finally he looked at the composer and said, "Lukas, what am I to do? Everybody says I am good and nobody *does* anything." Zubin was complaining to the right man.

Foss had been trained as a composer and a conductor by Serge Koussevitzky, the man who brought the Boston Symphony to preeminence. Koussevitzky was famous for his discovery of and friendship toward young musicians, a talent he passed on to his protégé.

"I suppose," says the composer, "that it doesn't really take talent to discover talent—all it takes is a little generosity and knowledge. Anyway, when Zubin spoke to me like that I said to myself, 'So nobody does anything . . . let's do something.'"

So Lukas Foss—who prides himself on his hand in the early careers of composer George Crumb and conductor Michael Tilson Thomas—got up from the table, went to a telephone, and called his manager in New York. "It's funny," he says, "I never really paid much attention to management. I just composed and took whatever conducting jobs came along. But I could tell that this was someone who could benefit from a good manager."

Foss's manager was Siegfried Hearst, a native of Germany, who for a number of years was the man in charge of conductors at National Concert Artists Corporation. A short, permanently vested man who could be as effusive with clients as he was brusque with artists, Hearst was in a somewhat defensive position as an artist's representative.

Much of the nation's orchestral work was born in New York, and for many years New York's musical life had been literally in the hands of Hearst's rival, Arthur Judson. As manager of the New York Philharmonic, Judson had controlled the most prestigious platform in America; as head of Columbia Artists, he had decided who stood on that platform. For a conductor not under Judson's aegis, work was seldom easy to come by.

Hearst was understandably reluctant to take on any new talent. "Listen," he said to Foss, "I can't bother with any students." And he hung up. Undaunted, Foss called him right back.

"It took three or four phone calls, but I was determined Siegfried was going to do something for this man. I pestered him and I badgered him until he finally said, 'Okay, okay, if it's the only way I can get rid of you, send him to see me.'"

On his way to the airport in New York, Zubin stopped at the address Lukas Foss had given him and was ushered into Siegfried Hearst's private office. The manager looked over the materials Zubin had with him, then asked about his previous experience and his musical background.

In all, the meeting lasted about twenty minutes, and at the end Hearst rose from his desk and stepped toward a window. "Look," he said in his thick accent, "I will confess I don't know that much about you, I have been to not even one of your concerts. But I think maybe everything is going to be all right with you. We don't need to sign contracts or anything like that. You just go on to Liverpool and do your work there and you will be hearing from me."

4

Stepmother
England

The flight to London was long and choppy but, for Zubin, no more
than a brief, smooth soaring above the clouds and into a stratosphere of
great expectations. A manager in New York. An orchestra in Liverpool.
Something of a name already in Vienna. There seemed to be no limits to
what he could accomplish, and it would be on a grand, international
scale.

The train ride north from London was something else again. There
were more questions than cows grazing in the tedium of the English
countryside.

How many concerts would he actually conduct? The contract had left
the number unspecified; perhaps there would be only one. Would he be
allowed to choose his own repertoire? From everything he'd read, there
seemed to be great variances in taste between Maestro John Pritchard
and himself. Would he be able to work harmoniously with the musicians
of the Royal Liverpool Philharmonic? He had assigned their aloof, pa-
tronizing attitude to a professional reluctance to be involved in competitions, but would they now accept him as a professional?

He met Carmen at his parents' flat in Manchester and they went on to
Liverpool, about an hour away by train, Zubin talking the whole way of

his experiences in America while growing more and more uneasy about the adventure ahead.

Perhaps it was the weather that made him see Liverpool in a different light the second time around. The encroaching gray of autumn gave the place a bare, monochromatic look it hadn't worn in May. Approaching the city, there were no flowers to be seen, no cheery buds on the hawthorn and lilac, no golden branches of laburnum. Blocks of dour flats flashed by, looking to Zubin like rows of condemned prisoners.

The towers of the Royal Liver building and the two cathedrals loomed above the city. Amid the clutter of residential, commercial, and institutional buildings he saw strange empty spaces, as though limbs or growths had been hacked away and never replaced.

He knew, of course, that the city had been bombed and burned during the war, that it was still in the process of reconstruction, but he felt none of Vienna's spirit of renaissance in the air.

Zubin saw in Liverpool an amalgamation of Bombay and Vienna. There was a certain vitality about the place, as well as an international feeling, as there had been in Bombay. One could walk the busy streets of the shipping district and hear smatterings of conversations in languages ranging from Chinese to Portuguese.

Liverpool was as consumingly commercial as Bombay, but it had none of the alternative charm of the city of his birth, none of the colors. The saris of paisley silk, the saffron robes of the swamis, the burkas of lavender, pea green, and maroon swirling among shades of white and fawn and oatmeal—these were replaced by gray work clothes, gray business suits, gray dresses, all lost against a backdrop of gray-black buildings. The architecture of Liverpool itself was a confusion of old and new, pre-Victorian and postwar, with no equivalent of Vienna's rococo obsession to lace it all together.

How such a place had come to have its own orchestra, and one with so pretentious a name as the Royal Liverpool Philharmonic, Zubin could not understand. Perhaps his burgeoning prejudices were nothing more than his own insecurities rising to the surface, a thing he could ill afford at so crucial a stage in his career. So, imprisoning any doubts he might have in the deepest dungeon of his soul, Zubin girded himself in the self-assurance that was his only armor and reported to John Pritchard.

In the early stages of their meeting, Zubin's positivism appeared to be paying off. He was to spend a good deal of time rehearsing the orchestra, said the maestro. He was to conduct not one but twenty concerts over the season, some in Liverpool and some "on tour." If all went well, Zubin would be invited back for another season as guest conductor, perhaps even as an associate.

The season was scheduled to begin in only a few weeks, and the music director was quite busy finalizing programs and meeting with the board.

So would Mr. Mehta be so kind as to work up with the orchestra a few of the pieces he, Pritchard, would be conducting in the first series of concerts?

Zubin tensed in his chair. He had seen this happen a few times in Vienna, the conductor leaving the preparation of his concerts to his assistant. Invariably this would involve a work the orchestra had played so many times that everybody—the conductor, the musicians, probably even the audience—was tired of hearing it. How could an inexperienced assistant conductor breathe new life into a work under those circumstances?

He watched Pritchard reach into his file cabinet with the sinking expectation that whatever scores he pulled out would already be in Zubin's collection, well marked and well worn from hours of study at the Vienna Academy. He needn't have worried on that account.

Pritchard handed him three scores, all looking brand new and free from the prejudicial scribblings of conductors long departed. It was immediately apparent that there was no *Surprise* Symphony or *Academic Festival Overture* in the batch.

They were, in fact, three scores Zubin had never seen. Only one of them, Richard Strauss's tone poem *Ein Heldenleben,* had he even heard. The other two, Edward Elgar's First Symphony and Arnold Schönberg's Variations for Orchestra, he had only heard of.

"Not to worry," assured the music director, showing Zubin to the door. The orchestra had played the Elgar a few years back, and recently they'd made something of a specialty of the modern stuff in their Musica Viva concerts, so neither the Strauss nor the Schönberg ought to give them much trouble. Zubin walked out of the meeting not knowing whether to laugh or to cry.

What was he supposed to make out of these scores in the few days of rehearsal allotted? There was barely time enough for him to learn them, much less teach them to the orchestra. He took the scores to his dingy flat and buried himself in them, letting Carmen serve his meals wherever she could find room on the table.

There was no time for historical research, no time for discovering what had influenced the composer in his writing or what his intentions had been. There was no time for anything but making whatever sense one could out of the notes on the page.

The Elgar, he saw soon enough, was late romanticism, with perhaps a good deal to recommend it had one the opportunity to interpret its nuances properly. The *Heldenleben* was a gigantic, epic triumph of postromanticism, of course. The sort of thing that was bread and butter for the Viennese. How the Royal Liverpudlians would play it, Zubin could not be certain.

The Schönberg was another matter altogether. Zubin saw little chance, in the time permitted, to come to grips with it himself, let alone instill its finer points in the musicians. It would certainly take the greatest amount of work of the three, and would require every ounce of cooperation from the orchestra. He soon learned that cooperation was one thing he could not assume from the Royal Liverpool Philharmonic.

From the outset he felt some orchestra members treated him as their inferior, giving him none of the respect a conductor requires from his players. Today, Zubin looks back on the experience with regret.

"I started very badly with the orchestra," he admits. "They really didn't seem to like me very much, and it wasn't their fault. I don't know, maybe it was Schönberg's fault. It all started when Mr. Pritchard gave me those Variations to conduct. It is something you simply don't give to an assistant on such short notice.

"I have discovered a great deal about that piece since then. I have discovered it is the hardest piece I know for orchestra, for a conductor to get together musically and hold together. Lenny Bernstein told me I was out of my mind when I took it on tour many years later with the Israel Philharmonic, though we had played it together by then so much that we were really actually *interpreting* it, as though it were the Beethoven Fifth or something. That, I must say, was a real accomplishment.

"But in 1958 I didn't know it nor could I prepare the orchestra for it. And the orchestra knew I had no place attempting it. Today I can listen to it as a normal piece of music, but at that time I simply did not have those sounds in my ears."

Rehearsing the Variations for Orchestra was just the beginning of what has proved to be a less than satisfying relationship between Zubin and the musical "system" of England.

He discovered that Pritchard and the Royal Liverpool Philharmonic had become known as specialists in music of the early twentieth century, the sort of music that might be described as "safe modern." Their recent concerts had included a number of works by Schönberg, Berg, and Webern.

This sort of specialization was a hallmark of music in England. Each orchestra and each conductor was expected to include a certain type of music on every program, which music became the "specialty" of that orchestra or conductor. The result, often enough, was that, as long as one stayed within the bounds of one's specialty, approval was assured.

"I didn't understand the English then, I guess, because it all seemed very much like snobbishness to me."

Though Zubin was to have later experiences that would contradict his own bias against "the English bias," at the time circumstances seemed to be conspiring against him in Liverpool. He saw himself as a twenty-two-year-old apprentice trying to drum into a hostile orchestra a piece as potentially bewildering as the Schönberg Variations, the first strictly twelve-tone composition ever written for orchestra and the first he had ever tackled, a piece full of rebellion against established order and accepted forms.

Under these circumstances, Zubin took his reluctant orchestra to such "important music centers" as Bedford, Rochdale, and Sheffield, traveling by bus through dots on the map with curious names: Newton le Willows, Snake Inn, Ashton under Lyne, and Ramsbottom. In fact, he spent more time traveling with the orchestra than rehearsing them.

"They would give me concerts to do, often with only one rehearsal, a program like the *Forza* Overture, the adagietto of Mahler's Fifth Symphony, the Glazunov Violin Concerto, and the Tchaikovsky Sixth Symphony—in one rehearsal. I said, I must have more time. They said, We have no other time. I said, Make simpler programs."

The one-rehearsal problem was only for the handful of concerts Zubin actually conducted in Liverpool. In the coal mining and manufacturing towns, where presumably the audience mattered less, Zubin was allowed to pick things both he and the orchestra knew, so that each "provincial" concert might not require its own full rehearsal. This tactic led to another problem for Zubin.

"The orchestra manager had a mania for *timing* in concerts. Every program must be the proper length. He didn't seem to believe that content and substance are as important as getting out of the hall on time. He wanted every concert to be exactly two hours and twenty minutes long."

Consequently, when a concert program was drawn up that came out to less than the prescribed length, the orchestra manager would suggest he stretch it out with his favorite old warhorse.

"He would say to me, in that accent of his, 'A bit shawt, are we? Well, why don't we put in an Oye-neigh Kloy-neigh? That should fill it up just fine.' So there was bound to be something like an *Eine Kleine Nachtmusik* in every concert."

Then there was the incident of the Late Lulu.

It happened during one of Pritchard's Musica Viva concerts. He had programmed the Orchestral Suite from Alban Berg's *Lulu,* which is sometimes performed with soprano aria and a piercing scream from the heroine. Pritchard dispensed with the aria, but he wanted the scream. Any woman could have done the backstage shriek, but he hired a beautiful actress for the occasion. Zubin's job was to cue the young woman at the appropriate point. The music builds to a climax, stops, the girl screams, and the music continues.

"But that girl was so beautiful," Zubin says, laughing, "I just got enraptured with her and started flirting with her backstage."

On the night of the concert, the music built to the climax, stopped, and . . . silence. It is doubtless difficult for a girl to scream while in the arms of a charming young assistant conductor.

Suddenly Zubin became aware of the absence of music. He looked up and saw Pritchard glaring in his direction. Pushing the girl away, he hissed, "Scream!" As so often happens when opera is heard and not seen, the audience missed the best part of the action.

Today John Pritchard maintains that he and Zubin had a very close, personal relationship in Liverpool, but Zubin feels he did not receive the guidance he required from his own music director, and searched elsewhere.

Whenever he could manage a few days off, he would board a train for Glasgow and Hans Swarowsky. He would take along any scores he happened to be working on and go over them measure for measure with his old teacher, the man who ranks second only to his father in influencing Zubin's early career.

His father, of course, was an even shorter train ride away, just under an hour. Zubin began spending less and less time in Liverpool and more and more time in Manchester, where he could be near Sir John Barbirolli as well.

As Zubin's dissatisfaction with the situation in Liverpool grew, so too did his enchantment with this venerable British conductor who had taken over the New York Philharmonic from Toscanini and who then went on to save the Hallé Orchestra from almost certain extinction.

The warehouselike building in which the Hallé rehearsed was, in Zubin's words, "an awful dump, right next to the railroad tracks. When the weather was warm, which it luckily seldom was, we would have to open the windows, and the smoke from the trains would blow in. In the wintertime we didn't open anything, but the wind blew in anyway. It was like an icebox in there. But I learned to love it."

A characteristically friendly man who believed strongly in the importance of close family ties, Sir John admired the obvious affection between Zubin and his father, who had become a trusted and important member of the violin section of the Hallé Orchestra.

"He adored my father, who by then was sitting right there in the front row of the first violins. Of course Barbirolli loved to take all the credit for his playing; he said my father learned it all from him. But he treated my father like a younger brother, and he immediately went out of his way to become friendly with me. He took me under his wing and taught me a great deal."

Yet, as Zubin sat in the drafty hall, absorbing Barbirolli's expertise, he became aware of a strange aura of disrespect that rose from the orchestra, no matter how lovely their playing might sound.

"Barbirolli was fantastic, a great conductor and a great man, but he seemed unappreciated there. Some of his musicians would talk back to him. That really incensed me. I knew I would never let a musician treat me like that.

"It didn't seem to bother Barbirolli. He was somehow above it all and cajoled the orchestra as though nothing had happened."

Zubin knew that his father felt unappreciated in the Hallé organization. Mehli corresponded regularly with his old teacher, Ivan Galamian, in New York, and in his letters there was always the question, "When are you going to find me a position in the United States?" Around the house they talked often of North America, and Mehli insisted that one day he would be playing his violin there, perhaps even in Philadelphia, but it was for Zubin, not Mehli, that North American opportunity knocked.

Zubin had all but given up on getting any work through his manager in New York when a cablegram arrived from Siegfried Hearst's office informing him that he was to conduct a radio concert of the Canadian Broadcasting Corporation Orchestra in March of 1959. That was hard enough to believe, but upon reading further Zubin discovered that the fee for this concert was to be five hundred dollars, no expenses paid. That wouldn't begin to cover his expenses. How was he supposed to get to Toronto?

At his father's suggestion, Zubin went to London to see Mrs. Vijaya Lakshmi Pandit, the High Commissioner for India and a sister of Nehru's. Mrs. Pandit received him warmly, having heard an Indian had won the international conducting competition in Liverpool. When Zubin explained his plight, the lady did not even pause to consider, nor to indulge in any of the red tape so natural to embassies.

"I couldn't believe it," says Zubin. "I just told her what I wanted, and she said, 'So, of course.' They paid for my entire trip. I'll never forget that."

There was still the matter of taking time off in March from his duties in Liverpool. What with travel and rehearsals, he had better ask for two weeks. The orchestra's manager came back with word that Mr. Pritchard did not mind if Zubin took off a week in March, the next-to-last month of his assistantship.

Since there was not much time to prepare a program and send it to the Canadian Broadcasting Corporation for approval, Zubin had to act quickly. There would be a pianist to perform the Beethoven C-minor Concerto. Something to open with, an overture perhaps, but nothing ordinary or in any way lightweight—there couldn't be anything of the student about him. The Brahms *Tragic Overture* was agreed upon for the opening. And for the featured work, something he knew, something the orchestra knew, yet not something the Canadian radio audience would know too well. Running down the list of works in the CBC Symphony's catalogue, he was delighted to find *Petrushka*. Not something one expects from a young conductor trying to make a good first impression, perhaps, but it had done the trick for him at the Liverpool competition. *Petrushka* it would be.

In the meantime, there was still the matter of finishing out his time with the Royal Liverpool Philharmonic. Among his remaining concerts was Tchaikovsky's Sixth Symphony, the *Pathétique*. It was during a rehearsal of this work that Zubin received a call from Manchester informing him that Carmen had given birth.

"I was working with the orchestra for a performance the following evening when I got the phone call. I had a daughter! First I felt so happy, then I was miserable because I could not rush to my wife's side. What could I do? I couldn't afford to let the orchestra go because it was my only rehearsal. Naturally. So I finished it off as quickly as I could and got on the next train for Manchester.

"I found my wife in one of these huge rooms, one of the horrors of socialized medicine, and there were about twenty beds all in a circle, with some women moaning in different stages of labor. Others, like my wife, were just coming out of the anesthesia.

"But where was my baby? I looked and looked and I couldn't find my child anywhere. In the big room where they kept all the babies, there was none named Mehta. I couldn't find my child anywhere. I began frantically looking through all the rooms, one after another, becoming more disturbed and more angry.

"Finally, in a small room off by itself, I found one little baby, all alone, crying. She was still covered with blood, and the cord was still attached to her. I found this card with my name on it. That's how I saw my child for the first time.

"For the first time in my life I knew what it was to be truly a victim of discrimination. In England, everybody knew that a child named Mehta must be an Indian. Maybe my thoughts on what I saw as discrimination were founded or unfounded. Maybe today I would take it differently. But that's how I took it then.

"I picked that child up in my arms and I ran out of that room into the hall, screaming at the top of my voice. Finally I found a nurse—and all she said was, 'Don't you know you're not supposed to be in here? Visiting hours are not for another fifteen minutes!'

"Well, they tried to make me leave, but I wouldn't go until they washed off the baby, cut off her cord, and brought her in to her mother. Then I went out to calm down. That was a rather traumatic experience, my first child."

The next morning Zubin returned to Liverpool, thinking of anything but the Tchaikovsky Sixth. By the evening's performance, his thoughts were still a long way from the work at hand.

The *Pathétique* requires a good deal of pulling together if the whole is to be greater than the sum of its parts. The bombast, the self-pity, the vulgarities and sentimentalities will prick away at the overall strength and beauty of the work if a conductor lets it get away from him, which is precisely what happened to Zubin that night. It turned into possibly the worst concert of his career.

"It was a terrible concert," he recalls with a groan, "just awful. I shudder to think what might have happened if I'd not had at least the one night between the birth of my daughter and the playing of that symphony."

Fortunately, neither the baby nor the symphony suffered any permanent damage from their neglectful treatment. Zarina—named after Zarin, of course—was a healthy little girl who went a long way toward getting Zubin's mind off the barbs he was suffering in Liverpool from both the musicians and the critics.

After Zarina was born, they moved back into the flat in Liverpool, where they received a visit from Carmen's parents. The Laskys were meeting their son-in-law as well as their granddaughter for the first time.

Zubin's buoyant candor charmed his in-laws as it did nearly everyone with whom he came into contact. Yet Carmen's father was uneasy about the marriage. Left alone with his wife, Lasky confided, "I must say, I like her fellow quite a lot. But I have a feeling it's not going to last."

Not long afterward, Zarin came to Liverpool for a look at his niece and namesake. Mr. and Mrs. Lasky were impressed by the comfortable, warm relationship that seemed to exist between brother and sister-in-law. In fact, Zarin made a deep impression on Carmen's parents.

The Laskys ended their visit and returned to Saskatoon, well in time to switch on their radio and listen to their son-in-law conduct the CBC Orchestra from Toronto. In Montreal the broadcast was heard by Zubin's old friends Eugene Husaruk and Eddie Kudlak, now both members of the Montreal Symphony Orchestra. Zubin had no time for reunions with family or friends, since it was a brief stay, crammed with rehearsals. But he did have time to extend his high opinion of United States orchestras to include those of Canada, although his first contact was not one to inspire confidence in a young conductor.

"I arrived at the theater alone and walked in the back just as the musicians were coming in and taking their instruments out of the cases. Of course nobody knew who I was. As I passed two violinists, one of them said to the other, 'Well, who's waving the wood today?'

"Waving the wood! I thought, Oh boy, they must really have no respect at all for conductors around here. I just wasn't used to that blasé attitude. Fortunately, the attitude vanished the moment they started to play.

"I suppose it took a lot of *chutzpah* for me to conduct the *Petrushka,* even though I knew that piece pretty well by that time. I don't think the musicians were expecting me to conduct it with such authority, and they were terribly impressed. I felt as though the people there appreciated what I could do. The concert went off very well, and I went away with a good feeling.

"It was morally refreshing for me to conduct like that after a year of giving second-rate concerts in Liverpool."

The Toronto concert was the high point in what had been a notably inauspicious first season for a young conductor. Even Zubin's few moments of happiness—Zarina's birth, attending Barbirolli's rehearsals— were tainted with bitterness. Looking back on the year, he could find very little good to say about it.

"The circumstances in Liverpool were all wrong, from beginning to end. It was supposed to be a stepping stone for me, but I knew it wouldn't take me anywhere.

"It must be pointed out that I really was not prepared, not experienced enough to handle an orchestra with so little rehearsal time, even though most programs consisted of the standard repertoire.

"All in all, their system of churning out concerts, coupled with my complete ineptness at rehearsing quickly, resulted in mostly quite mediocre music making."

Carmen seemed not to understand Zubin's dissatisfaction with Liverpool. Perhaps he was simply taking his own advice, not letting anyone see how upset he was.

"If he had any worries," she says, "he never voiced them to me. As his wife, I was unaware that he was having any difficulties in Liverpool."

Clearly, the sharing of musical experience that had brought them together was no longer a staple of their life. Even if Zubin had wanted to burden Carmen with his career decisions, she had problems enough of her own, caring for the baby.

Considering the financial pressures, Zubin might have agreed to put up with another season in Liverpool for the sake of an income. However, Destiny was hurrying him out of England with no more ado than his arrival had caused.

Nearly twenty years later, the two conductors, Mehta and Pritchard, would look back on that Liverpool season of 1958–59 from quite different vantage points. In the course of those two decades, the pupil has outdistanced the master in terms of public recognition, and to Pritchard, if not to Zubin, that success is due in some small part to the experience he gained as an assistant.

"I'm sure he did learn a good deal about the repertory," says Pritchard. "He was quick at it and so on. But," he continues, "I must be frank. The talent of Zubin Mehta didn't really need that year with the Royal Liverpool Philharmonic."

Confronted with that statement, Zubin shakes his head and says, "If you must know, I was not good enough for some of those things he threw at me. How would he know anyway? I don't think he attended one of my concerts."

"I often attended his concerts," counters the Englishman. "Why, I remember particularly a Beethoven Seventh he did very early on. That symphony is very difficult for young conductors, but Zubin did a marvelous job of it."

"I conducted my first Beethoven Seventh in 1961," Zubin says, "two years after I left Liverpool."

When the Liverpool season ended, Pritchard called his assistant into the office and said that, although he would have preferred it otherwise, he could not invite Zubin back the following year. The musicians, he felt, did not enjoy working under him.

"Well, I was not going to argue with him. I could have said, 'Why did you start me off the way you did? Why didn't you give me some help along the way?' But I didn't say any of those things. I only said, 'Thank you. Good-by.'

"There was nothing for me but to return to Austria. I had no work."

In the spring of 1959, Zubin and Carmen found themselves overwhelmed by melancholy in Vienna, the city that had given them so much happiness together. There was nothing different about the city; it was their own *Stimmung* that kept them from enjoying the budding limes and lindens, that made it hard to delight in reunions with old friends.

They had barely any money and no income in sight. The trust fund left by Zubin's grandfather was long used up, and the pittance remaining from his Liverpool salary was all but consumed by the price of their train tickets from England.

Some of their instrumentalist friends had found positions in orchestras and chamber groups and could afford to lend them enough to get by for a while. They moved back into the old apartment Carmen had lived in before they were married, expanded now to two bedrooms and a kitchen, thanks to the death of an old tenant. A third adjoining bedroom was rented out to an Armenian violinist named Haig Balian.

The rooms were spacious enough, but there were no laundry facilities, which made Carmen's diaper-filled existence all the more unpleasant. Worse, the building's decrepit elevator could only be ridden safely in one direction, so she had to carry Zarina down five flights of stairs any time she wanted to leave the house. As a result, Carmen stayed at home as much as possible.

In the first months back, Zubin could do little but make the rounds of his former friends and professors in an effort to get his name circulating again. He could not actually bring himself to ask for work, but only hoped that by seeing him again someone would be prompted to hire him. Since he had little more than programs to show for his year in Liverpool—there having been very few rave reviews—he could only trust to luck and to whatever remained of the ascending reputation he had left behind in Vienna after winning the Liverpool competition. The self-confidence that had supported him in the past was at its ebb.

His most realistic hope seemed to be the Jeunesses Musicales, whose directors were still quite certain that *der Inder* was a protégé. They invited him to "guest-conduct" one of their concerts. The fee was modest, almost to the point of embarrassment, but Zubin was in no position to refuse.

When Carmen presented him with the news that she was expecting a second child, he realized that the need for money would soon obliterate any artistic concerns when it came to career decisions.

What he could not do, however, was go back to his odd jobs as a bass player. His student and apprentice days were gone, and Zubin had to sever as many ties to that past as he could. He knew he could not play last-chair bass in an orchestra one week and the next week be invited to conduct that orchestra.

When summer arrived Zubin traveled to Salzburg for the music festival. The New York Philharmonic was making a number of guest appearances there under its young director, Leonard Bernstein, and he wanted to see what he might be able to pick up from watching this man who was making so many headlines in the music world.

At Salzburg he ran into Seymour Lipkin, one of the many American musicians who had befriended him at Tanglewood. Lipkin had come along to join the New York Philharmonic in Bernstein's *Age of Anxiety* Symphony, with its demanding piano part. When Zubin told the pianist of his interest in Bernstein, Lipkin said, "How would you like to meet him?" The offer delighted Zubin, though he would not realize until sometime later that the chance meeting with Lipkin was another of those curious "coincidences" that made it seem as though Fate, Ahura Mazda, or some other superhuman entity was playing an active role in the formation of Zubin Mehta's career.

From the first meeting, there seemed to be a rapport between the two conductors. "I only expected to meet him," Zubin recalls, "just to say hello. But he was very nice and started to ask me about what I had done. I'll never forget that meeting because he had every right to say, 'Here's another young conductor bothering me.' But he didn't.

"Then, after I heard him conduct, I went to him and asked him what possibility there might be of my becoming his assistant. He told me what kind of letter to write, where to send it, and to include programs, reviews, whatever I had. I thanked him very much and said I would do that as soon as I got back to Vienna. Of course, I never imagined anything would come of it."

Back in Vienna, Zubin's old professors in the Vienna Philharmonic introduced him to another conductor, Dimitri Mitropoulos, who had preceded Bernstein on the New York podium. As Barbirolli had done in Manchester, the Greek maestro developed an instant liking for Zubin and took him under his wing.

There was nothing official about their relationship, but Mitropoulos was ever ready to help with whatever musical advice Zubin asked him for. As for Zubin's feelings toward Mitropoulos: "I came to adore that man, as a conductor, but most of all as a human being."

But when he told Mitropoulos of having spoken to Bernstein regarding an assistantship in New York, the old man's eyes narrowed and he became very serious. "Listen to me," he said. "You may be starving now, but don't you ever take a job as anybody's assistant again. If you do, you'll regret it later." Zubin respected the advice but doubted he'd be able to follow it. Starving alone is one thing, but starving with one's wife and children is another matter.

Under the prodding of Mitropoulos and the directors of the Viennese Jeunesses Musicales, musical organizations outside Austria began to show an interest in Zubin's talents. There was an invitation from the orchestra of Trondheim, the capital of the Norwegian county of Sør-Trøndelag. Also, billed as the "leading young Viennese conductor," he was booked in Belgrade to conduct that city's orchestra for the Yugoslavian chapter of the Jeunesses Musicales. Both appearances were scheduled for the early part of 1960.

As for his American agent, Zubin was uncertain whether he would ever hear from the busy Mr. Hearst. Then, early one morning, he was awakened by a telephone call from the United States that proved Hearst had not forgotten.

On the contrary, Zubin was very much on Siegfried Hearst's mind in those days. In fact, attests the manager's former assistant, Joan Bonime Glotzer, "Mr. Hearst used to talk about Zubin Mehta to anybody who would listen."

One of those who listened was none other than Leopold Stokowski, the maestro who had provided Mehli with one of his most thrilling experiences in music, the man whose recordings Zubin had listened to in Bombay, hour after hour, as a surrogate for his father's music. In the late fifties, Siegfried Hearst was acting as Stokowski's agent in New York.

Although neither of the men had ever heard or seen Zubin conduct— indeed, Stokowski had never even met him—they shared a feeling that this unknown youngster from Bombay was destined for greatness. They agreed that the time was ripe for his debut in the United States.

Stokowski called an important friend in Philadelphia, Fredric R. Mann, the industrialist-philanthropist (later ambassador to Barbados) who was in charge of the Philadelphia Orchestra's summer concert season in Robin Hood Dell. There was a young conductor in Europe, said

Stokowski, who would be perfect for one of the Dell concerts.

"That's impossible," Mann pointed out. "We've got every concert committed already."

Stokowski paused for a moment, then said, "Look, you've got me down for two concerts, haven't you, Freddy?"

"That's correct."

"Well, just give one of them to this fellow Mehta."

Zubin never found out about that phone call, never learned that he owed his United States debut to the generosity of Leopold Stokowski. And when his telephone rang in those hours before dawn, he had no idea who Fredric Mann might be. As soon as he heard the words "Philadelphia Orchestra," though, Zubin was wide awake. It made no difference to him that the fee would be only five hundred dollars; there was simply no way he would turn down an opportunity to conduct one of the world's great orchestras for his first concert in the United States.

Sometime between the time he hung up the telephone and the sun rose, he was struck by the realization that he was going to have to reach the United States before he could raise a baton in Philadelphia. Where was he going to get the air fare?

The government of India had pulled him out of a tight spot once before, perhaps it would work one more time. He went immediately to see the Indian ambassador to Austria, who listened intently to his description of the importance of the Philadelphia invitation and how much it might mean to a young conductor from India. There was no need to point out that a certain amount of international prestige might be gained for his country as well as for himself.

It was not an unreasonable request, but this ambassador clearly did not pull the same strings Mrs. Pandit had been able to pull in London. For one thing, he was no relation to Prime Minister Nehru. For another, Vienna ranked far below London in ambassadorial status. This time there was protocol to be followed, there were letters to be written and telephone calls to be made. Perhaps the embassy would have an answer for Mr. Mehta in a few weeks.

For the Hindu ambassador, a few weeks meant only an immeasurable prick of time in one four-billion-year "day of Brahma." To the Parsee-turned-Westerner, a few weeks' wait was insult heaped upon an ego already bruised and scarred by the frustrations of delay in a career that seemed as though it would never begin.

The Hindus believe that anything a man suffers in this life, or anything he enjoys, is the penalty or fruit of some vice or virtue he had in a previous life. This is the law of karma.

If the Hindu belief is correct, then most conductors—like the majority of artists—must all have spent antecedent lives devoid of patience:

helter-skeltering about, gulping down their food, elbowing their way through crowds, and screaming at slow waiters. Impatience must have been a monumental vice in the justification for their present existences. How else to explain the endless periods of waiting this time around?

For Zubin, as for many artists, this was the "middle period," the seemingly inevitable letdown. After the years of youthful enthusiasm, of self-discovery, of recognition of his own peculiar genius, of eager development, he had come to the point at which further development was meaningless without some symbols of success.

Those symbols—public acclaim, critical recognition, and a viable income—seemed very slow in coming. In the meantime there was nothing to do but stretch the borrowed money as far as it would go and borrow more when that ran out. Since he didn't drink, Zubin could not even drown his *Zweifel* in cheap young wine at the *Heurigen*. He could only wait. Wait a few more weeks to hear from the embassy. Wait for tomorrow's mail to bring good news.

And suddenly there *was* good news. A letter from Siegfried Hearst's office announced that after his concert in Philadelphia's Robin Hood Dell Zubin would be required to stay in the United States through July, to conduct the New York Philharmonic.

Hearst's letter stated that the Lewisohn Stadium Concerts, the sanctified summer series in New York City, were in need of a conductor to fill in for Leopold Stokowski, whose health would permit him to conduct only one of the four stadium concerts he'd scheduled. Between the lines, Zubin read that Hearst had booked the dates knowing full well Stokowski would conduct no more than one. The dates were in July, just following the Dell concerts in Philadelphia.

Zubin could hardly believe it: the Philadelphia and New York orchestras in one summer! It was an opportunity he would never have dreamed of. Naturally, the fee would again be low, on account of the nature of the concerts, but no matter how badly he needed the money, the fee could not be a major consideration.

Zubin dashed off a letter to Hearst, thanking him and asking him for program suggestions. He thought of mentioning that he had no money to get to the United States, since that might prompt Hearst to lend him the fare, but he decided not to bring it up. The less anyone in the profession knew of his financial difficulties the better. Let him be thought of, especially on the far side of the Atlantic, as a rising star untarnished by experience.

Artists are notorious for failing to plan, to establish clear and attainable goals for themselves. Up until now, Zubin had been no exception. His life had gone where his career had taken him and the career path had been determined by chance encounters and blind steps. Now he began to perceive a direction and that direction was Westward.

He saw America—the United States and Canada—as the place where new standards for performance excellence were being set. Vienna, of course, was the epitome of acceptability. Presumably, whatever music succeeded in Vienna would succeed anywhere. Yet it seemed success could be attained in Vienna only *after* it had been proclaimed everywhere else. Perhaps America was no longer the Land of Opportunity it had once been, but it was still the place where opportunities seemed most likely to present themselves.

In early February, Zubin had a solitary concert in Belgium, once again courtesy of the Jeunesses Musicales. When he walked off stage to applause after conducting Stravinsky's *Pulcinella,* he was handed a telegram. Carmen had picked that night to go into labor. They had a son.

Word went through the orchestra quickly, and throughout the next work, Hindemith's *Der Schwanendreher,* every time he gave a cue to a musician Zubin was greeted with a silently mouthed "Congratulations."

They called him Merwan, an old Persian name that had been in the Mehta family for years, and while his arrival was a cause for celebration, the joy soon bent under the oppressive weight of their poverty and uncertain future.

Unprepared for the difficulties of bearing and raising children, Carmen had no family to call on for help, no money to make life easier. Her entire existence became "one round after another of washing the children, feeding them, and keeping them clothed."

Zubin regretted that his wife could no longer share the cheap and abundant music making of Vienna, but he was not about to deny his own pleasure. Carmen found herself growing resentful.

"He wanted just to pick up his student life where he'd left off. He wanted to continue going to concerts night after night and going out with his friends afterwards. All of a sudden he found himself saddled with a wife who was always tired, two kids, and no money."

If communication had been poor in Liverpool, it was nonexistent in Vienna. Zubin knew something was wrong, but he never quite fit the pieces together. Carmen had no thought at all of the self-doubt that was creeping over Zubin as a result of his failure to make any progress.

"Whatever difficulties Zubin was having, I was not aware of them. Probably I was not even aware of my own psychological difficulties because my life was so extremely physical."

At last, when Merwan was about ten weeks old, Zubin put forward a suggestion he'd been holding back for some time.

"What would you think," he asked, in his typically blunt way, "of going to stay with your parents for a while?"

Had she recognized the implications of that suggestion, Carmen would very likely have rejected it. But her answer came as quickly as if she had been toying with just such an idea herself.

"My reaction was one hundred percent physical. I was so tired that the thought of having my mother and father to look after me and my children was very agreeable. And for Zubin, the thought of being physically removed from the responsibility must have been very attractive."

Zubin watched Carmen and the children depart for Canada—on a ticket sent by her father—with a great deal of regret. Yet he'd convinced himself that, under the circumstances, this was the best way to meet his paternal responsibilities. He would rejoin them in just a few months, and meanwhile he would soak up whatever Vienna had to offer.

Vienna's musical cornucopia seemed truly inexhaustible. It was 1960, the year of the Mahler Centennial, and there was a great deal to be learned about Mahler, much of it from Bruno Walter. The redoubtable German conductor, close to his ninetieth year, had been a friend and disciple of Mahler's and had made the Bohemian-born composer's works one of his lifelong studies.

As he never failed to do, Zubin got himself admitted to the Musikverein for Walter's rehearsal of the Mahler Fourth Symphony. Sitting behind his old bass professor Otto Rühm, Zubin was entranced by the way the *dirigent* made the orchestra play this still-neglected music.

When the first rehearsal session ended and the musicians filed off stage for their break, Zubin stayed behind. He watched the old man move to a corner of the stage, where, wiping his brow, he slumped down on a bench. The two conductors were alone in the Musikverein.

"I don't think he even was aware I was there, and I wouldn't have disturbed him for the world. He was in a very pensive mood, completely lost to the world, as though he were communicating with Mahler.

"I tried to imagine what must have been going on in his mind. The things he had lived through in that hall, listening to Mahler conduct there, his own experiences. He just sat there for fifteen minutes, never moving, with his head tilted back. It was a moment I shall never forget."

After that rehearsal and the first concert, Zubin was introduced to Bruno Walter. As was the case so often in Zubin's early career, a rapport was established between the older conductor and the younger man, and as Zubin recalls, "As with Mitropoulos, a rather touching relationship started between us."

Halina Rodzinski recounts in her book *Our Two Lives* a story of Walter's attempt to destroy a rehearsal of her husband's Paris debut when Artur Rodzinski stayed four minutes more than his allotted time in the hall. Walter was certainly not famous for helping young conductors along. Yet he was ready to advise Zubin at any moment, immersing him in Mahler. The baptism was to have profound results on the course of Zubin's musical life.

He was forced to reassess the sophomoric criticisms of Mahler's music that he had heard so often from fellow students, and even from some teachers at the Academy. Gustav Mahler had been hailed in his lifetime as a great conductor, particularly of opera, but the Viennese had scoffed at his compositions. Even in 1960 it was not unstylish to call Mahler a *Spitzbube,* a common thief.

Not only was Mahler supposed to have stolen his musical ideas from other more "respectable" composers, but even greater ridicule was heaped upon him for "stealing from himself"—taking themes from his early compositions and working them into new forms. The Viennese seemed to forget that virtually every great composer has done the same. As a student, Zubin had made a game of detecting Mahler's "crimes"; now he went beyond the obvious in an effort to understand the composer in all his complexity.

Zubin remembered well a story told by his bass professor, Otto Rühm, handed down from *his* professor, who had played under Mahler. According to the story, whenever Mahler's assistant was seen carrying scores of Tchaikovsky or Wagner or other operas up to his master's room, someone would gibe, "Aha! The director must be composing again!"

But now, listening to Walter conduct the Fourth Symphony, he realized the truth of what others had said, that although the thematic inspiration may not always have been original, still, the craftsmanship with which Mahler developed those ideas was what made him a master.

He analyzed the music he was hearing in rehearsal and performance and found the man beneath. Mahler was the flame of romanticism's glorious self-immolation; his music expressed the mutually consuming duality of ecstasy and terror. It was all summed up in the brutally direct phrase of the *Song of the Earth: Dunkel ist das Leben, ist der Tod.* Dark is life, is death.

It was easy for Zubin to forget the agony of waiting and seal himself in the cosmic envelope of Mahler. For the first time he understood the man's genius for orchestration and precise coloring. He paid rapt attention as Bruno Walter pointed out to the orchestra Mahler's intricate indications of tempo and dynamics.

"He recounted for me the details of past performances, both his and Mahler's, and he analyzed the scores for me, but apart from that Bruno Walter gave so many of those terribly important details that one can never find in the printed score, details that a young conductor treasures for the rest of his life."

Finally the time came for Zubin's Jeunesses Musicales appearances in Yugoslavia and Norway. As luck would have it, the dates were only one week apart and separated by nearly the entire length of Europe. His memory of those concerts is one of trying to sleep in second-class compartments of railroad cars.

"Here I was going from Belgrade, near the southern end of the Danube, to this frozen place in Norway just beneath the Arctic Circle.

First it was the Orient Express, then a German train, then a Danish train. From Belgrade to Trondheim, all for the sake of two concerts that nobody would ever read about and which paid practically nothing.

"But at least it was an opportunity. I worked with two more orchestras, learned two different programs. I always did a different program for the sake of learning new repertoire."

When he returned to Vienna, there were two letters waiting for him. One was from the Indian Embassy, informing him that his request for transportation money to the United States would be granted. So he would be able to conduct the dates he had already accepted.

The second letter was from Leonard Bernstein, inviting Zubin to come to New York and work as his assistant in the 1960–61 season. It began to look as though the waiting was finally over.

He wrote Carmen in Saskatoon and his parents in Manchester to tell them the good news, and he was surprised to receive a prompt reply from England. Mehli had some good news of his own.

Ivan Galamian had gotten Mehli a position on the faculty of the New School of Music in Philadelphia, as well as the position as second violinist in the Curtis Quartet. At last he had made Philadelphia.

"My parents were ecstatic that we were all going to America," Zubin recalls. "My father was tired of the hardships of the Hallé orchestra, sick of the climate, tired of living on twenty pounds a week. My mother had grown up in a wealthy family with five servants in her house. I saw her in Manchester having to carry the heavy coal bucket herself from the cellar. And she just couldn't take the cold. The English didn't believe in central heating only little stoves with bricks in them. The only time my mother was warm was when she was sitting next to the stove. They were very glad to see the end of Manchester, even though my father and Barbirolli had a great love for one another."

Things were beginning to turn around. After the bleakest of winters, spring of 1960 found Zubin ready to conquer America. He had been there in 1958 as a student, but in 1960 he would be recognized as a professional conductor.

He would rejoin his parents in Philadelphia, his wife and children in Canada. He had already decided that his own best chances lay across the Atlantic; now his whole family would be there to see the waves he would make in the music world. His confidence returned, stronger than ever.

As for Vienna, it had given him things he would never forget, and he had no intention of leaving 'the city forever. Already he had been engaged for three concerts in Linz the following October. After that, who could tell? Maybe one day the Viennese might even invite him back to conduct the Strauss concert on New Year's Eve. For a young man of twenty-four, flushed with faith in his own ability, even the impossible seemed possible.

5

A Star Under the Stars

Upon his arrival in Philadelphia, Zubin was somewhat chagrined to find that he had been scheduled for only one rehearsal. But, as he soon learned, "with the Philadelphia Orchestra one rehearsal was time to spare." The musicians took to him almost instantly.

At first, when he walked onto the stage and set his scores down unopened, there were a few smiles; American orchestras were already fed up with boyish Toscanini imitators who felt constrained to ape his scoreless conducting—that was usually their only resemblance to the Maestro. But when the young Indian began conducting the Overture to Verdi's *La Forza del Destino,* slashing the air with the first three brass chords, they knew Zubin Mehta was something special.

The orchestra applauded him generously after the overture, listened to his corrections, then played it through again exactly the way he wanted it. The Brahms First Symphony—the same one he had listened to on that memorable first evening at the Musikverein—and the Beethoven C-minor Piano Concerto went just as smoothly.

Rudolf Firkusny was soloist in the Beethoven, and the musicians noted the spontaneous rapport that seemed to spring up between the young conductor and the veteran pianist. Zubin had heard him play in Vienna, but they had never met.

The program was, in some ways, quite conservative. There was nothing in the least bit "strange" to the ears of audience or orchestra. Yet the very fact that everyone involved knew the pieces, forward and backward, made the program risky for an unknown conductor.

Under Stokowski, the orchestra's records for the Victor Talking Machine Company dated as far back as 1917, when Zubin's father was only nine. Eugene Ormandy's tenure in Philadelphia began in 1936, the year of Zubin's birth. The two conductors had built the orchestra into one of the world's foremost music institutions. As a consequence, debuting in Philadelphia carried a potential for disaster, and, as Zubin admits, "I was scared stiff."

That evening, under the stars in the lovely Robin Hood Dell, Zubin Mehta made his professional conducting debut in the United States. As the critic for *Musical America* was to write later, it was "a sensational success" for the "youthful and unheralded conductor."

The audience cheered, calling Zubin back for bow after bow, and—as more than one reviewer noticed—the orchestra cheered, too. Mehli and Tehmina spent the next day clipping newspaper reviews, all of them raves. Most impressive, perhaps, was the evaluation of the city's dean of music critics, Max de Schauensee.

"His control of the orchestra was most impressive," wrote de Schauensee in the *Bulletin*. "His awareness of nuance and dynamics in an overall musical design showed him as a musician of already strong convictions. His music lives and has direction and purpose."

Of Zubin's future, he prophesied that "the sky might be the limit."

Even Zubin, his own worst critic, admits that "the concert in Philadelphia went quite well." But his stay in the City of Brotherly Love was brief; it was on to the Big Apple, which, as many performers have mixed their metaphors in pointing out, is a tougher nut to crack.

The Lewisohn Stadium Concerts were a New York tradition of long standing. Started in 1918 by wealthy arts patron and businesswoman Minnie Guggenheimer, the concerts had the double purpose of bringing good music to the people at low prices and of providing summer jobs for the otherwise out-of-work musicians of the New York Philharmonic. The Stadium, at 138th Street and Convent Avenue on Manhattan's Upper West Side was, for many years, New York's only summer concert hall.

The only musicians who got paid anything like their regular rates for the Lewisohn Stadium concerts were the members of the orchestra; soloists and conductors performed for pittances. Yet playing or singing in the Stadium had come to be regarded as prestigious, a summer event for the likes of Heifetz and Rubinstein, with the orchestra playing under big-name conductors. The Stadium season was eagerly awaited by music lovers and music critics as the high point of a season of cultural deprivation. Yet some were not so deprived as to settle for an unknown conductor from Bombay.

"Giuseppe Di Stefano, whom I had met casually in Vienna, was going to be my soloist. I was kind of looking forward to that, because I'd never conducted operatic arias before. But when I reported to Mrs. Guggenheimer's office in New York I found out that Di Stefano had suddenly canceled." Of course, the tenor had assumed he would be singing with Stokowski in the Maestro's first Stadium concert since 1940.

"Then, while I was standing in her office, Mrs. Guggenheimer telephoned Roberta Peters and asked her if she would do it. But Roberta said, 'Who?' Of course she had never heard of me, and she refused. Finally they talked Risë Stevens into it."

If opera singers could be choosy about with whom they appeared, the members of the New York Philharmonic could be just as particular. Only a few years before, New York Times critic Harold Schonberg had taken the orchestra to task for maltreating an inexperienced conductor during a Stadium concert he later remembered as "a disgrace."

"The musicians," wrote Schonberg, "clearly had a low opinion of the conductor, who was not very good, and they did everything but fall asleep on stage. Legs were crossed; musicians whispered to other musicians; they went through the motions, but the Girls High School Orchestra could have done better."

This was the lions' den into which Zubin walked on July 25, 1960, to rehearse such pieces as the Bartók Concerto for Orchestra, Till Eulenspiegel's Merry Pranks, Tchaikovsky's Fifth Symphony, and various operatic arias—all for the first time. More experienced men have crumbled under less pressure, yet with Zubin the greater the risk, the more forceful and winning his personality became. In the end, the New York lions were eating out of his hand, purring as benignly as had the musicians from Quaker City the week before.

"I don't know why, but the orchestra just seemed to like working with me. They even applauded me at the beginning of the concert."

Yet, by virtually all published accounts, the concerts just didn't seem to jell. "I never did understand that," ponders Zubin, "the reviews were uniformly bad. I must say, I certainly didn't know how to accompany those operatic excerpts, and they went very badly. Yet I seem to recall that Bartók's Concerto for Orchestra and Till Eulenspiegel went very well."

There were to have been three concerts, on the twenty-sixth, twenty-seventh, and twenty-eighth of July, with mezzo-soprano Stevens, pianist John Browning, and cellist Aldo Parisot the soloists for each of the three evenings. When rain canceled the second concert, most of that program was prefixed to that of the twenty-eighth, giving the stadium audience that night a musical bargain in quantity, regardless of what the critics might have thought of the quality.

The concerts were unquestionably not the disaster Zubin remembers, yet his New York debut was certainly less than the resounding success he'd had in Philadelphia, as far as the critics were concerned. The remarks of those New York critics are worth examining.

Musical America's John Ardoin heaped his greatest abuse on the Bartók: "I can find nothing good to say for his ideas of the Bartók Concerto for Orchestra. The tempos throughout fluctuated nervously and such spots as the big solo brass section in the first movement were overdriven."

For the *Times's* Allen Hughes, it was an overall uneasiness he had about the brash young conductor: "His faults result, perhaps, from overzealousness. He obviously knows the scores inside out; indeed, he seems to have x-rayed them. But the skeletal structures of musical scores are not very attractive to the listener."

The critics were uniformly distressed over Zubin's interpretation of the Tchaikovsky Fifth. "His ideas are expansive and romantic," wrote Ardoin, "but are frequently excessive... uncomfortably saccharine." Not so, declared Alan Rich in the *Herald Tribune,* "its emotional span could have been broadened without risking exaggeration." At any rate, huffed Allen Hughes, "Mr. Mehta would seem to have a long way to go before he becomes a satisfactory interpreter of the Tchaikovsky work."

"Never," bellowed Ardoin indignantly, "have I heard such strange accents and peculiar voicings of inner parts."

The reviews were certainly unfavorable enough, yet in each of them one can see the seeds of what many critics (including at least one of the aforementioned) were later to proclaim as the essence of Zubin Mehta's greatness: his ability to cull from a piece of music something new and revealing. He always had *ideas* about music.

The critical attitude that emerges most prominently is one of discomfort; they simply did not yet know what to make of Zubin Mehta. Apparently, they even doubted their own evaluations of him, else how could the same critics have written in the same reviews:

"He held absolute control over the orchestra and often produced rare excitement. He has a volatile musical temperament and it was evident that he possesses a solid rehearsal technique.... Mr. Mehta is obviously a very gifted young conductor" (Ardoin, *Musical America*).

"His conducting was often vigorous with decisive, sometimes far-reaching gestures" to a "responsive orchestra" (Rich, *Herald Tribune*).

"The newcomer is an individual of strong will and possesses the ability to impress his ideas on experienced orchestra players. His technique is fluent and the cues he gives the instrumentalists are precise" (Hughes, *New York Times*).

Solid rehearsal technique; respect and absolute command of the orchestra; the ability to extract his conception of the music from a potentially hostile group of players; excitement . . . these are the qualities the early critics saw, the qualities other critics would begin to see in every Zubin Mehta concert. And before long the roar of the crowd would deafen any grumbles of uncertainty about his musical ideas.

After the Lewisohn Stadium concerts, Zubin had a talk about his career with Siegfried Hearst, whose only advice was "Don't worry." He asked about Zubin's plans for the immediate future.

"I'm going to Canada to rejoin my family."

"Canada? Then you can stop in Montreal and say hello to my old friend Pierre Beique."

"But I'm going to Saskatoon."

"Stop in Montreal. Beique is the general manager of the Montreal Symphony. Tell him I sent you. Better yet, tell him Charles Munch sent you. He adores Munch."

"But Munch doesn't adore me. He's never even spoken to me."

"Then how do you know he doesn't adore you? Go and see Beique."

Zubin checked the bus schedules and discovered that traveling by way of Montreal was probably the simplest way to get to Saskatoon anyway. Besides, his two friends Eddie Kudlak and Eugene Husaruk were playing in the Montreal Symphony now. There was a stopover of several hours between buses, so he'd probably have time to look them up as well. Had it not been for them, he probably would not have agreed to call on the symphony manager. He had never so blatantly solicited work before, and found the very idea of asking for work repulsive. But the bus did go through Montreal. . . .

Pierre Beique had directed the operations of the Montreal Orchestra almost since its beginning in the 1930s. A businessman whose love of music had become obsession, Beique had succeeded in luring the cream of the world's conductors to his admittedly second-rate orchestra with admittedly third-rate fees. Charles Munch, Pierre Monteux, Otto Klemperer, Leonard Bernstein, even the great Bruno Walter—all of them had appeared with his orchestra in its high school auditorium.

Of course, with his limited budget Beique could not depend on a steady supply of stellar attractions. Nor was he even certain whether he could depend on his music director, Igor Markevitch, to handle the bulk of the season. It seemed Markevitch was in great demand as a guest conductor for orchestras far superior to Montreal's.

Beique kept an eye out for fresh talent that might improve the quality of a concert without emptying his small purse. When he read about up-and-coming soloists and conductors, he filed their names away for possible future use. One such file was labeled "Mehta, Zubin: Conductor."

"I'd been following his career ever since he won that competition in Liverpool," Beique declares proudly. "When he received the conducting award in Tanglewood, I had occasion to speak to my old friend Charles Munch, who was very, very complimentary toward him." (So Munch had been listening after all!) "I knew this was something special.

"Then Siegfried Hearst mentioned him to me as a young Indian conductor who had fascinated him. So I already knew his name when I came across that incredible review by Max de Schauensee in Philadelphia.

"Nearly twenty years later I can still remember almost his exact words, that the Brahms First Symphony has become a hackneyed work and it probably takes a young Oriental to give a new meaning to it. Coming from a sage of music like de Schauensee, that was quite a compliment. You don't come across that kind of praise very often. I clipped that review myself and put it in my file."

Had Zubin postponed his trip to Canada by one more day, a lot of things might never have happened. Had there been no delay between buses, had his friends from Vienna found jobs in some other orchestra... but, as usual, the stars were right for Zubin.

"I remember that day so clearly," says Beique, smiling broadly. "I was clearing off my desk, giving my secretary last-minute instructions so I could go home early, because the following morning I was leaving for the festivals in Europe, as I always did. Our paths almost didn't cross.

"Suddenly the telephone rang, and it was the receptionist outside. She said there was a young conductor here to see me. Well, I jumped all over her; I said, 'Didn't I tell you not to disturb me? I'm trying to get out of here!' And I hung up. A few minutes later she called back, rather sheepishly, and she said, 'This man insists he just wants to say hello to you because he is only in Montreal for a few hours.'

"I was about to hang up again—of course, I assumed it was just one of the local hopefuls—when she told me, 'He says Maestro Munch told him to look you up.' I said, 'Munch? Wait a minute, what's this fellow's name?' And she said, 'Zubin Mehta.' Naturally, she pronounced it all wrong, but I recognized the name immediately; I had just finished reading about him.

"'You mean that Zubin Mehta is outside my office right now and he wants to see me?' She said, 'Yes.' And I said, 'Well, I suppose you had better send him in.'"

Beique welcomed Zubin warmly, asking what brought him to Montreal, how the concerts in New York had gone, about the season in Liverpool.

"From the moment I met him, there was no doubt in my mind that this man was something more than your ordinary young conductor. His manner, his assurance, the way he was courteous, yet put himself on an equal level with me—I felt quite sure I would be reading much more about him in the future."

Zubin treated the meeting rather matter-of-factly, recalling later that "Mr. Beique had heard of my concerts in Philadelphia and New York and he was very friendly. But he said he had nothing to offer me because his season was only six weeks away and of course it was already filled. We talked for about an hour and I left. I had to get to Saskatoon to see my wife and children."

It was a delight to see the children again after nearly four months. Merwan was already crawling around the floor, and Zarina, almost two, was very protective of her baby brother. The reunion with Carmen was, in her own words, "rather strained."

She had let herself believe the pleasant fiction that everything would be fine once she recuperated from the pressures of early motherhood. Zubin, of course, would manage to keep them all fed and clothed when they got back to Vienna. But Zubin had reacquainted himself with freedom from responsibility and was not sure he was ready to pick up where they'd left off.

After two weeks in Saskatoon, Zubin decided they should all go to Philadelphia in September so Mehli and Tehmina could see the children. Playing the old and easy game of follow-the-leader, Carmen left the decision to her husband.

Once Zubin made up his mind to something, his enthusiasm for the idea infected everyone around him. A priest who was a friend of the Lasky family, as well as an art scholar, declared that he would drive them all to Philadelphia. He had always wanted to visit the Rodin Museum there, and this would be as good a time as any to make the trip.

Into an aging black Plymouth they piled, a priest, a Parsee conductor, a soprano turned housewife, two children, and their attendant baggage. Zubin, who hadn't yet the vaguest notion of how to drive, sat in the front seat with Zarina, reading maps. Carmen shared the rear seat with Merwan and his crib.

"What a terrible trip," she says now, laughing. "Nowadays I see these young girls carting around their babies on their backs from place to place and I think, They must be mad! Then I remember I did much worse."

More than two thousand miles they drove, from Saskatoon to Winnipeg, around the Great Lakes to Duluth and Madison and Chicago and Fort Wayne and Youngstown and Pittsburgh.

They drove off the main highways to find cheaper motels. Carmen fed the children in the back seat and washed out diapers in roadside streams. Zubin pointed out the scenic wonders in endless fascination.

Finally, after eight days of driving, there was the Pennsylvania Turnpike, with Philadelphia waiting at the end. Carmen felt more than prepared for the long air trip to Austria; it would be the height of comfort after this.

Zubin's concerts in Linz were not until mid-October, and his only work after that was another series of provincial concerts in Graz, in southern Austria. His plan was to spend about one month with Mehli and Tehmina before heading for Europe. Since the Philadelphia Orchestra's season was about to start, Zubin looked forward to eating his mother's cooking and to attending some of Eugene Ormandy's concerts.

Until that point, the assumption had been that Carmen and the children would be returning to Vienna with him, but Zubin was beginning to wonder if this was such a good idea. The hypothesis that two could live as cheaply as one had been disproven, especially when two became four. He was loath to separate again from the children, to whom he had grown firmly attached, but what would be the purpose of dragging the entire family back to Europe? At least in Canada they could be warm and comfortable and have enough to eat. Carmen's parents seemed willing enough to help for the time being, and he would send them money whenever he could.

For the first time, Carmen resisted Zubin's wishes. Vienna was the closest thing she had to a home now, and she wanted to return there with her husband.

"My leaving Vienna in the first place was a mistake. That probably was the beginning of the breakup of our marriage. How did it happen? I suppose it just *happened*. The same way we had drifted together, we drifted apart."

But at that point Carmen was not about to give up. Though even Mehli and Tehmina urged her to return to Saskatoon, she feared she might never see Zubin again. Neither she nor Zubin understood that their parting was inevitable, that his career was taking him away from her.

It was the same vicious circle in which so many young couples find themselves: the need for income and the excitement of a new profession takes one of them in a direction in which the other cannot or will not follow, resulting in an inability to share experiences, which was the thing that brought them together in the first place.

Tehmina looked on, remembering the *jotisi*'s caution that her son should not marry before this twenty-fifth year, but she did not remind

Zubin and he had never mentioned it to Carmen.

Two days before Zubin's scheduled departure for Vienna, Carmen was still arguing that he should take her along. It took a telephone call from London to convince her that if she stayed they would soon be reunited. The call was from the manager of the Montreal Symphony Orchestra, Pierre Beique.

In one of the earliest surviving fragments of Parsee literature, the *Gatha Ustavaiti,* an unknown writer describes the entrance of the prophet Zoroaster into heaven after a life of tribulation: "It shall be for him the best of all things. After his longing for bliss shall he be given bliss."

Since her visit to the *jotisi* in 1954, Tehmina Mehta had remained unshakable in her conviction that bliss in this life would be attained by her son. The difficulties she and her husband endured were made sufferable by the knowledge that Zubin would one day be rewarded with "the best of things."

"With my husband," she says, "there have always been stumbling blocks; nothing has been easy. Even now, if he wants to buy a pair of shoes, he must go to six shops to find a pair that will do. That has always been the pattern of his life. But not for my son.

"Always, always there has been some supernatural power behind me as far as Zubin is concerned. Whatever I have tried to do for his career I have succeeded in; there have been no stumbling blocks."

Having just come through the most difficult two years of his life, Zubin could have challenged her on that last point. But perhaps it had simply taken that long for the pieces of his cosmic jigsaw puzzle to fall into place. All of the things that had brought him to this point—the success in Tanglewood that prompted Charles Munch and Siegfried Hearst to recommend him to Pierre Beique; the dazzling success in Philadelphia's Robin Hood Dell that fixed Beique's attention to him; the presence of his two friends in Montreal, which had settled him on stopping over in that city; perhaps even the depressing poverty that had sent Carmen back to Canada and given Zubin reason to go there in the first place—all these things were factors in the telephone call from London. The final elements had to do with Beique himself and his poor relations with the music director of his orchestra.

The French-Russian Igor Markevitch was not Pierre Beique's favorite conductor. True, in his two years as Montreal's music director there had been moments of uncompromised brilliance. There had been a dazzling *Le Sacre du Printemps* under Markevitch, a Tchaikovsky *Pathétique* and a Haydn *Creation* that rivaled performances by the greatest orchestras and choruses. But, in Beique's estimation, the lows were far more numerous than the highs. The worst thing, to a man who had been a part of the

Montreal orchestra since the days when it was kind to even call it an orchestra, was the condescending attitude he felt the conductor demonstrated toward it.

Beique was therefore not overly shocked to receive a cable from Tokyo proclaiming Markevitch's regrets at having to cancel his first series of concerts in Montreal due to a severe ear infection. His first series included every concert of the first six weeks of Montreal's season.

Beique, who had made a stopover in London en route home from Bayreuth, began frantically searching Europe for conductors who might take over in Montreal. Since the beginning of his season coincided with the beginning of just about every other orchestra's fall season, he was almost totally unsuccessful. Only Vladimir Golschmann, former music director of the St. Louis Symphony and an old acquaintance of Beique's, was willing to spend part, but not all, of the time in Montreal. The first two weeks were out of the question for him.

Who, then, to open the season? The first concert was scheduled for the Montreal Forum, the home of the Montreal Canadiens hockey team, with more than eleven thousand seats already sold. He needed somebody with a big name, but there was nobody like that to be had, least of all for the niggardly fee he could pay. If not a "name," then a newcomer with a dramatic flare and good audience appeal, somebody like . . . Zubin Mehta. He wasted no time making the call to Philadelphia, where Zubin had mentioned he'd be spending some time.

Had Beique waited until he returned to Canada, Zubin would have been gone. The message might have been a week getting to him, and Beique would very likely have found someone else. Zubin told him it would be difficult, that he would have to do some rearranging in Linz—he refused to cancel—but with the flexibility of those provincial orchestras, he thought it might be possible to free the two weeks.

Cables were exchanged, and the management at Linz agreed to move Zubin's concerts up a few days, with his final performances scheduled the afternoon and evening of the same day. That was the only way it could be arranged for him to be in Montreal on time. After the three concerts there he would have to fly back to Austria to conduct in Linz. Carmen and the children would join him in Montreal and they would return as a family to Vienna.

Before he left the United States, Zubin had one final piece of business to attend to in New York. He had to speak to Leonard Bernstein about his still-open offer as assistant conductor.

Zubin remembered well the advice of Mitropoulos against hiring on as anyone's assistant; for the first time he felt he might have the luxury of considering that advice. The concert fees in Linz and Montreal would give him an appreciable, if not lordly, income for the next several months. After that, there would be a tour of Yugoslavia, a result of his success with the Jeunesses Musicales in Belgrade. Perhaps he could work his way into a musical directorship of one of those small central European orchestras and thereby be assured of a salary. That seemed to offer greater possibilities than the New York position.

Bernstein received Zubin at Carnegie Hall, then suggested they go for a walk in nearby Central Park. It was a lovely Sunday afternoon, and the park was filled with bike riders and dog walkers and tourists in hansom cabs. The first blush of autumn color was on the elms and sycamores.

"I could have three assistants if I wanted them," said Bernstein as they walked along. "But I don't want three assistants. Only you. There is tremendous opportunity here in New York, and you and I are going to accomplish great things together."

Perhaps, but Zubin found himself wondering how long it would be before he found himself chafing at the bit of assistantship, how long before the glamour of New York turned into the nightmare of Liverpool. Besides, he wanted to do what he had seen his father do in Bombay, he wanted to build something. What could an assistant hope to accomplish in the way of building? There was also the matter of guest-conducting stints, offers for which were beginning to trickle in from Europe.

Looking back on that moment from the vantage point of today, Leonard Bernstein says, "It was really a terribly important decision for him." Not wanting to force Zubin into something he might regret later, Bernstein gave him until after the Montreal concerts to make up his mind.

6

~~~~~~

Spiritual and
Artistic Growth

MEHTA CREATES SENSATION

That headline appeared in the December 1960 issue of *Musical America* above an article that was a paean to three astonishing concerts in Montreal, concerts that marked the arrival of Zubin Mehta on the North American musical scene.

Had it been left to the sponsors of the Forum series, Zubin's first concert might have been canceled. It took a good bit of persuasion from Pierre Beique to convince them that they should trust the opening of the season to an unknown, twenty-four-year-old conductor from Bombay. John McConnell, the principal sponsor and publisher of the Montreal *Star,* had his doubts and could have said no. But, as it happened, McConnell had only the previous week returned from a visit to India and thought that the gesture of good will between the two "Common-wealth" countries would be worth the risk.

"Besides," Beique told them, "we have no other choice."

Beique knew he was going out on a limb, since the Forum concerts were the most valuable assets his orchestra had at the moment, but he did not have long to wait to realize he'd made the right decision.

"Zubin arrived for rehearsal," recalls the French Canadian, "and I was very curious to see how that would start. Well, in the first fifteen minutes of the rehearsal, there was no doubt that he had conquered the orchestra professionally, with authority and with serious musicianship."

Beique does not consider himself a musician, yet he has spent a lifetime listening to and working around music. He had been with the Montreal Symphony twenty-five years and had heard virtually every rehearsal of the orchestra under resident and visiting conductors that included every famous name of that era, with the sole exception of Toscanini.

"You develop a mysterious, indefinable sense of how things go and how the personality of the conductor is projected and how the body of musicians react right away. There's some kind of a surge and contagious reaction when things are right. This time things were right."

That first rehearsal began with Berlioz's *Symphonie Fantastique,* one of the crowd-rousing giants of symphonic literature and a severe test of any conductor's skill. It provides plenty of opportunity for a conductor to let the reins slip away from him and have the orchestra go tearing off like a runaway team of horses. Not surprisingly, it was the first time Zubin had conducted the *Fantastique,* except for a rehearsal in Liverpool.

After those first fifteen minutes, Beique felt so certain of his choice in Zubin that he left the Forum and attended to some business back at the Symphony office. Returning in time for the rehearsal intermission, he found himself swamped by excited musicians.

"What are you going to do about this guy?"

"Where did you find him? Keep him here."

Beique did his best to temper their enthusiasm for the young conductor. "Look, boys, just carry on and play," he advised them. "After all, this is only the first rehearsal."

But the musicians came to him again after the second and third rehearsals, showing what was for them extraordinary interest in a conductor. There was no doubt in anyone's mind that the concert in the enormous arena was going to be an experience that Montreal would be talking about for seasons to come.

"Conductor Zubin Mehta created a real sensation," reported *Musical America,* "when he made his local debut October 25 with the Montreal Symphony. News of the illness of Igor Markevitch, regular conductor of the orchestra, obliged the management to find replacements and it was fortunate to find Mr. Mehta and Mr. Golschmann available."

The reviewer was half right. Zubin did create a sensation. The Forum that night rocked with cheers as loud as any that ever greeted a victory for the Montreal Canadiens hockey team. "People had the same intuitive reaction that I did," says Beique. "He had a tremendous ovation; the people went wild."

The reviewer was also half wrong. Igor Markevitch may have been convalescing from an ear infection, but according to word received by Pierre Beique and the Montreal board of directors, Markevitch was conducting in Paris.

Beique was livid. He decided that this would be the last season for Markevitch, determining on the spot to offer the job to Zubin Mehta. "When a comet passes through your life," he says, "you do not have to be any sort of a genius to realize it.

"I was immediately conquered by this young man who was personable, who was willing to work, and who needed an orchestra. I had known and developed friendships with some of the world's greatest conductors, but Zubin's attitude, his professional approach, was surely the purest I had ever encountered. Maybe in the beginning the diamond was rough, but it was still a diamond. And I could see that later on it would become more and more polished. The talent was unlimited."

Zubin, astonished at the compliments he received after that first concert, forced himself to wait until after the next performance to take it all seriously.

The initial concert in the Forum was a one-time-only "dollar concert," and could hardly be compared to the experience of conducting the orchestra in its regular hall, a high school auditorium that seated twelve hundred people. The main work on the November 1 and 2 program would be the Bartók Concerto for Orchestra, a more sober piece than the Berlioz, and the audience would be the supposedly more reserved season subscribers.

But by the time that second concert came around, those subscribers had been worked up into a feverish anticipation both by the press and by firsthand reports of the Forum concert. Those who had not attended were kicking themselves, and those who had were beaming at their own perspicacity.

Montreal's first-nighters have been known to sit on their hands and to give polite but cold receptions to unimpressive strangers, but there was none of that for Zubin. They cheered him from the moment he walked onto the stage. They applauded the *Barber of Seville* Overture and *La Valse* as though they'd never heard them before. They loved their first-chair violin and viola players in Mozart's *Sinfonia concertante,* as though they had been doing the *1812 Overture.* The Bartók concerto was a revelation. And when it was over they were left, as the *Musical America* critic observed, with "an overwhelming impression" of Zubin Mehta.

So impressed was Pierre Beique, that the morning after the second concert he contacted every member of his executive board and asked for their concurrence. Having received it, he waited until after the final concert and then made the offer. Zubin did not have to consult anyone before accepting.

As of the 1961–62 season, he was named music director of the Montreal Symphony Orchestra.

No one could have been happier at the news than Carmen. The relief she'd felt on his winning the Liverpool assistantship paled beside the elation of knowing they would settle down in Canada, in a home of their own, supplied by the orchestra. No more shuffling from place to place, depending on the ill health of other conductors; now they would have a chance to rebuild their life together. From that moment, Montreal would be her home.

It was long after midnight when they finished celebrating the final concert and Beique's offer. Back in their hotel room, Zubin had a call to make, to Siegfried Hearst in California.

During the first week of rehearsals in Montreal, Hearst had phoned to say that Georg Solti was interested in Zubin as assistant conductor in Los Angeles. Somewhat reluctantly, he had let Hearst talk him into flying out for an audition between the final Montreal concert and his departure for Linz and Yugoslavia. Now, of course, there was no need to make the trip. Or so he thought.

"Dat's ferry gut," Hearst grumbled, his German accent broader on being called up from a sound sleep. "So now you got an orchestra of your own. Ve discuss it tomorrow ven you get here, ja?"

"Wait a minute, Siegfried, don't hang up. Why should I go out to California? I don't want to be Solti's assistant. I don't want to be Bernstein's assistant. I don't want to be anybody's assistant. I'm going to be the music director of the Montreal Symphony Orchestra."

"So a big-time music director can't afford a lousy airplane ticket? Besides, nobody out here knows about your appointment. It didn't make the front page of the *Times* yet, so come audition for Mr. Solti."

"But it's not ethical . . ."

"You just come and let me worry about that, okay? Now I'll go back to sleep."

Flying in from the east, Zubin's first glimpse of Los Angeles was an aurora of orange-brown haze rising behind movie-set purple mountains. Beyond the mountains loomed a stretch of desert, empty until, out of nowhere, roads appeared. They were solitary highways at first, then roads crossing roads crossing roads in a cobweb spun by a drunken spider. Silver cables strung at crazy angles seemed to thicken toward an unseen center.

Suddenly, trapped in interstices, he saw green groves of orange and lemon trees that shimmered under rainbows formed by the perpetual water sprays that kept them alive. Finally the houses began to appear— someone lived here after all, Zubin thought—one at a time, then in bunches on hillsides. With virtually every house came a blinding reflection of blue, which it took Zubin a moment to recognize as swimming pools. Factories, clusters of commerce, communities came into view; they all seemed to struggle in that mindless web of roads and highways.

Without warning, the plane was over the ocean, blue and, from the air, serene, with its shifting paisley pattern of breakers. The plane circled, and at last the city itself came into view.

Zubin was unprepared for the seemingly endless reach of the place, block after block of buildings, looming above streams of traffic that wriggled through the morning rush. As his field of vision turned toward the east, he could see the orange-brown haze disappearing back over the mountains. He'd been impressed by the bird's-eye view of New York, but compared to the constrained, insular mass of that eastern city, Los Angeles seemed a boundless place where one might expand to the limits of his own imagination.

The airport was just as confusing as Idlewild and Heathrow, worse because it seemed impossible to find a taxi. Finally, he was in a Yellow cab that somehow began finding its way through the morass of freeways, past main streets of timid little towns whose inhabitants all seemed to shop at the same stores and watch the same movies. At some undefined point the suburbs ended and the city began, looking so much cleaner than New York, Philadelphia, or London. It was more like Montreal, uncrowded, greened with lawns and trees—only the evergreens were not firs but palms.

Siegfried Hearst helped Zubin settle into his hotel room and at the same time settled his misgivings about auditioning under false pretenses.

"Look," he said, "what is it costing them to listen to you? You paid your own way here; they are out nothing but a little time. I just want Solti to hear you, and some of the people who run this orchestra. You never can tell, it might develop into something for the future."

Zubin relented and asked how he was supposed to audition. It would be during a rehearsal the following morning, and Hearst had suggested the Brahms First Symphony and Mozart's *Prague* Symphony to audition. At least, Zubin thought, he was on safe ground with the music.

But the audition went no further than the first movement of the *Prague*. When that was over, Solti called Zubin over to where he was sitting, beside Siegfried Hearst.

"Well," said Hearst to Solti as Zubin sat down, "what do you think? Was I right or wrong?"

Solti nodded his head gravely and turned to Zubin. "Yes," he said, "I would like you to be my assistant."

Zubin started to speak but, for once, could not find the right words. At last he stammered, "Thank you, sir, but . . ." and his voice trailed off. He looked at Hearst for help, thinking that the man who'd got him into this jam ought to be able to get him out.

The manager jumped into the breech, choosing his words carefully but explaining precisely what had happened. The only alteration to the facts was Hearst's declaration that Zubin had received the offer from Montreal only yesterday, after he had arrived in California—at his own expense, Hearst was quick to add—so there had been little point in his going away before Solti had had a chance to hear him. Again, Zubin was struck by Siegfried Hearst's gift for manipulation.

"Except for Sol Hurok," he recalls fondly, "I never met any manager who knew the ins and outs of how to speak, how to negotiate, like Siegfried. He was a master.

"Solti understood completely. He gave me a bit of advice on my choice of tempi in the Mozart symphony, wished me well, and sent me away to Linz and Yugoslavia. And I thought, Well, at least I got to see Los Angeles and say I conducted there. I never figured I'd get back there again."

In New York, between flights, Zubin reached Leonard Bernstein and told him the news about Montreal. Bernstein congratulated him on his good fortune and said he knew Zubin would be a great success in Canada, although he was sorry they would not be able to work together.

So, in November of 1960, Zubin flew to Europe to see if his streak of luck would continue. In two days he had turned down two assistantships under two esteemed conductors; but come the following season, he would have an orchestra of his own to conduct—and to build.

Measured in terms of public acceptance, the Yugoslavian tour was a resounding success. Zubin expanded his repertoire as usual, though he was less than satisfied with the playing he got from some of the local orchestras. Indeed, his patience and charm were often put to the test as he rattled along Yugoslavian rails from the poppy fields of Macedonia, through the pig farms of Serbia, to the sophisticated charm of Zagreb. He found it difficult to believe that only a few weeks before he had been plummeting along the avant-garde freeways of Los Angeles.

Soon enough, though, there was the welcome sight of the Austrian border. The week before Christmas he was back in Vienna—this time in a hotel. He was not exactly rolling in money yet, but his Yugoslavian dinars were enough to afford a good room and a decent meal at Liesinger's. However, he had little relish for living alone in hotel rooms and dining alone, particularly at Christmas time, with two jobless months ahead.

He returned to his hotel one evening, after sitting in on a Philharmoniker rehearsal, to find a cablegram waiting for him. It was from

George Kuyper, the manager of the Los Angeles Philharmonic.

"Reiner ill," it read. "Can you come for rehearsals January 15? Details will follow."

So Siegfried Hearst had been right after all: the California audition trip had paid off. When Fritz Reiner canceled at the last minute, the Los Angeles management had Zubin Mehta on its mind and knew he'd be available. Quickly he dashed off a reply, "Will be delighted," and handed it to the desk clerk. October in Montreal, December in Yugoslavia, January in California . . . he suddenly felt for the first time a sense of urgency about his career that was never to leave him.

Within a week he received the dates of the four concerts he was to conduct, along with the programs Reiner had scheduled. Schumann's Second Symphony, Beethoven's Seventh, *Le Rossignol* by Stravinsky, and Richard Strauss's *Don Quixote* were the featured works; Zubin had never conducted any of them.

It would have been a colossal opportunity to expand his repertoire, but he wisely decided on a few substitutions. He was not very familiar with the Schumann Second Symphony, so he substituted the Fourth, which he knew well though he'd never conducted it. Though he'd never performed the Beethoven Seventh either, he was eager for a chance to conduct it, so that stayed. *Le Rossignol* and *Don Quixote* were new to him, so he got scores from the library and looked through them.

With some regret, he let prudence dictate a change in Stravinsky, from *Rossignol* to *Petrushka,* which, of course, was an old warhorse for him. Since the orchestra had already scheduled the cello and viola solos for their first-chair musicians and since he felt an immediate liking for the music, he decided to have a go at the *Quixote.*

Except for the Stravinsky, then, and for the *Coriolanus* Overture and Webern's Six Pieces, which he added to round out the programs, he would be performing all the music for the first time. What's more, he had less than a month to study and learn the difficult *Don Quixote.*

On January 15, 1961, Zubin returned to Los Angeles, the city he'd supposed he would never see again. He was twenty-four years old, dripping with confidence. In two years he had leapt from the crowded ranks of students and apprentices to the status of international artist.

Again he strode onto the stage to confront the Los Angeles musicians, but this time it was the stage of Philharmonic Hall, not a high school auditorium; he was auditioning for no one but himself. Several years later, a member of the L.A. Philharmonic administrative staff looked back on the day with a sense of awe.

"He came on stage carrying a baton and a score of *Don Quixote,*" she remembered. "Fritz Reiner had programmed that, and I remember everyone was a little bit surprised that Zubin had kept it in. He set the score down on the music stand and never opened it! He just smiled at the orchestra, lifted his baton, and gave the downbeat. It was as though he struck a spark with that downbeat that electrified the orchestra. And out in the auditorium we could feel it, too."

Zubin, too, recalls the moment: "What a rare, marvelous experience it was to hear the music of *Don Quixote* coming out of that orchestra for the first time. It was obvious that the musicians and I were going to get along."

After the first concert, Zubin greeted enthusiastic well-wishers and autograph seekers in the dressing room, still wearing his one-and-only full dress suit, purchased for twenty-five dollars in Vienna. Since the suit still had no pockets, he had to borrow a pen every time someone presented him a program to sign—a ritual to which he had not yet grown accustomed.

Looking up from one such program signing, he found himself staring into a face he recognized instantly from photographs on dozens of record jackets. It belonged to the violinist his father idolized, Jascha Heifetz.

"I couldn't believe it. Here was this man my father revered as a god. He had come to my concert and now he was congratulating me. Heifetz was congratulating Mehta! As soon as everyone left I picked up the phone and called my father in Philadelphia. I said, 'You'll never believe this, but "god" was at my concert tonight.'"

There was another important person in the audience that night, someone who was to have a direct hand in the molding of Zubin's immediate future and, ultimately, of his entire career. Her name was Mrs. Norman Chandler. Known in social circles as "Buff," Mrs. Chandler had shared the power as publisher of the Los Angeles *Times* since 1944. Earlier, in 1960, she and her husband, Norman Chandler, had handed over the publication to their son Otis. Now she could devote full time to her first love, the arts in Los Angeles.

In 1961 Mrs. Chandler was president of the Hollywood Bowl Association, executive vice-president of the Southern California Symphony Association, a guarantor of the Los Angeles Civic Light Opera, a regent of the University of California, and, since the previous summer, chairman of the Music Center Building Fund Committee. Her twofold aspiration in 1961 was to see the Los Angeles Philharmonic in its own permanent home with its own permanent music director. As matters stood, she realized, her orchestra was without leadership and losing quality.

The eventual interweaving of Dorothy Chandler's destiny with that of the young Indian conductor was not yet apparent at that first concert in Los Angeles's Philharmonic Hall. However, there was a hint of things to come in the conversation that took place backstage afterward.

"Tell me, Mr. Mehta, exactly when were you born?"

"April 29, 1936," Zubin answered. "Why do you ask?"

"You're a Taurus, then," and Mrs. Chandler smiled, curiously. "I might have known. I'm a Taurus myself."

Zubin's initial program of *Don Quixote* and the Schumann Fourth was given twice, on January 19 and 20, to warm but not overly enthusiastic receptions. The Los Angeles audiences were noted for an attitude of "show me," and they may have been waiting for confirmation of their first impression.

As Ernest Fleischmann was to write after taking over as executive director of the Philharmonic in 1968, "Los Angeles audiences . . . cannot be easily categorized like, for example, the Viennese (conservative), the Londoners (middle-of-the-road) or the New Yorkers (liberal). Reputations are not easily established in Los Angeles."

Perhaps not, but the reputation came soon enough for Zubin. By his second series of concerts, on January 26 and 27, it seemed apparent that he was on his way to becoming (quoting Fleischmann again) one of the "six to ten musical heroes here who can do no wrong."

Those concerts of *Petrushka*, Webern's Six Pieces (heard for the first time in Los Angeles), and Beethoven's Symphony no. 7 were magical nights for the orchestra, for the audiences, and for the Philharmonic's board of directors. Even Zubin felt hard pressed to recall them with his typical matter-of-factness.

"I must say I learned a lot at those concerts. The orchestra and I got along. The public reacted very nicely. Everything jelled. I came away completely enlightened."

Before the last concert was over, though, there was more adventure in store. Igor Markevitch—whose ill health and career prerogatives seemed fated to propel Zubin's career—would not be able to conduct the next week's concerts. Could Zubin possibly stay? Why not? answered Zubin. Markevitch had programmed the Bartók Concerto for Orchestra—just as he had in Montreal—along with Tchaikovsky's Piano Concerto no. 1, with Byron Janis as soloist. He'd heard the Tchaikovsky dozens of times, but had never conducted it.

By now the Los Angeles press—egged on by Mrs. Chandler—was treating Zubin as an Event. There were newspaper articles, radio and television interviews, all portraying him as a dashing young Hindu (of course, everyone from India must be a Hindu) who had flown from the East, perhaps on a magic carpet, to rescue the city from cultural despair.

Rumors began to circulate, as rumors do in the thick Los Angeles air. Zubin was a playboy, a glamour boy, a roué, a ladies' man, a "swinger." He was "seen" doing the night spots with various female celebrities. In fact, whenever he was not with the orchestra rehearsing that week, he was alone in his hotel room feverishly studying the scores for the Friday and Saturday night concerts.

No matter what the facts might be, however, Zubin Mehta was an overnight public hero in the city that was built on its own publicity. When Zubin walked on stage the evening of February 2, the spark he had struck three weeks earlier with that first downbeat was running like sheet lightning through the theater.

With uncanny appropriateness, Zubin opened the program with the Overture to Verdi's *La Forza del Destino,* almost as though he were paying tribute to those "unseen powers," as his mother would describe them, which had somehow brought him to this moment. Again came the first three notes, splitting the air of the old theater like staccato thunderclaps, and the second three, just as startling, leading to the Destiny motif.

Waiting backstage, pianist Byron Janis felt the excitement and knew he was going to be part of a special evening, if he could do his part to sustain the almost unbearable level of energy. When the applause for the overture finally waned, Janis walked to the piano and, with barely a pause, signaled the young maestro that he was ready.

Like two cobras, Zubin's arms struck, down and out, making the horns cry out with an urgency that no one in the audience could have thought the hackneyed old concerto still contained. Then the pianist's hands crashed down on the keyboard like Thor's hammers, and Zubin called up the soft rain of the strings—the elemental duality, the Yang supported by the Yin. The arguments stated, the piano and orchestra then entered into a dialogue that flowed and ebbed and climaxed in a surge of spirit and sound at the end of the long first movement.

There seemed hardly a breath from the audience in the pause between movements. Zubin could feel their eyes glued on him as he leaned forward, summoning the strings to tiptoe in, almost imperceptibly, out of the silence. The flute entered, like the faraway piping of a shepherd at night, then the piano, and Zubin urged them all into a tinkling nocturnal dance.

The rondo finale began with the feeling of another kind of dance, like a festival in a Russian village, until simple joy turned to passion and passion to almost violent vehemence. The collaboration between soloist and orchestra was brilliant, flawless, and when Zubin's arms whipped them all into the final, desperate chords, it was like the dying delirium of one enormous creature. The audience exploded.

Zubin felt like a man trying to stand against a tidal wave. He was weak, he wanted to collapse and let himself be swept away by the roaring, cheering crowd. He gathered his strength and followed Janis offstage; both men were sweating and trembling. They walked on again to see the orchestra members applauding, stomping their feet, the audience on its feet, yelling and bravoing. They walked off again, but it was the same when they came back on. Suddenly, Zubin was moved to do something he'd never done before. He leaned over and shouted into Janis's ear, then walked over to the concertmaster. He was going to repeat the last movement.

In her box, Dorothy Chandler was also leaning over to shout in the ear of the woman next to her, even as they both stood and applauded. "We can't let this Indian get away," she said.

"I thought he'd turned down the assistantship offer."

"I'll think of something," said Mrs. Chandler.

The next day Mrs. Chandler did think of something. She contacted most of the other board members by telephone and secured their approval. There was little time to waste, since Zubin was scheduled to leave the following morning for Vienna. She sent a car to his hotel that afternoon.

Zubin arrived at the Chandler home to find, on the table, a typewritten contract between the Los Angeles Philharmonic and Zubin Mehta.

"They offered me something they called an 'associate conductorship,' not Solti's assistant, but his associate. It was something I could accept without being anybody's *shammash*. My first question was, 'How does Mr. Solti feel about this?' But they said not to worry; they would deal with that side of it and it would be okay.

"Next I telephoned Montreal. There was a bit of grumbling there, but finally they agreed. After all, I was only contracted for a twelve-week period in Montreal. They wanted me in Los Angeles for nine weeks. Twenty-one weeks of my own concerts—wonderful!

"We came to a tentative agreement, pending Mr. Solti's approval, and I penciled my name on the contract. Nobody seemed to have any doubt it would all be settled amicably. My first scheduled appearance as associate was to be that summer in the Hollywood Bowl, so I told them I would see them then and I went back to Vienna."

Hardly had Zubin landed in Vienna than he received an urgent telephone call from Egon Hilbert, the former cultural diplomat whose moral scruples Zubin had offended in Rome. Now Hilbert was director of the Vienna Festival and offended only by bad performances and conductors who failed to show up. He made Zubin an offer that seemed too good to be true.

"Ormandy has canceled his June concerts," said Hilbert. "Are you available?"

"You can't mean the Vienna Philharmonic?" But that was just what Hilbert did mean.

The dates were prior to the start of the Hollywood Bowl season, so

Zubin was able to accept. He'd never dreamed he'd be conducting the Vienna Philharmonic at age twenty-five.

Almost immediately on the heels of Hilbert's call, a cablegram arrived from something called PALPHILORC, in the shorthand international cable address system. The message inquired as to his availability in the closing weeks of May for twelve concerts.

Puzzled, Zubin made some quick inquiries concerning the identity of the "Palphilorc" before he accepted any engagement with it. He learned that the letters stood for Palestine Philharmonic Orchestra, which had changed its name, but evidently not its cable address, to Israel Philharmonic in 1948.

Eugene Ormandy had been scheduled to conduct in Israel just prior to his concerts in Vienna and had canceled the entire tour. Delighted at the prospect of visiting the Middle East, Zubin cabled his acceptance.

Suddenly, another request, this one from Lies Askonas, a British agent who'd heard Zubin the night of the final Liverpool competition. She could get him an engagement with the Royal Philharmonic if he could come immediately.

Zarin Mehta, now a full-fledged London accountant and rising rapidly in his firm, took an afternoon off from work to attend his brother's rehearsal with the Royal Philharmonic. He'd been moved many times by this orchestra's playing, but never had he felt anything like the mixture of uneasiness and pride that swept over him as Zubin walked onto the stage.

What were they thinking, he wondered, an upstart Indian *bhisti?* Just another boy conductor? Certainly this would not be any easy relationship.

But Zubin went about his work methodically, using his knowledge of the music and of each instrument to win the musicians' respect. It took longer than it had in Toronto or Philadelphia or New York or Montreal or Los Angeles, but by the end of the rehearsal the members of the Royal Philharmonic were won over. The evening's performance took on an added dimension when the orchestra learned that its beloved former music director, Sir Thomas Beecham, had passed away during it.

After the successful concert in London, Carmen joined him and they traveled to Israel together, hoping to recapture whatever it was that had escaped from their marriage. Their problems could no longer be blamed on a lack of money, but in two years Zubin's life had undergone many dramatic changes. Carmen's, on the other hand, seemed only to have drifted slowly, and in a quite different direction. Still, they were closer in Israel than they had been for some time.

They were met at the Tel Aviv airport by Enrique and Aida Barenboim, Daniel's parents, who took them out on the town for their first night in Israel. To Zubin, it was like coming home.

"On Dizengoff Street, I thought I was walking again in Bombay. The same heat, the same confusion, and the outdoor cafés, each with its unique smells, the same as in Bombay."

Besides the sights, sound, and smells, there was a feeling of brotherhood he'd experienced in no other place. Jostling in a human river of people from all corners of the earth, nearly all of them Jews, Zubin was as much in the minority as he'd been in Vienna or at Tanglewood. Yet, with the so-called Oriental Jews outnumbering their European-born countrymen, his complexion went unnoticed. Seated at the sidewalk tables, nursing their coffees or reading the poster-filled kiosks, were Jews from Morocco, Yemen, Iraq, and Egypt, whose skin tones included every shade of brown.

What moved him most, however, was the reception the orchestra gave him, not at the first rehearsal when they felt each other out with a healthy skepticism—neither having heard of the other before—but at the second rehearsal.

"As soon as I walked into the room they started applauding, and I could tell they meant it from their hearts. This was for a young man a very great boost."

The program for the Israel concerts was one of the most demanding Zubin had ever chosen, consisting of the Dvorak Symphony no. 7 in D-minor, Kodaly's *Dances of Galanta,* and the Symphony in Three Movements by Stravinsky. There were three rehearsals, followed by concerts in Tel Aviv, Haifa, and Jerusalem.

"The orchestra loved me, but I'm afraid the concerts did not go very well. The Dvorak D-minor Symphony, especially, did not get enough rehearsal. It is one of the more difficult of all the romantic works for orchestra. The Stravinsky I worked the hardest on because it was my first encounter with it." And also because he would be conducting it again in two weeks, not in Israel but in Vienna, where one could not afford to make mistakes.

"That first rehearsal in Vienna was the worst rehearsal of my career." Zubin groans, shaking his head as though to get rid of the painful memory. For the first time he was facing many of his old professors, not as a student but as their *Dirigent.* Worse perhaps was the experience of directing some of the younger players, with whom he had shared rather puerile experiences hardly more than a year before. And he had to go and program the Stravinsky Symphony in Three Movements. To the Israelis it had offered relatively few problems; to the Los Angeles Philharmonic it would have been duck soup; but to the Bruckner-bound

Viennese it was tortuous and largely incomprehensible.

After the first rehearsal Zubin dragged himself back to the Imperial Hotel for a night's sleep he knew would be filled with awful dreams. In the lobby he almost bumped into Josef Krips, on his way to conduct a performance at the Staatsoper.

"Professor," Zubin moaned, "I've just done one of the most awful rehearsals in my entire life. I'll never be called here again."

The older conductor did his best to calm his worries and set his mind at ease, but Zubin feared the worst. Disgrace at the Vienna Festival could mean banishment from the regular Vienna Philharmonic season as well. Matters were not much helped by a thoughtful speech the orchestra president took it upon himself to deliver to his musicians.

"Gentlemen [there were no ladies in the Philharmoniker], we have to start thinking of the younger generation of conductors." Zubin wanted to hide somewhere. The president, Prof. Otto Strasse, seemed to like him, but what kind of thing was this to say to an orchestra?

"There are not so many of the older ones around any more," the violinist-president went on, "so why not give one of these young ones a chance?"

With a broad smile, he turned and waved the "young one" to the podium. Like a dutiful guinea pig, Zubin thanked Strasse for his kind words and rapped his baton. Maybe moments like this were what made conductors cancel.

But the worst was over. Perhaps recalling his own admonition to the contralto in *Pierrot Lunaire,* Zubin called up his reserve confidence and let the orchestra think he knew precisely what he was doing. After a number of small corrections they began playing the Stravinsky as though it were as Viennese as apple strudel.

Rounding out the program was the more appealing *Don Quixote* by Richard Strauss. That gave the festival audience something to cheer about, which they did. The concerts went extremely well, and the press hailed the return of "Vienna's own Indian" in glory. As one critic wrote, "A great career is sure to lie ahead of Zubin Mehta."

A year before, Zubin might have taken that as fatuous flattery, but now it had the ring of truth. The Vienna Philharmonic management was talking about asking him back for the regular season, and there were suggestions that he might be a good candidate for the Salzburg Festival.

In exactly one year he had conducted seven major orchestras of five nations. Including Stokowski in New York (and in Philadelphia), four important conductors had canceled appearances and bequeathed him a total of eighteen important concerts—and that in the space of only nine months.

The following season, Zubin would extend his record of accomplishments even further, becoming the youngest conductor ever to lead the Berlin Philharmonic. That distinction so agitated Zubin that he cut himself shaving and walked bleeding onto the stage of the old Hochschule.

The first half of that memorable evening's program in Berlin included the Schumann Cello Concerto, played by Enrico Mainardi. The concerto proceeded smoothly, Zubin growing progressively surer of himself, when suddenly, as he turned to give Mainardi a cue, he saw a look of anguish come across the old man's face. Zubin could see he wanted to speak, but could not. At last the concerto was over, and Zubin stepped off the platform to grip the cellist's hand.

"*Maestro,*" Mainardi whispered, "*i tuoi pantaloni sono aperti!*"

Zubin looked down to see that, indeed, his fly was open. Quite a debut, he thought. Back in the dressing room, between halves, members of the orchestra filed in one by one to tell him in discreet, hushed tones, "*Herr Kapellmeister, die Hosen . . .*"

Fortunately, his brilliant conducting of the Mahler Symphony no. 1 in the second half took the minds of musicians and audience off the *Unglück* of the first half. At last Zubin could put into practice the invaluable education in Mahler he had received from Bruno Walter in Vienna.

Many of those international guest appearances during 1960 and 1961 came about as a result of cancellations by other conductors. Several years later Zubin would tell a magazine reporter, "I made half my career by jumping in at the last moment. Sometimes I think my success was due almost entirely to the misfortunes of my colleagues."

But as Zubin hopped from continent to continent, he never imagined that another conductor's cancellation would lay much more than a concert in his lap. In Los Angeles, Zubin Mehta was about to inherit an entire orchestra.

7

⁓⊰⊱⁓

The Profession
of His Father

To trace the history of music in Los Angeles, one does not have to reach back very far in time. It was the railroad that brought music, as it brought so many things, to the little American-Mexican-Indian town dozing around a plaza church. It was not until 1885 that the railroad arrived, though California by that time had been a state for twenty-five years. But once Los Angeles stirred, there was no holding it back.

The railroad brought Emma Albert's English Opera Company, and Angelenos who had been musically exposed to little more than saloon piano rolls were suddenly hearing *Mignon* and *Lucia di Lammermoor*. In less than a decade, four concert halls, an oratorio society, an organ factory, and any number of performing groups sprang up. Los Angeles was on its way to overtaking the big city, San Francisco, as music center of the West.

Opera was first to take root and flourish, though it was always treated as an exotic import, rather than as an indigenous art form. Many stage-struck youngsters, who would become actors in the not-so-distant film industry, got their early lessons in histrionics from such stars as Enrico Caruso, Nellie Melba, and Emma Calvé.

They all performed in Hazard's Pavillion, which seated roughly four

104

thousand humans for opera performances and about half that number of cows, pigs, and horses for the more profitable livestock exhibitions. In 1906 a million dollars changed Hazard's Pavillion into Temple Auditorium, and the Lombardi Opera Company gave its production of *Aïda* as the grand opening program. In a second-floor auditorium on nearby Spring Street, the thirty-odd musicians of the Los Angeles Symphony Orchestra gave their less lavish concerts.

There had been several attempts at organizing a full-scale orchestra for the city, including the first all-female orchestra (twenty-five strong) in the United States; but the orchestra that was to metamorphose into today's Los Angeles Philharmonic was not formed until 1897.

The Los Angeles Symphony was founded by Harley Hamilton, violinist and part-time conductor of the Women's Orchestra. Hamilton's chief problem—the problem that would keep coming back like a bad penny to future generations of Los Angeles music directors—was how to provide enough money to keep his musicians fed and clothed without their having to moonlight in the saloons and dance halls. Part of his problem was solved by the intervention of Mrs. John C. Mossin, the first known "angel" in the City of Angels and spiritual ancestor of Dorothy Chandler. Mrs. Mossin is cited in local history as "the Mother of the Los Angeles Symphony" because it was largely due to her money and energy that the orchestra kept its head above water for twenty-three seasons.

Hamilton's other problem was getting the musicians he needed in the first place. Los Angeles was still the boondocks as far as serious music was concerned, and it was not much easier for Hamilton to recruit bassoonists and French horn players than it would be for Mehli Mehta in Bombay forty years later. Hamilton was forced to rearrange and transpose parts so that the music he wanted could be played by the instruments available.

Thus the Los Angeles Symphony could offer its audiences a taste of the symphonic literature "in a harmony which was satisfying," as an early Los Angeles *Times* critic kindly observed, "even if somewhat different in tone color than that which Beethoven had conceived."

As Hamilton's orchestra struggled along, however, it was beset by local dissatisfaction and resultant financial difficulties. The musicians themselves were so unhappy that in 1919 nearly every single one of them jumped ship to join a new orchestra, the Los Angeles Philharmonic. They had been made an offer they could hardly refuse: more money.

The money belonged to one man, William Andrews Clark, Jr. Wealthy lawyer, son of a Montana copper baron, dilettante musician, Clark put up one million dollars of his own money and in 1919 became the second of only two men in American musical history to establish an orchestra single-handedly. (The other was Boston's Major Henry Lee Higginson in 1881.) For the first time, Clark promised the press, Los Angeles would have an orchestra whose players would all be "salaried men removed from any participation in cabaret shows, parades or fatiguing employment."

Fifty-five of those musicians came from the briefly mourned Symphony. In four months' time, forty-three others were recruited on the East Coast by Clark's chosen conductor, Walter Henry Rothwell.

Clark was looking for a big-name conductor, and, when Sergei Rachmaninoff and several others turned him down, Rothwell was the closest he could come. A London-born piano prodigy, Rothwell became a composition student at the Vienna Music Academy under Anton Bruckner and later studied conducting under Gustav Mahler—associations that tie him rather curiously to the man who would inherit his position nearly half a century later.

When he stepped off the Santa Fe Limited on September 26, 1919, Rothwell told the waiting Los Angeles press, "In New York I found the heartiest interest in our undertaking. . . . I found musicians keen to come West. . . . Most of the eastern conductors were deeply interested. They did all in their power to further my efforts in getting the right people for the right places."

One month later, the largest orchestra ever assembled in Los Angeles, ninety-eight players, gave its first concert in Trinity Auditorium to a crowd of twenty-four hundred. That such a feat could have been accomplished in four months under such circumstances attests to the power of a paycheck in the world of musicians.

The Los Angeles *Examiner* called the orchestra "the most prodigious infant in symphonic history . . . a musical Minerva, sprung into life full grown and in all its panoply of equipment." The somewhat awed reviewer went on to predict that the orchestra would grow into a "really great organization . . . which will improve with associations and custom."

The reviewer was correct in her prophesy. Over the years the Los Angeles Philharmonic did grow and mature, though the graph line was to be jagged, not straight, with downs as well as ups. Conductors came and went, some famous, others only local heroes.

Georg Schneevoigt took over from Walter Rothwell and he was followed by a succession of passing stars: Artur Rodzinski, Otto Klemperer, Alfred Wallenstein. The sixth permanent conductor was Eduard van Beinum, who was perhaps the most beloved of the musicians themselves. After his death in 1959, the orchestra was left without a permanent conductor, to be guided and misguided by a string of guest conductors, including Bruno Walter, Igor Stravinsky (both of whom made their last recordings with the orchestra), Leopold Stokowski, and Eugene Ormandy. They conducted programs of their choosing, either at the old auditorium in the winter or in the Hollywood Bowl in the summer.

Neither place provided a decent home for music. The auditorium was a barnlike structure that served nearly as many purposes as had Hazard's Pavillion in 1887. The Bowl, a natural amphitheater in the Hollywood Hills, is an outrageously immense valley with seating for seventeen thousand that four orchestras would be hard pressed to fill with sound.

Still, attendance at Philharmonic concerts was good, and the Bowl was nearly always packed. The only imminent danger to the orchestra after Eduard van Beinum's passing was an absence of leadership and a resultant loss of quality.

Mrs. Chandler and the other members of the board saw that many of their musicians were becoming lax about their playing. Between the various sections there seemed to be very little rapport. Moreover, too many of the players were devoting too much time to studio work in the movie and recording industries. William Andrews Clark's ideal of a self-sufficient symphony organization had gotten lost over the years.

So it was with a sense of relief that Mrs. Chandler announced to her board in late 1960 that Georg Solti, one of the most successful guest conductors, had agreed to take over the orchestra as music director the following season. Almost instantly, morale among the musicians began to perk up. Solti was a distinguished conductor with an international reputation who might at last elevate the Los Angeles Philharmonic to the level of a world-class orchestra.

If there was any apprehension on the part of the board, it was due to Solti's insistence that he could spend only twelve weeks of the year in Los Angeles, only about one-third of the entire season. The rest of the time, including nearly all the summer season, the orchestra would once again be given over to guest conductors. This gave Solti most of his year to continue his work with the Royal Opera House in London and other, presumably more prestigious orchestras in Europe and America. Dorothy Chandler foresaw difficulties in the arrangement.

It was then, in February 1961, that Mrs. Chandler hit on what she thought was the ideal solution. Zubin, as "associate conductor," could provide a continuity for the season, taking over the orchestra for a full nine weeks.

The board accepted the proposition enthusiastically, Zubin accepted enthusiastically. Unfortunately, the incoming music director was at the music festival in Lucerne and could not be reached by telephone to gauge his enthusiasm.

At this point in what Zubin regretfully looks back on as "a dirty business," the stories conflict. To this day, the musicians in Los Angeles who were there at the time refuse to talk about it. As then-concertmaster

David Frisina says, "It's nice to think of what might have happened to the orchestra under Solti. On the other hand, look what's happened to us under Mehta. I'd just as soon not even mention the whole affair."

The starting point of what became a much-publicized controversy was the board's negotiating and signing a contract with Zubin without consulting the man they had just appointed music director, the man whose "associate" Zubin was supposed to become.

Solti himself refuses to speak of the incident today. However, even though the break with Los Angeles left him free to take over the Chicago Symphony, the wound has never completely healed. As he tells it—or as he told it at the time—Solti heard nothing of Zubin's hiring until American newspapers reached him in Lucerne.

On the other hand, Mrs. Chandler and the board members maintain that they immediately cabled Solti, seeking his approval. According to Mrs. Olive Behrendt, who later took over as president of the Southern California Symphony–Hollywood Bowl Association, the board tried for three weeks to reach Solti before announcing Zubin's appointment to the press. Then, having read of the board's action in the newspapers, it was to the newspapers that Georg Solti fired off his reply. It was unconscionable of the board, he raged, to make such an appointment without consulting him first.

Charges and countercharges were fired across the Atlantic, escalating from the theater pages of newspapers to major articles in national magazines. In Vienna, Zubin stumbled onto the story in the European edition of *Time* Magazine.

"I had no idea that all this was going on, that Solti had offered to resign. I tell you, today I would pick up the phone and call him. But in my young days in Vienna I just never thought of calling anybody long distance. Neither did he contact me and say, 'Look, I wanted you as assistant, but why did you do this?' There was no contact. The next thing I hear, he has resigned. Now they have an associate and no music director."

It seemed then to Zubin that whatever career he might have had in Los Angeles was stillborn. Hearing nothing further from the management, he went back in July to conduct his promised concerts at the Hollywood Bowl. He assumed the pencil-signed contract had been forgotten. The orchestra would be looking for a new resident conductor, and certainly the board would not repeat its mistake by telling him, whoever it might be, that he already had an associate before he started.

Zubin could afford to be somewhat fatalistic about the Los Angeles job. After all, he still had the Montreal Symphony, and suddenly he was gaining a great deal of recognition in Europe. His mother kept telling him to trust to fate, and perhaps she was right. There were plenty of other orchestras in the world to conquer; perhaps a lasting relationship with the Los Angeles Philharmonic just wasn't in the stars.

Not unpredictably, Buff Chandler had other ideas about destiny. She had no intention of letting her fellow Tauran get away.

"We had a crisis," she recalls. "There was no permanent music director. I'm in no way a professional musician or qualified as a critic, so what do you do? You turn to people who are best qualified to give advice. I asked Jascha Heifetz, Gregor Piatigorsky, John Vincent of the U.C.L.A. Music Department, Dr. Raymond Kendall of U.S.C., and Wayne Griffin, who was then president of the Bowl, to make up a list of top conductors.

"I stressed that this was not New York, Boston, or Chicago but Los Angeles. And our orchestra was about to enter a new phase. We needed not only the best person musically, but the right man at the right time right here. Because of age, health, or other commitments, our list of esteemed men was narrowed down to two. At that point I had to choose and make my recommendation. It was Zubin Mehta."

But now that Los Angeles wanted Zubin, did Zubin want Los Angeles? He wondered whether indeed the board had acted capriciously, as Solti maintained. Perhaps Mrs. Chandler and the others would think nothing of going over *his* head in the future.

Had Zubin acted on impulse, as he so often did, the course of musical history in the last decade and a half might have run much differently. Certainly it would have in Los Angeles and quite possibly in several other of the world's music capitals as well. But instead of turning down the offer, he expressed his doubts to Siegfried Hearst, who worked out a contract with general manager George Kuyper that spelled out Zubin's independence from the board in artistic matters.

That stumbling block removed, Zubin Mehta was named music director of the Los Angeles Philharmonic.

Zubin would have to wait a whole season before officially taking charge in Los Angeles, but the management encouraged him to put any changes into motion as soon as he liked. Since he had conducted the orchestra already more times than he had any other professional group, he had a fair grasp of its strengths and weaknesses.

"A good orchestra without much character," is how he assessed it. "The orchestra had a huge repertoire and was very flexible. Of course, they had played under a lot of fine music directors and guest conductors before I came along.

"There had been van Beinum, with whom they had been very happy making music. Some of the concerts were very good, I'm told, others,

with guest conductors, not so good. But sometimes even the great orchestras give below-par concerts. Sometimes the Montreal Canadiens
lose hockey games, too.

"If you want to compare how the orchestra played when I came to the
way it is now, put on the Bruno Walter recording of the Bruckner Ninth
Symphony. That was my old orchestra. They had to call it something else
(the "Columbia Symphony") because of contractual problems, but it was
the entire Los Angeles Philharmonic. They played well, but not with the
warmth and richness I knew they could have. My first preoccupation was
how to build this up."

How to *build*. Zubin clearly had no intention of treating the Philharmonic as a given quantity in his musical equation. He did not plan to
settle down with his three-year contract, content to be known as the
music director of a semiprestigious organization. He wanted to build the
Los Angeles Philharmonic into something better, something it had never
been before.

"Since my earliest days with my father in Bombay, I was brought up on
orchestra *building*. He was always training and trading, switching players
around and getting new instruments. That's what I wanted to do in
Montreal and Los Angeles.

"It's like an apprentice automotive engineer who has worked for years
on Rolls-Royce blueprints. The only thing left when he strikes out on his
own is to design and build his own car. So he asks himself, What's the
ideal car? That's what I wanted, the ideal orchestra."

In Zubin's mind and in his ear, the most ideal orchestra situation he
knew of so far was that of the Vienna Philharmonic. That, to him, was
the Rolls-Royce of orchestras. His "ideal orchestra" would not only have
to produce a sound like the Viennese, but must go much further in those
departments in which he felt the Viennese were lacking.

"In the Viennese approach, there is no harsh-sounding instrument.
Whatever the music, an ugly sound is wrong. As a result, the abject
harshness of, say, Stravinsky is foreign to them. That is the weakness in
Vienna.

"But the Los Angeles Philharmonic already knew how to play
Stravinsky. And the French music that gave the Viennese so much trouble, they played that beautifully. They could also play Shostakovich
wonderfully—but you don't need a special sound to play Shostakovich.

"Now if I could give this orchestra the right sound for German music,
the Viennese sound, it would be the ideal orchestra. Certainly it would
be *my* ideal orchestra."

Zubin's method of achieving the desired result was twofold. First,
there was the simple matter of programming music that would help him
mold the sound he wanted. He chose the most direct, yet in some ways

the most treacherous, route, the music of Anton Bruckner. If he could show the musicians how to play Bruckner the way he thought Bruckner should be played, then they could handle anything in the post-romantic German repertory.

The second step was more difficult. He had to get rid of certain players who were not up to his standards, players the critics callously referred to as "deadwood."

This would have been an ideal moment for Zubin to seek advice from a more experienced conductor, something he later learned to do. Instead he acted, as he so often did, on impulse, and he came very close to destroying the warm conductor-musician relationship that had served him so well with this and other orchestras in the past. He was assisted in his error by well-meaning friends who did not foresee the consequences.

"I had no intention of sacking at random, but I knew at least ten players who shouldn't even be in the orchestra. I was asked to make a list, which I promptly did. I was very uneducated in these matters."

It must be remembered that this was in the early sixties, when the American Federation of Musicians still had rather lax firing laws. Now, as Zubin points out, "the musicians' union is very strong, and it is only because of such mistakes."

Zubin had a healthy respect, indeed compassion, for the orchestra members as individuals. Yet he knew there was no dearth of precedents for sacrificing inadequate individuals for the sake of the ensemble.

"People like Fritz Reiner in Chicago—I am told he once hired a principal cellist, then, after one day, he fired the poor man. Or Stokowski, building a great orchestra on the backs of hastily unemployed musicians. Today we are paying the price with strict rules as to what we can and cannot do."

To soften the blow beforehand, Zubin decided to appoint a new personnel manager for the orchestra because, he felt, the present man was not doing the best job of representing the orchestra's interests. He took Joseph Fishman out of the second oboe chair, where he had been since 1948, and made him personnel manager. But Fishman quickly saw there was nothing he could do to keep the ax from falling.

"There was really no choice," Zubin reflects, with perceptible sadness in his tone. "You can't tell them, 'Please resign, but if you refuse you can stay on.' Sometimes an entire section will be featured in one solo passage, and if that is not played well the standard of the entire orchestra is reduced."

Zubin's greatest difficulty was with the wind players. Many of them were in their mid-fifties, old enough to have become seemingly permanent fixtures in the orchestra, but also old enough to have "lost their lips" or the lung power they needed to sustain long passages. It was only slightly easier in the critical string section, where there were musicians in the front rows who belonged in the fourth, and others who did not belong in the orchestra at all. There was a great deal of shuffling, a great deal of compromise.

"When the musicians heard of my list of nine players, all hell broke loose. The orchestra really loved me, but now they thought, He's turning into a monster. This was never my intention. I only wanted to get going on my job as quickly as possible."

The orchestra committee intervened and it was only with the passage of time that the nine players left, through attrition. Nevertheless, Zubin's attempt at housecleaning was the first decisive step toward instilling a sense of pride, a pride that has since grown steadily in the Los Angeles Philharmonic.

As personnel manager Joe Fishman puts it, "It used to be we were just happy to fill a chair. Now we have a choice of the best. We can offer fifty-two weeks' pay, including vacation pay, and a chance to play in one of the best orchestras in the world. They come from all over just to audition, from Colombia, from Korea, from Italy. There's a real international interest in this orchestra.

"You have to build something and then strive to make it better. And there's the feeling of always getting better, not like just trying to hold on to what you have. It's a lot like being a world champion—everybody's gunning for you. Even if we've gotten there, we're still trying to get there, we still have that feeling it's going to be better next year."

Zubin's critics insist he acted too hastily in trying to force the Philharmonic into the mold of his "ideal orchestra." Yet it can be argued that he took great pains to make the best use of the material he had.

For instance, he was struck by the orchestra's penchant for playing twentieth-century music. As a guest conductor, he was impressed by their ability to make music out of the difficult Six Pieces by Webern. After the Webern there had been a number of condescending and uncomplimentary remarks from board members and patrons alike, who let Zubin know they would be pleased if he would steer clear of such stuff in the future. But in his first address as music director, Zubin made his intentions on this score quite clear. "I will," he told the board, "introduce as much modern music to you as I possibly can."

The Montreal Symphony had essentially the same problems as the Los Angeles Philharmonic: a few incompetent musicians, and neither sufficient pay nor good enough instruments for those who belonged.

In Montreal, however, there was a shortcoming that overshadowed all others, the shortcoming that had afflicted the orchestra since its conception in 1934, and which Zubin had little hope of ever solving. There was barely enough money to keep the orchestra going, let alone build it into something better.

The city's first symphony had been the Montreal Orchestra, founded and conducted by an English composer, Douglas Clarke, and supported by McGill University. Clarke and his orchestra were undone by their own shortsightedness in neglecting the tastes and opinions of the overwhelming French-speaking majority. The neglect included a failure to recognize French-Canadian artists and extended to an unwillingness to program the French repertory.

Unhappy at being overlooked, the leaders of the French community decided to form their own orchestra, giving it the typically impossible name of Les Concerts Symphoniques de Montréal, thus daring their English-speaking brethren even to pronounce it, let alone subscribe to it. Not surprisingly in a city of 800,000, there were not enough musicians to supply the second orchestra, so Les Concerts shared those of the Montreal Orchestra. The English orchestra played on Sunday afternoons at His Majesty's Theater, and the same musicians traveled to the French East End of the city to play their French concerts in a high school auditorium under the direction of Wilfrid Pelletier.

In 1937 the Montreal Orchestra collapsed under the weight of the Depression, leaving Les Concerts Symphoniques de Montréal to struggle on, luring any English-speaking citizens who could still afford the price of a ticket to their high school auditorium.

Two years later, Les Concerts found itself in the grip of a management crisis, needing new blood. The man who got the job of running the orchestra was Pierre Beique, a recent commerce graduate of McGill University and an employee in a perfume and pharmaceutical firm who'd been drawn to the orchestra by his consuming love of music.

There was, of course, no salary for a managing director—his first year's budget was only $17,000—but Beique's father agreed to "grubstake" his determined son. He supported him for three years before the younger Beique had the orchestra back on its feet enough to write himself a paycheck.

With no money and little incentive to offer, Beique traveled to New York and consulted with a man who had once been a resident of Montreal and later became one of the top artists' managers, Siegfried Hearst. In those days, Hearst managed such luminaries as Artur Rubinstein, Mischa Elman, Josef Szigeti, and Emanuel Feuermann.

"We are poor as rats," said the infant impresario, "but I would like to have some of your people as soloists. Would you give me a minimum and a maximum figure for them?"

Hearst agreed, allowing some of his biggest artists to go to Montreal for fees that seem ludicrous by today's standards. Rubinstein, for example, was guaranteed $750; if the house sold out—which of course it did—that figure skyrocketed to $1,000. Immediately Montreal was established as a forum for international artists.

Beique's second, and perhaps more difficult, achievement was to unite the French and English factions of the arts community in Montreal. The orchestra became a bilingual operation, and former officers of the Montreal Orchestra's board accepted invitations to join the reorganized board of Les Concerts Symphoniques de Montréal.

The problem of the orchestra's name took longer, and it got worse before it got better. By 1950 it was customary to refer to it as *L'Orchestre* des Concerts Symphoniques de Montréal, thus assuring another line of newsprint in every concert review but making it extremely difficult to write checks. Finally, in 1952, everyone agreed it should be called the Montreal Symphony Orchestra, or MSO. Or L'Orchestre Symphonique de Montréal, or OSM. In Montreal it is rare to please everyone at once.

Yet, as Zubin found out from his first performance at the Montreal Forum, it could be done. He knew he would have the support of the public and of the musicians; if anything could be considered lacking in Montreal, it was financial support.

Montreal had no wealthy benefactors and little thriving industry to support the arts. The federal, provincial, and local governments all contributed to the orchestra's upkeep, but most available funds were being drained off by the construction of a new civic center and arts complex.

At least by 1963 the new Place des Arts would provide a decent hall for the orchestra, and would seat nearly three times the capacity of the current theater. Old Plateau Hall, the East End high school auditorium the orchestra had used since 1934, could accommodate only thirteen hundred and had miserable acoustics.

Until the larger hall was completed, Zubin's only hope for increasing the musicians' take-home pay lay in lengthening the season. After long tugs of war with Pierre Beique and his administrators, he extracted a promise that over the next several years the season would be expanded from twelve to twenty-six weeks.

To further raise the orchestra's morale, Zubin instituted a pension fund, stretching the Symphony's shoestring budget almost to the breaking point.

Other than making personnel changes, there was little more he could personally accomplish in the first season to elevate the orchestra's international stature. Because of strict rules imposed by the Montreal Musicians' Union, he was not even allowed to hire musicians from outside the province of Quebec.

To improve the situation any further, he needed help. He got it from one of the most unlikely sources imaginable, the Soviet Ministry of Culture.

It began as one of those absurd casualties of the cold war. The Congress of the United States ruled out a proposed American tour by the Red Army Chorus, whose beautiful music might have served in those days to melt some of the ideological ice. As a responsive gesture of ill will, the Russians sent their chorus to America's closest neighbor, Canada, where it was received with open arms.

That tour went so well, the Soviets decided to send another chorus to Canada, this time planning ahead. The Georgian chorus would be flown by special Aeroflot plane to Montreal, whence it would travel by Air Canada to other Canadian cities. It would be a shame, the Commissar of Culture declared, to let that big plane return to Moscow empty; why not fill it with a representative performing group from Canada for a tour of Soviet cities?

So it was that, in the spring of 1962, Zubin found himself flying across the Atlantic and Iceland with an orchestra that had never been off the island of Montreal.

"It was a tremendous emotion and made for an enormous change in our attitude toward ourselves," Pierre Beique recalls. "Sitting in Tchaikovsky Hall, draped with the red flag and the maple leaf, it was a great thing for this little band of hometown musicians. It was also a great thing for Zubin."

The audiences were enthusiastic in their reception, and all the big names of contemporary Russian music turned out for the concerts—David Oistrakh, Emil Gilels, Leonid Kogan, and others. After four days in Moscow they flew to Kiev, then on to Leningrad for three more concerts, which were sold out. Wherever they went on the streets, they were followed by throngs of curious Russians, eager to exchange violets for autographs.

By the time they reached Leningrad, Zubin had mastered the Russian language well enough to give a short speech during each concert. The speech was nothing unpredictable—declarations of mutual understanding and peace through music—yet the Russian intelligentsia must have marveled at a native of India appointing himself the cultural bridge between Canada and the Soviet Union.

There is a story, often printed in American newspapers and magazines, that during one of these speeches Zubin uttered the brief hortatory sentence, "ВОССТАНИЕ," pronounced "vas-sta-nye." In English the word is "revolt."

"Not so," declares Zubin with finality. Then comes that tell-tale wrinkling around the eyes. "I never said that to an audience. It was to a group of autograph seekers backstage."

As soon as the Russian tour was announced, the enterprising Viennese impresario, Rudolf Gamsjaeger, had invited the Montreal Symphony to play his Musikverein. Gamsjaeger had witnessed Zubin's success with the

Vienna Festival and knew a good publicity ploy when he saw one. Using the press and word of mouth, he parlayed a visit by an unknown orchestra under a twenty-six-year-old conductor into the sold-out event of the season.

Entering Vienna with his own orchestra, Zubin felt like Pompey returning to Rome. By the sheer force of his personality, he transformed the Canadians into something more than they had been. The performance that evening towered over anything the orchestra had done before, and for Zubin it was the summit of his achievements to that point.

Out in the theater, in that glittering jewel box Zubin had first seen from a seat behind the basses, were friends, professors, and colleagues from student years, along with many of the old-guard Philharmoniker subscribers in their gowns and full dress.

As Zubin brought the encore, Weber's Overture to *Oberon,* to its rousing conclusion, one stately gentleman paused before applauding with his white gloves. He leaned over to his wife, nodding in the direction of the young conductor, and barked something that sounded very much like "Foot-vonkler. Foot-vonkler." To those who know the Viennese dialects and the Viennese taste in music, it was the ultimate compliment: "Furtwängler. Furtwängler."

If the 1962 tour marked the beginning of prominence for Zubin's Montreal Symphony, it also signaled the end of his marriage to Carmen Lasky.

The end had been coming for a long time. They were living comfortably enough in Montreal, sharing their love of Zarina and Merwan—but that was all they shared these days. They had stopped being a family. Moreover, Carmen suddenly had the luxury of time to think about her own fulfillment as a woman, time to realize she wasn't happy.

Still, she went along on the Russian tour, supposing, as always, that being together would somehow heal the wounds. But when she saw that the pleasure Zubin found in others was so much greater than any pleasure they could feel together, she knew it was over. Worst of all was his obvious attration to another Canadian soprano, a witty, vivacious young singer named Teresa Stratas.

That Stratas was even along on the tour, that she came to meet Zubin at all, was another of those curious conincidences which dominate the landscape of Zubin's career.

The soloist's berth was originally assigned to a Montreal tenor named Richard Verreau, a pupil of Beniamino Gigli and a protégé of Pierre Beique. Almost as the Aeroflot plane was about to leave for Russia, Verreau took ill and sent Beique scrambling for a replacement. Forsaking Montreal, he telephoned Toronto, where he located the Greek-Canadian soprano.

Still a relative unknown in international operatic circles, Teresa Stratas was described by Beique in 1962 as "a little Callas. A dynamic personality and a glorious voice." Her temperament was such that she was bound to be drawn to the equally charming, equally volatile conductor.

What ensued was, according to Beique, "only a little flirtation. After all, Zubin was an intelligent man, was not about to cause a *scandale*. Besides, his wife was right there, along with a prominent member of the Canadian Parliament, who was also dating Teresa."

It was enough of a straw, however, to break the back of his marriage. Carmen left the company as soon as they emerged from Russia, flying back to Montreal to start a complicated round of divorce proceedings. First there would be a separation, then a settlement, then a Mexican divorce, then finally an Ottawa annulment. It was a harrowing process for both of them, yet neither emerged with any feelings of bitterness.

"There was never a war," Zubin remembers, "never any dirtiness. My lawyers warned me about injured women changing their personalities overnight, but that never happened with Carmen.

"There had been a great deal of sacrifice on her part, and my traveling didn't help. I don't know whether I grew or she didn't grow or what, but at some point it just wasn't right. I felt it would be better to do it now, rather than wait for the children to grow up, because I didn't want hatred to set in."

Nor has there ever been hatred between them.

"When I think of Zubin now," Carmen reflects, "I think of him as a musician, not as my former husband. I think I always thought of him that way. Probably it sounds very strange, but since I was a young child the strongest element of my life has been music, and Zubin was a part of that. Sometimes the children and I become angry with him for things, little things. But then we see him conduct and we forget Zubin the father, Zubin the husband, and think of him as Zubin the conductor. He is a *great* musician, you know."

8

❧◆❧

Jupiter, Ruler of the
Tenth House

When Zubin took over the orchestras of Montreal and Los Angeles, he inherited two theaters that were impractical, unattractive, and ill suited for the purposes of symphonic music. Yet once again fate was on his side, for in both cities the wheels of progress were already in motion. The season 1964–65 would see Zubin established in the newest and most lavish arts centers in the United States and Canada.

Montreal had been pining after a home for its orchestra since the late 1940s, when its grandly named high school auditorium, Plateau Hall, began to sell out. The more operating costs rose, the less satisfactory the thirteen-hundred-seat facility became. Management did all in its power to program special events in cathedrals, parks, and skating rinks, but playing a concert in Plateau Hall became more and more expensive as the years went by and the old seats wore away.

In the 1950s, a number of half-hearted attempts were made to buy one of the city's huge old movie houses, in order to convert it into a symphony hall, but cinema was still big business and the owners were not inclined to sell. Various building and fund-raising committees sprouted up, only to shrivel and die in the long Canadian winters.

At last, in 1958, the orchestra was befriended by Montreal's cause-espousing mayor, Jean Drapeau. Over his several terms in office, Drapeau would mount other bandwagons—such as trade, sports, and public transportation—to build Expo 67, the 1976 Olympic City, and the Montreal subway system. But in 1958 the cause was culture and the edifice became Place des Arts.

The plans grew like mushrooms under the snow, until at last Montreal was promised a dazzling downtown complex of three theaters, seating three thousand, fifteen hundred, and eight hundred fifty respectively. They would all be joined by interlocking foyers, and each would have an entrance to the new subway system, to promote easy coming and going. La Grande Salle, the largest theater (and since renamed for Wilfrid Pelletier), would be a multipurpose arena, suitable for opera, ballet, and of course symphony. Its principal tenant would be the Montreal Symphony Orchestra. The plans were well under way when Zubin signed on as music director, and, by the time he returned from the Russian tour, construction on Place des Arts had begun.

The single disadvantage of the city shouldering the burden of construction was that management of the theater complex operated according to the rules of politics, not of the arts. This disparity between artistic ideals and political reality became apparent early in 1963. Long before construction was finished, but as plans were being laid for the grand opening of Place des Arts the following October, someone hit upon the idea of a gala "festival week" of opera. After all, what could be more extravagantly demonstrative of Montreal's commitment to artistic excellence than a week of opera?

That Montreal had no opera company of its own was no more than a passing concern. Seek help from Mother England and she would provide her forces from the Royal Opera House at Covent Garden. In what seems today a classic example of provincial inferiority complex, the theater management prepared to book an opening night *Lucia di Lammermoor*, featuring Joan Sutherland and her conductor-husband Richard Bonynge. Before these arrangements were finalized, however, word of them leaked to Montreal's French-oriented press.

"*Pourquoi* Covent Garden?" asked the newspapers. Was Montreal so ashamed of its native talent that it should pay outrageous amounts of money to hear British singers in an opera about Scotland? Did not the honor of opening La Grande Salle belong to the orchestra whose home it would become?

There being no reasonable answers to those questions, the French partisans won. As they generally do in Quebec. The honor of opening La Grande Salle fell to L'Orchestre Symphonique de Montréal and its Indian *chef d'orchestre*, Zubin Mehta, with the opening selection "guest conducted" by the beloved former director, Wilfrid Pelletier. The Place des Arts opening festival would continue with a variety of performances, including another by the orchestra, this time with Rudolf Serkin, under an old friend and frequent visitor to Montreal, Charles Munch. Because he would be in town for his own rehearsals, Munch was invited to be Pierre Beique's guest at Zubin's opening concert.

Except in cities like Vienna and New York, where a great variety of music is constantly performed, conductors rarely get a chance to hear other conductors conduct. Munch had not heard Zubin since Tanglewood in the summer of 1958, when his only comment to the young Indian had concerned the spacing of his feet on the podium. In the ensuing six years, however, Munch had had a great deal to say about him.

He had discussed Zubin on several occasions with Siegfried Hearst and early on suggested him to Pierre Beique. What most people in the music world did not know was that Munch also recommended Zubin to the board of the Boston Symphony Orchestra.

The BSO had been a well-beloved home for Charles Munch since 1949, and he prided himself on having kept the orchestra at the peak of perfection it had attained under his predecessor, Serge Koussevitzky. Even compared with the New York Philharmonic, which, as he was fond of saying, still played "under the ghost of Toscanini," Munch considered his Bostonians the equal of any orchestra in the world.

Because of his love for the Boston Symphony, Munch gave considerable thought to the matter of a successor when he announced his retirement in the winter of 1960–61. Out of all the available conductors, who would be the one most capable of leading the orchestra to perhaps even greater heights? The name he settled on, the name he proposed to the board, was that of a still unheralded beginner, Zubin Mehta.

Almost simultaneously, Zubin was being considered for the top posts in Montreal and Los Angeles. Perhaps he was not ready to take on so prestigious an orchestra as the BSO. Certainly the "Brahmins," as the Bostonian elite are known, did not think they were ready for a twenty-four-year-old Parsee.

They made what seemed to them a logical and properly conservative choice, though many of the Boston Symphony musicians would come to regret it; they offered the job to fifty-year-old Erich Leinsdorf. The Viennese-born music adviser of the Metropolitan Opera had made his name guest-conducting orchestras throughout the world. Besides, he was a prolific recording artist for RCA, which also had the Boston Symphony under contract, a coincidence that held the promise of even more recording income for the orchestra.

Munch went into semiretirement at the end of the 1961–62 season, Zubin's first triumphant year in Montreal and one season after had been hopping from country to country as a last-minute replacement for his indisposed colleagues. Munch knew then he'd been right about Zubin, but he didn't know *how* right until the night of the opening concert at Place des Arts as he sat in Pierre Beique's box, watching and listening to Zubin conduct the Mahler First Symphony.

It was a glowing, fiery performance, made warmer by the acoustics of the new hall, all red and silver gray with a honeycomb ceiling. But Munch knew it was not just the improved acoustics giving a new sound to this orchestra he'd conducted so many times in the past. It was Zubin, Munch realized, driving and cajoling the musicians through the shifting colors and moods and tempi like a man possessed, yet a man who saw clearly the way before him.

Just after the overwhelming collapse of the symphony's final bars, in the half moment before the audience collected itself and began to applaud, the white-haired conductor put his arm around the shoulder of his old friend Pierre Beique. Munch's words, in French, were all but swept away in a torrent of cheering and shouting, but Beique heard them and still remembers.

"Pierre, when Toscanini died, we all thought, Now the brightest light of our profession has gone out forever. But you have found Toscanini's successor."

That, Beique realized, was the highest praise he would ever hear of a conductor. He had known, almost since the day a travel-weary young man stumbled into his office, that he was a witness to something rare in the annals of music. Now his own opinion had received the ultimate confirmation, from the man he respected above all others in the trade.

Had he been the worrying sort, Beique might have paused to wonder how long an orchestra such as his, with its rather inadequate funding, could hope to hold on to "Toscanini's successor," particularly when he already had another orchestra, bigger and richer, in Los Angeles. But this was not the moment for such concerns.

La Grande Salle was a success, the conductor was a success. It seemed only logical, then, that the manager must be a success as well. Pierre Beique leaned back in his comfortable red velvet seat and joined in the frenzied applause that belonged partly to him. At least, he thought, Montreal had stolen some of the Los Angeles thunder by opening its hall first.

Since 1945, Los Angeles had seen a number of sporadic efforts at building a decent home for serious music, but bond issue after bond issue failed to get enough votes. The majority of Angelenos seemed to think that old Philharmonic Hall was plenty good enough for their orchestra. At any rate, the only time anybody really enjoyed those high-brow concerts was during the summer, when you could eat and drink in shirt sleeves at the Hollywood Bowl.

Then, in 1951, it looked as though the Bowl itself was about to go under, with no cash or credit for paying musicians or Bowl employees. A woman who had just that year joined the Hollywood Bowl Association was chosen to chair the emergency Save the Bowl Committee. Using the clout of her newspaper and her influence on the influential of southern California, Dorothy Buffum Chandler rallied enough support to save the Hollywood Bowl from disaster.

Having once succeeded, she decided to build the momentum. If she could make enough noise to keep the public giant from dozing off again, perhaps she could get the support for a music center. On Saint Patrick's Day, 1955, Mrs. Chandler made her loudest noise. It is recorded in the cultural history of Los Angeles as "the Eldorado Party."

The party's theme came from an automobile, which one of Mrs. Chandler's co-conspirators, Mrs. Grace Salvatori, wheedled away from General Motors, for free. The champagne-colored 1955 Eldorado convertible with white leather interior was raffled off at $1 a ticket, $5 for a book of six. On top of that, tickets for the party were sold at $50 a person. The goal was $250,000 to start what was to become the Music Center Building Fund.

On March 17, 1955, the only place in Los Angeles in which to be seen was the Ambassador Hotel's Embassy Room—which had been enlarged gratis for the occasion. Among the celebrities in attendance were Bob Hope and Samuel Goldwyn. Entertainment included a multi-million-dollar fashion show, Danny Kaye leading the ninety-six-member Philharmonic in a Rossini overture, Dinah Shore and her troupe doing a retake of their television show, and Jack Benny playing *Zigeunerweisen* without cracking a joke but cracking lots of notes.

It was called "an evening of improbabilities," and among the unlikely happenings turned out to be an administrative employee of the Philharmonic, with only $30 worth of tickets in the huge 400,000-stub raffle drum, driving away in the Eldorado. Most improbable of all was that the party earned not $250,000, but more than $400,000 for the Music Center Building Fund.

The fund grew by fits and starts until 1959, when the Los Angeles Dodgers won the World Series and civic pride boomed in the City of Angels. By 1960 the fund had climbed to $4 million—all in privately donated funds, for a public building. Not to be outdone, the County of Los Angeles gave Mrs. Chandler a site—the top of a hill overlooking a planned civic center—and an architect, Welton Becket.

In July of 1960, Becket presented his plans to the County Board of Supervisors: an elegant, floodlit plaza (which the newspapers immediately dubbed "the Acropolis"); a stately auditorium, the Music Pavilion ("the Parthenon"), with gently curving walls of glass and granite, embraced by slender fluted columns, rising nearly one hundred feet to a sculptured, overhanging roof.

Eight months later, Mrs. Chandler and architect Becket surprised everyone (and pushed the Philharmonic-Solti controversy off the front pages) by presenting another set of plans to the County Board.

Buff had been to London in the interim and was so smitten by the London theaters that she made up her mind Los Angeles must have drama as well as music. Two theaters, one large and one small, would join the Music Pavilion atop the hill. She assured the board that her volunteers would raise another $7 million toward the cost of the augmented Music Center, so how could the county say no?

"If Mrs. Chandler pledges it," said board chairman Ernest Debs, "the money is practically in the bank."

It began to seem that boards and committees in Los Angeles were formed for the purpose of acquiescing to Dorothy Chandler's will. By the end of that summer, she had also wrested a unanimous vote of approval for her choice to lead the Symphony into its new home, Zubin Mehta. By November 21 all the plans were approved. Construction began March 12, 1962.

All during construction, Mrs. Chandler and her volunteers never let up on their fund raising. Gifts poured in from celebrities such as President and Mrs. Kennedy, Cary Grant, Nat King Cole; Hollywood's most expensive motion picture in history, *Cleopatra,* had its gala opening night as a Music Center fund raiser and brought in a million dollars; Walt Disney designed and manufactured "Bags for Bucks," and Mrs. Chandler organized a "Bucks Brigade" to solicit contributions from the man on the street.

The entire nine-year campaign cost only $152,000 and raised more than $18.5 million. In December of 1964, billboards went up throughout the city, proclaiming: "Thank you, Mrs. Chandler, for our new Music Center." The first building, the Dorothy Chandler Pavilion, became the first public edifice in California named in honor of a person still living.

They called it the Parthenon, but the finished Dorothy Chandler Pavilion bore little resemblance to that bare Greek temple. It seemed more like an Egyptian pyramid, furnished with such extravagance as to provide adequate comfort and splendor to the Lords of Culture on their journey to immortality.

Welton Becket had the carpets custom woven in Hong Kong and sent designers to Bavaria just to oversee the casting of crystal for the twenty-two chandeliers and fifty-six wall sconces. There were twenty-four thousand individual pieces of hand-polished crystal alone in each of the three immense, cascading chandeliers dominating the Grand Hall. The interior walls contained Mexican onyx the color of honey, white Byzantine tiles from Italy, black beanwood paneling from Australia, and beige silk curtains from Japan.

Several of the city's music heroes were simply declared immortal and commemorated in works of art. There were busts of Otto Klemperer and Alfred Wallenstein (by Anna Mahler, daughter of Gustav) and Gregor Piatigorsky (by Jane Ullman); and, in the Founders Room, portraits of Buff Chandler (by William Draper) and Zubin Mehta (by Marion Pike).

To summon worshipers to service, there was a custom-built carillon consisting of 149 symphonic bells, a full complement of orchestra, celeste, and harp bells, a chime of tubular bells, and 28 bells of cast bronze.

The glory of its trappings notwithstanding, the one thing that really mattered about the Pavilion was the way music sounded in it. Two years before, in New York, Philharmonic Hall had been slapped into life by outraged critics, who declared it unfit for human ears. Even before that hall was officially opened the nation's most widely quoted music critic slashed it to ribbons in the *New York Times,* declaring that "no multipurpose hall can have fine acoustics."

Since the 3,250-seat Pavilion was also intended as a multipurpose hall—for symphony and chamber music, recitals, and opera—the administrators elected not to let any critics into the hall for rehearsals before opening night, a decision that Zubin endorsed wholeheartedly. At least the opening night audience would arrive expecting the best, not the worst.

The week prior to opening, however, the hall was crawling with acoustical experts, engineers, and technicians from RCA Records. RCA had decided to use the debut of the Pavilion as a demonstration of the company's still new Dynagroove recording process, providing the cost would be subsidized by the orchestra.

Both Zubin Mehta and the Los Angeles Philharmonic were still fairly unknown quantities on disc, but the grand opening of the Pavilion was expected to provide enough fanfare to ensure adequate publicity for the recording. Moreover, RCA would be delighted if the lion's share of critical attention went to Dynagroove rather than to Mehta.

The morning of December 5, the orchestra played its first rehearsal in the hall. Zubin had decided to start the opening night concert, after the "Star Spangled Banner," with a fanfare by Richard Strauss. He had intended the opening number to be *Elytres,* commissioned from Lukas Foss, but the composer had given him a rather quiet, pensive piece that did not seem to fit the occasion, so he substituted the Strauss.

After the first reading of the fanfare, Zubin turned to the principal RCA engineer for his comments on the "acoustic cavern," as the experts called the hall. Up in the boxes on the Founders' Level, architect Welton Becket did not wait for an expert opinion. Becket had been criticized for spending a quarter of a million dollars on acoustic consultants' fees, but as the music sounded in his ears he knew he was vindicated. He swung around in his seat to Mrs. Chandler and the few others who were there to reap the first harvest. "Well," said Becket, with as much relief in his voice as triumph, "we really did it, didn't we?"

The self-congratulation was short lived, for out in the foyer something of a row was going on, and Becket was called to quell it.

The Symphony's public relations man was doing his insufficient best to placate a music critic who had traveled all the way from New York to review the opening of the Pavilion, only to be told there would be no "acoustical previews." The critic was introduced to Becket as Harold Schonberg, the man who had written so devastatingly about New York's Philharmonic Hall.

As the voices rose and echoed through the intentionally hollow-sounding domed lobby, Schonberg remarked, "I hope you don't have this inside the hall."

Finally Schonberg was assured that the New York press was not being discriminated against and he settled for a tour, sans music, conducted by the PR man and Becket, who sent a message in to Zubin that he should call a recess.

As he entered the rear of the auditorium, the critic was astonished to hear clearly every syllable of Zubin's instructions to the orchestra on stage. That would have been impossible at Lincoln Center's new hall.

"I suppose," said Schonberg when the hurried tour was over, "that tomorrow night you'll try to confine me to the best acoustic areas as they did in Philharmonic Hall."

"You can go anywhere you like," Becket said with a smile. "I'll see that you get a pass. You can listen from the catwalks if you like." The two men backed away from each other, neither quite satisfied with the compromise.

The following night, December 6, the Pavilion opened. In true Hollywood fashion, there were floodlights and camera lights everywhere; everybody who was anybody and ambulatory in the worlds of entertainment, culture, society, and finance was on hand.

On his way to the stage door, Zubin passed a group of pale young men wearing red silk *sherwanis* and Nehru caps; there was no mistaking them for Indians.

"What's this?" he asked. "Are we also having a masquerade ball?"

"We're ushers," one of the group spoke up. "These are our uniforms."

Zubin groaned. Nobody had consulted him about the costumes. He felt a little bit like the host at a catered cocktail party, but he decided not to complain, since he had already incurred the ire of some of the Symphony dowagers by telling them at a pre-opening party that their condescending attitude toward his musicians was not appreciated. "Just because they wear bow ties," he said, "you don't have to treat them as though they were all waiters." On occasion, his patience with the moneyed gentry of Los Angeles could wear a bit thin.

He was all smiles, though, as he stepped onto the new stage, acknowledging the emotional ovation. It was the moment he had been chosen for, he knew, the moment Dorothy Chandler had had in mind when she selected him as her music director. He waited for the applause to die down, then addressed the audience.

"Ladies and gentlemen, this evening we are going to usher in a new era . . ."

Then, after the National Anthem and the Strauss fanfare, he turned to the audience again and shouted: "Ladies and gentlemen, we *like* the acoustics!" A laughing cheer went up in the hall; the audience liked the acoustics, too.

As Zubin welcomed the evening's soloist, Jascha Heifetz, architect Welton Becket saw a movement along one of the side aisles in the orchestra seats. Harold Schonberg was on the move.

Becket felt his stomach tighten. No matter how much he and Zubin and most of the audience liked the acoustics, public opinion—possibly even future financial support—could be vastly affected by what the critics wrote. It was not like reviewing a performer or even a play, in which changes could be made or locales could be changed. This was the most important element of an immovable, largely immutable $35-million-dollar investment, which he just happened to consider the crowning glory of his architectural career. That so much of his work now hung from the ears of a few taste makers, to be shunned like cheap jewelry if it didn't strike their fancies, was a bit unsettling.

By and large, Becket had no cause for concern. Fortunately for the Pavilion's and the Philharmonic's immediate future, the Los Angeles *Times* had not yet hired as its music critic Martin Bernheimer, who never learned to love them with the same fervor that native Angelenos seemed to lavish on both the building and the orchestra.

In Bernheimer's later judgment, "The acoustics in the Pavilion are overbright, overresonant. Also there are some dead spots. Nobody else seems to agree, but I still maintain that in the center of the orchestra section, if there's a piano concerto you can't hear the piano, the sound just isn't defined."

Reminded of this criticism by the man who would become Zubin's self-appointed nemesis in Los Angeles, the conductor becomes angry. "Anything Bernheimer says about acoustics, you had better take with lots of salt, because—even though we have tried and tried to give him better seats—he insists on sitting in the same place for every concert, the extreme left aisle, where he can be close to an exit and the first one to leave."

At any rate, in southern California newspapers on December 7, 1964, the reviews were, in general, highly favorable and in many cases glowing. The following day Schonberg's evaluation appeared in New York, not the wrecking ball Welton Becket had feared, but a pat on the back for him and Dorothy Chandler and all the others who had put their reputations on the line with the Music Center.

"By any standards, a success," Schonberg had written. "A live hall with a remarkable throw for so big an auditorium . . . even under the balcony overhangs the sound comes through with clarity and presence. . . . Probably the most beautiful concert hall of its size erected anywhere in the United States. Becket has grandly succeeded in his interiors, rich and lavish without being vulgar . . . a brilliant success."

That was the sort of praise that would continue to pour in for the Dorothy Chandler Pavilion. "Playing a recital on that stage," said Rudolf Serkin, "is like playing inside a Stradivarius violin." Said Beverly Sills, "It's a joy, one of the best halls for a singer. I adore it." And RCA's John Pfeiffer wrote, "The Pavilion is one of the most beautiful and acoustically satisfying of the world's great theaters."

Pfeiffer's engineers were very much in evidence during opening week, getting a feel for the acoustical cavern, running more tests, even recording one of the orchestra's live performances for a better evaluation.

The following week, Zubin began rehearsing the two pieces RCA intended to record, Respighi's *Feste Romane* and Strauss's *Don Juan*. Both were big, full-bodied works that would exploit the rich sound of the hall and the orchestra. Unfortunately, the recording would also lock into place an impression that many critics around the world were beginning to form of Zubin: that his repertoire consisted solely of big, full-bodied compositions in a narrow, romantic range that began with Mahler and ended somewhere around Strauss and Respighi.

It was, at any rate, the sort of music RCA expected from Zubin. As the recording date neared, Zubin was quite clear about what he expected from RCA. "I do not want cold, mechanical perfection," he told the engineers. "Rather, I want a warm, expansive tone, without the explosive attack one hears from some of the famous orchestras."

Difficulties in capturing that "warm, expansive tone," along with the "acoustic ambience" of the Pavilion, became evident from the start. To avoid the "mechanical" sound, the RCA engineers wanted to use a minimum of microphones, but what these few microphones captured was something less than the true presence of the orchestra. The engineers felt the strings sounded muddy, and in broad passages they were completely overwhelmed by the brass and percussion.

Most of the problems were ironed out by alterations in the physical placement of the musicians. The movable floor that was designed to become an orchestra pit for operas and musicals was raised to the height of the stage, and the strings were brought forward on this. The percussion and trombone sections were exiled to the rear of the stage and elevated on special platforms so they could see Zubin conduct. An intermediate-height platform held the woodwinds and basses. In addition, a number of baffles were placed to direct and partially deaden certain instruments. All of this was supposed to increase the effectiveness, in respect to the strings, of the gold-leaf acoustical panel that extended out into the hall from the top of the proscenium. These adjustments having been completed, the recording sessions proceeded smoothly, and, after the first mix, the test tapes were pronounced satisfactory by chief engineer, producer, and conductor.

Several months later, when RCA at last released the first recording of Zubin Mehta conducting the Los Angeles Philharmonic, its handsome fold-out jacket promised the buyer "a fuller musical-aesthetic involvement than has ever been possible via records before" and that Mehta's interpretation of Strauss and Respighi would be "projected into your sound consciousness as on no other recording."

Yet for all the puffery and hoopla, the record was not a particularly big seller. With notable shortsightedness, RCA failed to sign the Philharmonic to a recording contract, though Zubin himself was to record some operas for RCA in later years. It was also the last time Zubin and the Philharmonic recorded in the Music Center Pavilion. It was, however, far from being their last recording.

The publicity attendant on the Pavilion's opening—including a fourteen-page color spread in *Time* Magazine, with Dorothy Chandler's portrait on the cover—did serve to project Zubin into the consciousness of the American musical establishment. Stories on the "twenty-eight-year-old, Bombay-born conductor" began to spring up in national publications from *Newsweek* to *Vogue*.

A full-column story in the *New York Times* proclaimed: "Mehta Paves Way for Music Center." Included among its feuilletonic observations—women diners dropping their forks at the conductor's approach, Zubin drenching his food in Tabasco sauce "in sweepingly dramatic gestures"—were several salient points.

During the 1964–65 season, observed the *Times,* the Los Angeles Philharmonic doubled its highest previous gross, doubled the previous season attendance record, and doubled its number of season ticket hold-ers. In its first year in the Pavilion, the orchestra played to 125,000 persons, 10,000 of them season subscribers, grossing about $225,000. The *Times* divided credit for these astounding accomplishments evenly, between the new Music Center and Zubin Mehta.

If Zubin had yet to arrive at "household word" status, his name was at least to be found on the tongues of administrators and directors in the nation's most prestigious music institutions. Indeed, it seemed that the only accomplishment missing from the Mehta career was success in the opera pit. It would not be missing for long.

9

⌁⌁⌁

Opera: Facets
of a Diamond

Since his first brush with opera in Vienna, Zubin had wanted to conduct music drama as well as the symphonic literature. The symphonies he enjoyed most were always the most dramatic, and the addition of singing actors and stage directions would be only a short step from such dramatically structured works as the tone poems of Richard Strauss. Moreover, the bulk of the standard operatic literature fell within Zubin's familiar spectrum of romantic and post-romantic music.

The first opera he'd attended was Beethoven's *Fidelio* in 1955. Eight years later, Zubin conducted his first performance of the Beethoven Ninth Symphony, something he considered a necessary preliminary to the task of managing a full-scale opera. It was the Czech Philharmonic that asked him to conduct it.

There is a tradition in Prague that the annual Spring Festival ends with a performance of the Beethoven Ninth in the Cathedral of St. Vitus, the fourteenth-century masterpiece that dominates the skyline of the ancient capital. Like the Viennese with their New Year's Eve *Fledermaus,* the Czechs knew how they wanted their Beethoven Ninth.

Zubin's problem started when his connecting flight in Frankfurt was an hour late taking off. Since he had managed to cut things as close as possible, he arrived at rehearsal thirty minutes behind schedule. He rarely arrived anywhere early, but he did like to be on time, so there was a bit of nervous flutter in his stomach as the driver turned onto a fantastic bridge, filled with spires and statuary, that crossed Smetana's Moldau. The car started up a hill, at the top of which Zubin saw a medieval acropolis, the Hradčany Palace, with a green cathedral lurking at its center like some gothic vulture. At that moment Zubin wished he had somehow managed to conduct his first Ninth Symphony in Montreal or Los Angeles.

He was ushered through massive bronze doors into the narthex of the cathedral, and he could hear his footsteps echoing through the nave as he walked toward a distant altar, feeling just a bit like Isaac entering the temple with Abraham. In the chancel, arranged around the central altar, were the members of the Czech Philharmonic and an enormous choir, all sitting stock still, their three-hundred-plus eyes fixed on the tardy, dark figure coming toward them.

Zubin smiled, but his voice sounded hollow as he spoke to the orchestra manager walking beside him. "Shouldn't they be playing Mendelssohn's 'Wedding March' or something?"

But the manager was all seriousness. "It is too bad," he said in his oddly accented German, "that you could not get here on time."

Reaching the altar railing and the podium, Zubin suddenly realized the chorus and soloists should not be there. They were not needed until the final movement of the symphony, which would certainly take him several hours of rehearsal to reach.

"It is customary," said the orchestra manager gravely, "to begin with the finale at rehearsal. That way the chorus and soloists can be released. We always do it that way."

His confidence was nowhere to be found, so Zubin saw he would need all the charm he could muster to get through the day. "I'm afraid there's been a mistake," he said, smiling broadly for the benefit of the choir. "You see, I always rehearse a piece from beginning to end. I'm sure you can see how logical and necessary that is."

From a pew behind him, Zubin heard the chorusmaster growl something in Czech, a language he, gratefully, did not understand. Looks of astonishment and disbelief crossed the faces of the choristers as, with much guttural grumbling and a good many severe glances toward the podium, they got up to leave.

"If only I had known how to handle myself better," Zubin says now, sighing. "Of course, I should have just gone along and started with the finale. But it was my first time ever conducting it, and I wanted to build myself up to that incredible conclusion, from the beginning to the end. It turned into an unhappy experience in my life. I lost my confidence and the rehearsals were horrendous. If ever an orchestra has drained me of my confidence, it was that one. From the minute I stepped onto the podium, I had such bad vibes I wanted to go home."

But he was there, so he went through with it. And, after an immeasurable rehearsal period, the evening of the performance arrived.

Looking out from the "backstage" sacristy, Zubin saw the front pews of the great cathedral filled with officials of the city and the resident diplomatic corps. Ambassadors from India, Canada, the United States, and Austria were there, he knew. Would there be any nation on earth he could safely call home if he made a mess of things here? Behind the seated diplomats were perhaps eight thousand people, all of them standing.

As he hunted inside himself for the courage to step out and face them, one of the Spring Festival directors whispered, "By the way, they did tell you there will be no applause?"

"You mean when I go out or when we finish?"

"None. It is against tradition to applaud in the church. Not allowed."

Maintaining his aplomb that night was one of the most difficult assignments Zubin ever had, but if ever music had been written to inspire confidence, it was the Ninth Symphony. By the time he led the assembled forces into their final *Freude, schöner Götterfunken,* and spurred the orchestra into the prestissimo coda, he was feeling some of that "divine spark" of joy himself, remembering the musical ecstasy of his first night in the Vienna Musikverein. It would have been nice to hear a thunderous, spontaneous ovation after the crisp finale, but there was at least a glow inside him from knowing he had pulled it off.

He waited for the murmuring audience to file out, receiving polite congratulations from the festival directors and the leaders of the orchestra and chorus, then went out a side door to a waiting car. As the car rounded the cobblestone street to the front of the cathedral, Zubin was greeted by an incredible sight. The eight thousand members of the audience, diplomatic corps and all, were lined along both sides of the street that curved down the hill to the Moldau. When his car came into sight, they began to applaud and cheer.

Like a visiting monarch, he waved to the crowds that stretched from the cathedral steps, out the gateway of the Hradčany, and onto the old bridge. Letting the car find its way across the river, the driver looked into his rear-view mirror and observed a curious sight. The Indian conductor was stretched out, his head thrown back against the seat. He was sobbing, tears streaming down his face.

In the 1970s Zubin would return to Prague, to salvage "my love affair with the Czech Philharmonic" in such massive works as *Le Sacre du Prin-*

temps, the Bruckner Eighth Symphony, and the Mahler *Resurrection* Symphony. Yet, after that Beethoven Ninth, he was not surprised it took the Czech Philharmonic eight years to ask him back. He was not satisfied—it was a public practice.

In May of 1963, Zubin returned from Prague to North America, convinced that he had weathered one of the worst storms of his career. After that Beethoven Ninth, he felt prepared for anything that might happen in the unstable atmosphere of opera. Immediately, he put forward his plans for a season-ending *Tosca* in Montreal and entered into negotiations with the Maggio Musicale festival in Florence to do an *Il Trovatore* there.

Pierre Beique, a dyed-in-the-wool opera buff, was more than receptive to the idea of staging and opera in the new hall, where there was a large orchestra pit and sufficient backstage depth to accommodate sets. As always, the problem in Montreal was funding, so *Tosca* would have to be produced on a shoestring.

Zubin threw himself into the task, working with Montreal set and costume designers to come up with what they hoped would look like a lavish production. He put together a good cast of American and Canadian singers, headed by American soprano Ella Lee as Tosca and as Cavaradossi Richard Verreau, the Montreal tenor who had canceled the Russian tour. And he considered himself fortunate that George London agreed to sing the role of Scarpia.

The performances, in February 1964, were evenings to remember in Montreal. Place des Arts glittered in a fresh snowfall, and La Grande Salle was filled to overflowing with local and foreign dignitaries, as well as the Symphony's subscription first-nighters, unaccustomed to finding opera on their bill of fare. It was the first time the orchestra had tried anything so daring.

The opening performance went off without a hitch—something that can be said of relatively few operatic first nights—and the Montreal papers were filled the next morning with *Tosca* stories from front page to society gossip columns. A Symphony board member who was an old-world acquaintance of Rudolf Bing's telephoned New York and so belabored the Metropolitan Opera's general manager with glowing descriptions that he finally agreed to fly up to Montreal to see what all the fuss was about. After the second performance, he appeared backstage to compliment Zubin and the singers, then returned to the Metropolitan, secure in the knowledge that opera was alive and well in the provinces.

Things went so well with *Tosca* that Zubin talked the Montreal board into two operas for the 1964-65 season, *La Traviata* and *Carmen,* along with an *Aïda* the following fall. Among the many sopranos he auditioned for the demanding role of Violetta was a still less-than-famous coloratura from the New York City Opera, whose top notes Zubin found dazzling in the first act "*Sempre libera,*" but who seemed less suited for the highly dramatic second and third acts. So, though he was impressed with her personality and agility, Zubin declined to give the role to Beverly Sills— another of those hasty decisions he regrets to this day. Instead, he settled on a dramatic soprano he'd met in Florence, Virginia Zeani. She would sing *Traviata* and return the following season as Aïda.

Zubin's operatic success was less notable in Los Angeles, the city whose history of opera goes as far back as its musical life. That history, which began in 1885 with Emma Albert's traveling opera company, is nothing more than a long succession of visiting troupes. The early Angelenos heard Caruso, Melba, and Calvé, as their descendants would hear Sutherland, Horne, and Treigle, as visitors from distant planets who arrived, made their mark, and disappeared, leaving the city without an opera company of its own. Since the early 1920s, the welcome mat had been laid each fall for the San Francisco Opera Association, scheduled to put in its first appearance at the Dorothy Chandler Pavilion in September and October of 1965.

This arrangement was less than satisfactory for society-conscious Los Angeles. Somewhere it had been decreed that any proper "social season" begins in November, with several weeks of opera. Since the people of San Francisco had read the same book, their opera company was not available on rental in November. By the time the Pavilion opened, therefore, Mrs.Chandler and her troops were shopping around for an alternative.

Zubin had what he considered a proper suggestion, opening the Symphony season with *Salome* by Richard Strauss. Though there was some grumbling at his choice of operas, the plan was adopted. *Salome* would be the first staged and costumed opera ever produced in a Los Angeles Philharmonic subscription season.

But even as Zubin's preparations went ahead for *Salome,* the local music czars were doing their own Dance of the Seven Veils to promote the beheading of any real hopes Los Angeles might have for a resident opera troupe. The sword fell with the creation of the Music Center Opera Association, which the Center's directors proclaimed "one of the finest achievements in the first decade of the Music Center."

The Association quickly ended the arrangement with the San Francisco company and established a new one with the New York City Opera. Since the City Opera fall season in New York terminated in early November, leaving most of its employees with nothing to do, the offer of a trip to sunny California was welcomed and, three years later, solemnized as tradition.

Since New York City Opera traveled with its own conductors, notably Julius Rudel, and since he knew Los Angeles could only support a certain amount of opera per year, Zubin saw right away that he would not be able to make his operatic reputation in Los Angeles. But by the summer of 1965 that reputation was building, and by the start of 1966 he would be recognized in Europe and America as an emerging giant among opera conductors.

Rudolf Bing had apparently been sufficiently impressed by the Montreal *Tosca* to invite Zubin to conduct a total of ten *Aïdas* at the Met in December and January, following close on the heels of his Montreal *Aïdas*. The second hint, or more than a hint, was the reception his *Abduction from the Seraglio* received at the Salzburg Festival that same summer.

In Austria, Zubin was rapidly becoming a celebrity, his reputation in that small but musically dominant nation growing with each guest appearance, not to mention his triumphant tour with the Montreal Symphony. His Salzburg debut had been in 1962, enough of a success for him to be asked back the following year. After the second festival appearance, the Salzburg directors accorded *der Inder* the signal honor of asking him to open their festival with a new production of Mozart's comic opera *Die Entführung aus dem Serail*, starring Fritz Wunderlich, Reri Grist, and Anneliese Rothenberger.

The *Abduction* went as well as anything Zubin had ever done. The fact that it was in the delicate style of Mozart, a style his early and late detractors have maintained is foreign to him, did not seem to matter. No amount of conducting grand-romantic Bruckner or *übermenschlich* Strauss had clouded his recollection of or dimmed his love for the classics. So moved was the visiting critic from the Chicago *Tribune*—who perhaps had not heard of Zubin's already established career in the wilds of Montreal and Los Angeles—that she called him "the most promising young Mozart man the festival had found in seasons."

The European music critic for *Time* Magazine was even more impressed. Instead of a story on the entire festival, he talked his editors into a full-page story on a single conductor. It was headlined, "The Next Toscanini?"

"Seldom has the Salzburg Festival witnessed such an ovation," *Time* reported. "After the festival's opening concert last week, a capacity audience of 2,200 stomped, clapped and bravoed in a demonstration that verged on Beatlemania." The article went on to quote acclaimed Mozart stylist Josef Krips as declaring, "The next Toscanini has been born!"

The *Time* writer called the Salzburg *Abduction* "the height of Mehta's career to date," although he was credited also with "rejuvenating Montreal's faltering orchestra almost overnight." After lengthy descriptions of Zubin's conducting style ("clean, precise beat," "a pitcher unfurling a fastball") and his sex appeal ("brutal charm," "catnip gaze") the article concluded with a prediction that the next ten-year period of Zubin's life "promises to be some decade."

That decade began with a return to Philadelphia in October, the first time he had conducted that city's orchestra since his smashing Dell success.

There were four concerts in Philadelphia on four consecutive nights, from October 28 to November 1, followed by the opening of the orchestra's Carnegie Hall engagement in New York City. For his program, Zubin chose the *Coriolanus* Overture of Beethoven, Schönberg's Five Pieces for Orchestra, and the Bruckner Symphony no. 9. Not an easy program for conductor, orchestra, or audience.

The Bruckner Ninth had been Zubin's first recording for London/Decca, with the Vienna Philharmonic, and from nearly all reports that interpretation was considered highly successful. But in the two intervening years he had given the long and tortuously complex symphony a good deal of thought, coming to several new conclusions as to its proper interpretation, especially after a meeting with George Szell, who heard Zubin conduct it in rehearsal with the Vienna Philharmonic. He saw nothing unusual in these second thoughts about the symphony, considering that Bruckner himself spent seven years revising the first three movements and never did get around to completing a fourth. Still, many of the musical intelligentsia attended those concerts expecting to compare the Vienna recording with the Philadelphia live performance, the same conductor with the same interpretation.

After the Carnegie Hall performance, the *Herald Tribune*'s Alan Rich found himself fascinated more by the Mehta viewpoint than the Bruckner design. "The recording by Mehta and the Vienna Philharmonic is more straightforward, terse and compelling," he wrote. "Here we are faced with the essence of Mehta's art and his problem: 29 years old, enormously gifted, but still in the process of trying things out.

"Better this, however, than the easier way out. Mehta's future growth, of which there is not the slightest doubt, is going to be a tremendous thing to watch. Even now, he is clearly a man to conjure with."

Rudolf Bing might have read those reviews and smiled; his gamble on Zubin, an operatic unknown, was about to pay off. Almost on the heels of this much-written-about Bruckner would come the Indian's debut at the Metropolitan opera. Very likely the theater would be sold out and the reviewers there in force, with full columns set aside in the next day's papers.

Before the reviewers, though, there were the Met's resident critics to face, and Zubin encountered them at his first rehearsal. It was a rude awakening to the glamorous world of Opera with a capital O.

"All through my younger years, my colleagues couldn't have been nicer to me, especially the older ones. They always had words of encouragement and were ready to answer any of my questions. But when I started at the Met they all swooped down on me like vultures. Not Lenny, but all the other Met conductors.

"They would sit behind me at rehearsals and criticize me. They would even talk about me to the musicians, right behind my back" . . . and he pauses to shake his head, sighing. "That Met!"

Though working with the orchestra was very pleasant, Zubin discovered for himself all the problems about which he had read: insufficient rehearsal time, the practice of letting the second cast perform without an orchestra rehearsal, and uneven casts.

But, with all its shortcomings, there was still something marvelous about the old house, something magical in the soft gold glow of it, with its patina of immortal performances, something that seemed to give access to greatness without ever promising it. Zubin's opening night was December 29, in that week between Christmas and New Year's when New York is always poised on the brink, tensed and anxious for beginnings, like the critics, all fidgeting in their seats fifteen minutes before curtain.

Backstage, just inside the Fortieth Street entrance, where they were allowed to wait out of the cold, were three people Zubin had invited to share the excitement of his Met debut, Pierre Beique, Carmen, and Zarin. They could not take their seats until Zubin arrived with their tickets.

"Where the hell is he?" Beique muttered, checking his watch for the hundredth time.

(He was standing in the cold on West End Avenue, trying to hail a cab.)

"He should have been here half an hour ago," observed Zarin.

Carmen, stoic as ever, said, "Stop worrying. You know he'll be here. He's never missed a performance yet."

Behind them paced the gaunt, imperious general manager, Rudolf Bing. He also was consulting his watch with increasing frequency. The last musician had straggled in from Bill's Bar across the street more than ten minutes before.

Beique already blamed the graying and loss of his hair on moments such as this, waiting at airports for Zubin's plane to bring him from places like Los Angeles and Tel Aviv with only minutes to spare for a Montreal concert. "With the schedule he keeps," said Beique, "it's no wonder he's never early. But why did he pick tonight, of all nights, to be late?"

At three minutes before curtain time, as Zarin recalls, Bing looked at his watch again and said, almost shouted, "Well, we shall just have to start without Mr. Mehta." With that he stepped over to a telephone and picked up the receiver.

No sooner were the words out of his mouth than the door opened and in walked a smiling Zubin, pretending to be calm. Sliding off his overcoat and gloves, he tossed them on a table, shook hands with the scowling, silent Bing, and handed a ticket envelope to Zarin.

"I think," he told his brother, "you all had better get to your seats quickly because the performance is about to begin."

"Good luck," Carmen shouted. As his coattails disappeared through the doorway that led to the orchestra pit, Carmen shouted the traditional good-luck wish, "*In bocca al lupo,*" and indeed it may have seemed that Zubin was walking "into the mouth of a wolf."

But when he emerged again, after an unexpectedly prolonged first-act ovation, the scowl had disappeared from the general manager's face. Bing realized, as did the critics and the paying public, that Zubin Mehta was the find of the season. And nothing happened in the ensuing three acts to change anyone's mind.

"One name emerged," wrote Alan Rich in the *Herald Tribune,* "writ large and clear, as one of the great events of the year." The name, of course, was that of Zubin Mehta.

The critics were unanimous in their praise of Zubin's command over all the elements of the huge opera. Yet for all the control he exercised, they saw a remarkable flexibility at work, in letting the singers expand when a luscious phrase deserved expanding or pause when pausing gave dramatic emphasis. This last point was something that Zubin had taught himself from the standing room sections of the Staatsoper in Vienna—that the "moments" in opera must belong to the singers.

As he told an interviewer from *Opera News* Magazine, "It's unfortunate, but people don't care" about all the difficulties a conductor has holding an opera together. "They've come only to hear the high note. Especially in some of the famous Italian operas, one high note is worth a thousand bars of music."

But the New York critics had heard their share of high notes over the years. They were looking for a conductor whose commanding presence might turn an average Metropolitan performance, with its moments of brilliance separated by often interminable lapses into dullness, into the unified work of art that a composer like Verdi surely must have intended. In Zubin they found their man, and for weeks to come they would write about those *Aïda*s.

Reviewing a Saturday afternoon broadcast performance, the *Times*'s Howard Klein found it "one of rare completeness." And, even though the cast had been changed to an all-star group for the radio audience—Leontyne Price, Richard Tucker, Irene Dalis, and Robert Merrill—the reviewer proclaimed that "the major role belonged to the conductor, Zubin Mehta.

"He brings to the pit," wrote Klein, "a dictator's control, a demonic possession of every note and phrase (without a score) and an incandescent musicality that blazes where most flicker."

Alan Rich declared that Zubin's pacing of the opera, adjustments of balance, and control over all the elements of the production were "on a level to beggar description."

Hubert Saal, the critic from *Newsweek* Magazine, also devoted his entire column to Zubin, who "was like a man intoxicated. The passions of love, hate, jealousy and self-sacrifice flickered across his face like images upon a screen. His body rolled with the operatic punches. His hands stabbed, pierced, slashed . . . with the aplomb and showmanship of a Roman policeman." No matter that no one could possibly have seen those things unless he was sitting in the orchestra pit. The writer was trying to make the point that he and everyone else in the Met had been *moved,* and moved not by high notes or histrionics, but by a conductor who was all but invisible to most of the audience.

One is struck by the uniformity of praise in the reviews of these years. Gone is the uncertainty that marked the New York critics' observations of Zubin's Lewisohn Stadium concerts in 1960. Perhaps because he had already made a secure place for himself in Montreal, Los Angeles, Vienna, Salzburg, and Israel, these New York critics could themselves feel secure in letting down their armor of diffidence and simply exulting in a great performance of great music.

Often the most thoughtful critiques come from the magazine writers, who have several days, often as much as a week, to consolidate impressions and consider their meaning, not having to rush to a city desk and hand their reviews, page by page, to a breathless copy boy. In the case of Zubin's December 29 debut at the Met, the most interesting review did not appear until the January 22 issue of the *New Yorker* magazine hit the newsstands. The half-page account by Winthrop Sargeant deserves attention for its astute analysis of the Mehta conducting style.

Sargeant began on a note of self-congratulation, pointing out that he was the only one of New York's major critics to appraise Zubin's talents correctly two years earlier. (That was a hurriedly-put-together appearance with the American Symphony Orchestra in Carnegie Hall to benefit the United States Jeunesses Musicales.) "Since then," continued Sargeant, "he has become more widely acclaimed, and finally Mr. Bing has seen fit to hire him, though, owing to Mr. Bing's habits of extreme caution in regard to everything except scenery and costumes, he has been given merely a string of *Aïda*'s to conduct."

Yet, continues Sargeant, even in so familiar an opera, Zubin's is "a remarkable job of conducting—the finest I remember in any Italian opera during the Bing administration." He goes on to say that "Mr. Mehta is probably the most important find among conductors that Mr. Bing has made during his career here."

Analyzing the Mehta style, the *New Yorker* critic calls attention to the fact that Zubin, unlike virtually every other conductor to come along in the last twenty years, had not been influenced by Toscanini to the point of imitating him. Such mimics, he writes,

> follow the most obvious and superficial aspect of the Toscanini style; namely his adherence to rigid and speedy tempo. Now Mr. Mehta has a musical personality of his own, and the tradition it springs from is Central European, coming from men like Furtwängler, Walter and von Karajan. He is not a rigid-tempo man, as is nearly every other younger conductor now before the public. He knows when to give a little, when to let a singer breathe, when to permit a slight deviation from the steady pulse of the music—things that are matters of taste and artistry rather than of rules and regulations.

> Moreover, Mr. Mehta has a phenomenal sense of musical line, by which I mean an intuitive feeling for the form of musical phrases, their interconnections and the relative stress to be placed on their component notes. In addition, he has a way of displaying the texture of a score as a jeweler displays the facets of a diamond. Elements one never particularly noticed before suddenly come to life in his interpretation as he lifts one or another into prominence.... And beyond everything else I have mentioned, Mr. Mehta has a degree of authority—an ability to rouse the eighty or hundred men under him to special efforts—that is found only in born maestros.

There is more, a good deal more, and one can read the entire article several times without finding the slightest qualifying phrase, word, or even suggestion that Zubin is anything less than a great opera conductor. All this for a man who until two years before had never conducted an opera.

Magazines such as *Time, Newsweek,* and *Opera News* sent interviewers to Zubin's hotel room in New York to find out how he had managed such a feat, thinking, perhaps, that he confronted an opera in the same way he confronted a symphonic work.

"When you conduct a symphony," he told *Opera News,* "you are sole master of the situation. If that symphony is not recreated with sincerity, it falls flat on its face. In opera this is not always so. Usually you and the singers begin together and end together, and in between is not really a conducted opera but an improvisation.... Occasionally you do feel you've recreated a masterwork. In *Salome,* for instance, where you build piece by piece, as you would a Brahms symphony."

On the other hand, Zubin says, "Beethoven's Fifth sounds good with a lousy conductor, but opera just doesn't hold its own under mediocre leadership. There's so much to control, so many things happen at the spur of the moment. That's why I conduct without a score. I don't have to look down every two seconds to see where I am." As for *Aïda,* "it's the *Eroica* of operas. You feel that everything functions; you can find no fat."

It was unquestionably a high point in the career of a twenty-nine-year-old conductor. "Frankly," Zubin said, "I'm glad I made it to the Met before I was thirty." But he had no intention of quitting while he was ahead. "What do I want in opera? Everything! I've still fifty years to do opera."

10

1967: By Dint of Hard Work

Nineteen sixty-seven was a convulsive year for America's symphony orchestras. In New York, Leonard Bernstein announced his imminent abdication of the prestigious Philharmonic throne. Jean Martinon left his post with the Chicago Symphony. Erich Leinsdorf, who had been awarded the Boston position Charles Munch wanted for Zubin, decided not to renew his contract when it expired two seasons later. Even Eugene Ormandy was rumored to be fidgeting in Philadelphia.

In Montreal, the Symphony's board of directors watched the turmoil across the border and wondered how much longer they could hold onto their own dynamic leader, whose current contract would expire at the end of the 1966–67 season.

Not so in Los Angeles. Pride in and of the Philharmonic was soaring, confidence in Zubin at its peak. His love affair with the Israelis might have stung a bit at first, but the Los Angeles board still saw that as a passing flirtation. As executive board member Olive Behrendt told an interviewer, Los Angeles was still Zubin's first love and most likely vehicle to stardom. "To Zubin, the challenge is right here," she said. "He can do anything he wants, he has all kinds of recording possibilities." Indeed, his Los Angeles recording possibilities were among Zubin's most exciting prospects at the start of 1967.

Decca/London officials had been highly pleased with Zubin's leading of the Vienna Philharmonic in the Bruckner Ninth. He followed that up in 1966 with an album of opera preludes by Wagner and the Liszt *Les Preludes,* again in Vienna; then, with the London Symphony Orchestra and Vladimir Ashkenazy, a recording of the Brahms Piano Concerto no. 2. Since all three records were artistic successes, and beginning to look like commercial successes as well, Decca/London officials let Zubin talk them into a contract with his own orchestra in Los Angeles.

This had been one of Zubin's highest priorities since he took over in Los Angeles, feeling strongly that recordings—quality recordings of important music on a good label—would boost the Philharmonic's international reputation. He had signed his contract with Decca on the condition that he be allowed to record with his own orchestra, as soon as he determined the orchestra was ready. Decca officials went along, providing the musicians would be paid European scale, not American. This gave Zubin the added headache of finding benefactors in Los Angeles who would make up the difference. It took some doing, but at last a contract was signed between Decca and the Los Angeles Philharmonic.

The four-year exclusive contract was momentous for a number of reasons. First, it signaled the arrival of the Los Angeles Philharmonic on the international scene, with a recording industry giant willing to make a long-term investment in its future. As for marketability, clearly Decca was counting on the emerging prominence of Zubin Mehta to boost record sales. Historically, this was the first exclusive contract ever signed between an American orchestra and a major European recording house.

Before they could begin recording, however, Zubin had a date with television cameras. The *Bell Telephone Hour,* lured by the maelstrom of publicity that seemed to swirl about him, was planning a TV special devoted to the conductor "whose sable locks, honey-colored aquiline features and voracious energy give him the appeal of a matinee idol and make him a kind of culture hero." Or so said *Time* Magazine.

The television crew invaded the Music Center to film Zubin rehearsing, eating lunch, going over programming details with administrative personnel, working with the sections, talking to the camera, and finally playing a concert. They crowded their lights and sound gear into Mehli and Tehmina's Los Angeles home for a glimpse into Zubin's personal life. They interviewed players, board members, and office workers for their opinions of their favorite Parsee. When they had everything they wanted, they packed their equipment into cases and went away.

The film company was hardly gone when the recording crew arrived from London, with fifty-six crates that weighed more than two and a half tons. The Music Center staff was delighted to see the crates go not to the Pavilion, but to the campus of the University of California at Los Angeles, where the Philharmonic had found a new recording home.

Three years earlier, RCA had wanted to capture the "acoustic ambience" of the new Dorothy Chandler Pavilion. But the London engineers insisted the Pavilion was all wrong for recording, that what sounded good to the human ear bore little resemblance to what sounded good to a microphone. After digging around Los Angeles for a couple of weeks in January, London's John Culshaw and Arthur Haddy made the surprising announcement that henceforth all Philharmonic recording sessions would be held in Royce Hall at U.C.L.A.

University officials and local music critics were astounded. For years it had been taken for granted that the acoustics at Royce Hall were deplorable. It was all right for lectures, but got little praise from the visiting concert artists and ballet companies who used it for their campus appearances. Culshaw and Haddy were firm in their decision, and, when he arrived the first week of April, chief engineer Gordon Parry concurred: with a few alterations, Royce Hall would do admirably.

The principal alteration turned out to be the erection of a new stage platform. Parry wanted to get virtually the entire orchestra out from behind the proscenium. The platform had to be strong enough to support the musicians, instruments, and mike booms, but able to be broken down and put up again between takes, since the hall was booked solid for evening lectures and performances by the American Ballet Theater.

Time was a tremendous pressure, since the orchestra had only two weeks between the end of its subscription season and the start of a spring tour in the East. The musicians would be unavailable for the necessary week of setting up the hall prior to the recording sessions. To solve this last problem, Zubin enlisted the aid of a youth orchestra to give the engineers some music to place their mikes by. (This was the American Youth Symphony, which recently had come under the direction of Mehli Mehta, who had moved to California the year before.)

To further complicate matters, Zubin had to break away in the middle of the recording period for a one-night stand at the Metropolitan Opera in New York. That would cut three days out of the recording schedule.

Then there was Zubin's insistence that the U.C.L.A. music students be allowed to attend recording sessions. The engineers relented, providing the students would stay in the top balcony seats and not make any noise.

The biggest noise, however, turned out to be that made by the cymbal player in *Pictures at an Exhibition*. No matter where the engineers situated the man, no matter how they segregated him from his cohorts, the crash of his cymbals got into everybody else's microphone and there was no way to achieve a proper balance. He couldn't simply bang them together more softly, since that made a sound altogether different from the one Zubin required. After much experimentation, the percussionist was stationed up among the students in the far reaches of the balcony. There he sat, listening to the music on a headset, awaiting Zubin's cue on a closed-circuit television monitor. He spent the better part of two weeks there.

The actual number of recording days was ten. During that time the orchestra taped the Mussorgsky/Ravel *Pictures at an Exhibition, Petrushka* and *Circus Overture* by Stravinsky, Scriabin's *Poem of Ecstasy,* Schönberg's *Verklärte Nacht,* and the Fourth Symphony of Tchaikovsky.

By the end, Zubin's easygoing manner and exuberance for the music had infected everyone. The London executives, the engineers, even the students felt caught up, the way the orchestra already was, in Zubin's almost delirious joy in making music. Musicians and students crowded into the makeshift control room to share with the engineers the experience of hearing the takes played back. When it was over, the music students pitched in to help the small recording crew load up and carry out the heavy cases of recorders, cables, mikes, and booms. The closing sentence on the liner notes for *Petrushka* seemed to be speaking for everyone concerned: "Needless to say, we are all looking forward to next year's sessions."

There was no time to look back on those first recording sessions, however. The orchestra had to pack up its own twelve tons of paraphernalia and head East.

The Los Angeles Philharmonic would later play the concert halls of Europe and Asia under Zubin, and there they would benefit from their identification with Hollywood and the American West. Now they were crossing the Rockies for the first time, going where those labels spelled "provincial" and "small-time" to the cultural elite. The thing Zubin feared most was condescension from the eastern critics.

The tour was scheduled to take them to Washington, D.C., Detroit, Fort Wayne, and several other midwestern cities, but it would begin in New York with the orchestra's Carnegie Hall debut. The tour was financed by a grant from the Michael J. Connell Foundation, and John Connell went along to see how his money was being spent.

The Carnegie Hall concert was booked by Sol Hurok, who paid the orchestra all of two thousand dollars for the evening, conductor's fee included. "You want to play New York?" Hurok asked. "So don't expect to get paid for it." The musicians' union would not permit their playing for pennies, so the fees were picked up by John Connell.

Amid frenetic last-minute preparations for that first concert, Zubin had managed to leave his tails at the apartment of a current girl friend, with whom he was staying while in New York. The tails—no longer the pocketless Viennese bargain, but one of several dress suits he was buying and wearing out at the rate of two a year—arrived by taxicab in time for the second half of the program. The first half he conducted—with Van Cliburn playing—in a tuxedo borrowed from a second violinist.

A number of such misadventures occurred on the tour. In Fort Wayne, Indiana, the librarian was the culprit. Zubin had scheduled the Prelude to *Die Meistersinger* as an encore, but in putting out the music the librarian had neglected to place a *Meistersinger* part on concertmaster David Frisina's stand.

The error was not discovered until Zubin was about to begin the encore. He saw panic on the face of the new assistant concertmaster, who shared Frisina's music stand. Frisina whispered to the boy, "Just keep on playing C major," and nodded to Zubin that he would manage. Zubin was astonished, after starting into the Prelude, to hear Frisina playing his part perfectly from memory.

The personal highlight of the tour, for Zubin, came in Washington. There, in the capital of his adopted nation, he was presented the highest civilian award of the nation of his birth. The Indian ambassador to the United States, B. K. Nehru, came onto the stage at the concert's conclusion to give the conductor the Bhusan, the Order of the Lotus. It meant a great deal to Zubin, particularly since it came from the country in which his father had struggled half his life just to get people to listen to his music.

At least from the critics' point of view, the tour was a resounding success. The Los Angeles papers proudly carried all the favorable reviews from each of the cities visited, letting Angelenos know that their orchestra had indeed made the big time. Yet among the more reputable of the critics the lasting impression was left not by the orchestra but by its conductor.

New Yorker critic Winthrop Sargeant took the opportunity to analyze what he saw as the Mehta style:

> He has the capacity to control every sound made by an orchestra and he does this with the simplest of gestures, every one of which has an immediate and perceptible effect. He has a talent for conveying a mood of serenity, or of serene grandeur, to both orchestra and audience that is rare indeed in the younger generation of conductors.

Sargeant's description bears an uncanny resemblance to violinist Eugene Husaruk's recollection of Zubin standing before the student orchestra in his first conducting class at the Vienna Music Academy. Asked to describe his friend's conducting technique in 1978, violinist Pinchas Zukerman would use almost identical words. Zubin's entire body was his instrument. With it—with the slightest gesture or glance, with the broadest arc of his arms—he could so illuminate a composer's manuscript as to make it almost impossible for anyone to mistake his intention. There were still those who took issue with those intentions, just as there had been at Lewisohn Stadium at 1960, just as there will always be, but no one could argue that Zubin did not get what he wanted from an orchestra.

The only review that sticks in his mind—or, one might say, in his craw—from that bold journey East, came from a newspaper critic somewhere in the Midwest.

"We were playing the *Mandarin* [Bartók's *Miraculous Mandarin Suite*] which opens with an atmosphere like that of Gershwin's *An American in Paris,* like downtown, with traffic and automobile horns—but much more brutal. So what did they say? They said it was like Hollywood Boulevard. Someone was tempted to write that and just couldn't resist. It's this kind of wiseacre remark that I find revolting. For five years I'd been working for a central European sound. But they said we had a Hollywood sound. It makes me rather angry when I hear that."

The logistics of an orchestra tour are hectic enough without the conductor flying off to other cities between performances. But this is exactly what Zubin was doing, conducting the touring Metropolitan Opera's production of *Otello* between stops on the Los Angeles Philharmonic tour.

He'd managed to arrange Monday nights free from the orchestra, so that he could lead the Met in its opening night in Atlanta, Dallas, Detroit, and Cleveland. On the orchestra's day off, Zubin traveled.

In Cleveland the *Otello* performance was given in a huge old municipal auditorium of the sort musicians disparagingly refer to as a "barn." The barn having no orchestra pit, the orchestra and conductor were crouched beneath the apron of the stage, crowding into the first row of audience seats.

The opera went as well as might be expected until Zubin began conducting the restless but lovely introductory music to the second act. Suddenly he felt himself being elbowed out of the way, leaning at a dangerous angle toward the woodwinds.

"Excuse me," huffed a matronly voice.

Mercifully, the orchestra kept playing as Zubin righted himself. The jostler was a hefty middle-aged woman clearly distressed at his having started up before she had taken her seat.

Immediately after the opera, Zubin hired a private plane to take him to Montreal, where he would rejoin the Los Angeles orchestra for the gala opening of Expo 67. The Philharmonic joined forces with the Montreal Symphony in a performance of the *Symphonie Fantastique* ("It's the way Berlioz dreamed of it!" says Zubin), Ravel's *La Valse,* and Respighi's *Pines of Rome.*

Incredibly, all of this—recording, tour, Met, Expo—took place in less than six weeks, from late April until the first of June. Zubin could be forgiven if he hurried off to the calm of a Caribbean island for a few weeks' rest. But he did not go there to rest. He was engaged to conduct a concert in May at the Pablo Casals Festival in San Juan, Puerto Rico.

Also at the festival was the cellist Gregor Piatigorsky. "Grischa," as he was known, had become a great friend and ally of Zubin in Los Angeles, where he made his home. He had been a supporter of the Philharmonic for many years and was always free with his advice to the young music director. The two men were disappointed that they had no concerts together at the Casals festival, but in their time off they could share the sun and the ocean at the beach of the Caribe Hilton.

Piatigorsky was worried about recent developments in the Middle East. As they waded into the surf one day, he squinted eastward, as if he could see all the way to Israel, and said, "What do you think about Nasser?"

"You mean throwing the United Nations troops out of the Sinai? Maybe he just wants to show them who's boss in Egypt."

"Maybe."

"You don't think there's going to be a war, do you?" Zubin asked.

There was a look of deep concern in the old musician's eyes. "Maybe," he said.

Inevitably, the conversation drifted back to music and the regrettability of the two "Angelenos" having no concert together. Zubin came up with an idea. He would ask to postpone the Bruckner Fourth he was supposed to conduct and substitute the Strauss *Don Quixote* for cello and orchestra.

"That's a marvelous idea," said Piatigorsky. "Do you know the Old Man was the first one to play it in America, and under Strauss's direction?" He was speaking, of course, of Pablo Casals, who thought the program change was indeed a grand idea.

Don Pablo was sitting in the wings on the evening of the concert to see his two friends perform the German composer's idealization of the legendary Spanish hero. At one point, during the F-sharp major variations, which depict Quixote lost in reverie, Zubin turned to cue the basses and saw a movement of white in the wings, a handkerchief. The Old Man was weeping.

The morning after the concert, Zubin picked up a Miami *Herald* in the hotel lobby and read the disturbing news that Nasser had moved heavy tanks and artillery into the Sinai. It began to look as if Grischa was right about war.

Making a joyful noise with Merwan and Zarina.

Seeing the sights of Montreal with his children, Zarina and Merwan; his first wife, Carmen Lasky; and (*front seat, left*) brother Zarin.

Relaxing at home with a technique the Parsees picked up from the Hindus.

The principals in Christopher Nupen's film, *The Trout*. *Left to right:* Jacqueline du Pré, Zubin Mehta, Pinchas Zukerman (*viola*), Christopher Nupen, Daniel Barenboim, Itzhak Perlman (*violin; back to camera*), London, 1969.

Taking lessons from his friend Danny Kaye in rehearsal for the Music Center's Tenth Anniversary Concert, Los Angeles, 1974.

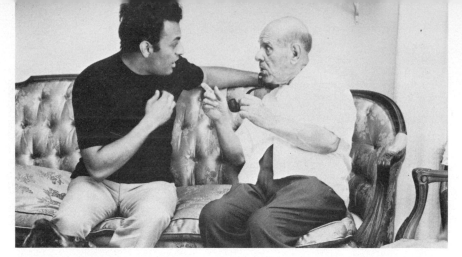

With Pablo Casals, 1967.

Photograph by R. N. Khann

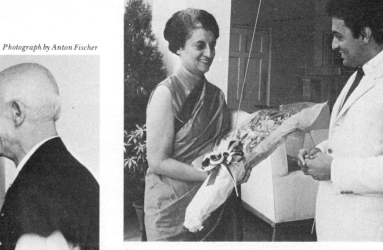

With Prime Minister Indira Gandhi, 1967.

Photograph by Anton Fischer

With Dimitri Mitropoulos.

With Pierre Beique, 1961.

Photograph by Zev Radovan

With Teddy Kollek, 1973.

Photograph by Christina Burton

With baritone Hermann Prey.

Photograph by Christina Burton

With soprano Kiri te Kanawa in London.

Photograph by Eugene Cook

With Nathan and Therese Milstein.

With Gregor Piatigorsky in Los Angeles shortly before Piatigorsky's death in 1976.

With friend Isaac Stern at a secret air force base in Israel during the Yom Kippur War, 1973.

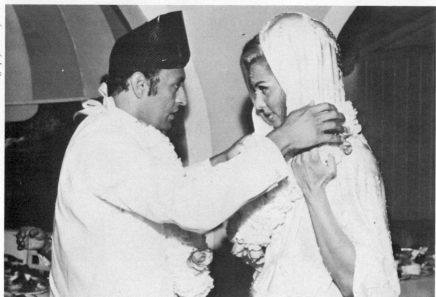

Nancy Kovack becomes Mrs. Zubin Mehta, according to the Parsee rite, in Los Angeles, 1969.

Tehmina and Mehli Mehta with their grandchildren. *From left*: Rustom, Merwan, Rohanna, and Zarina.

Zubin and Yehudi Menuhin enjoy a chat during a reception given at the Royal Opera House after a performance of Verdi's *Otello*, 1977.

Under the stars and laser beams at the Hollywood Bowl "Star Wars" concert, November 1977.

In the days that followed, word from the Middle East grew ever grimmer. Nasser closed the Gulf of Aqaba, Israel's only outlet to the east since he nationalized the Suez Canal. There were reports of Jordanian troops staging mortar attacks on New Jerusalem. On the streets, and in the synagogues and homes of Israel, the people were preparing for war.

After five years of conducting there, Zubin had developed a deep affection for Israel. It was almost his second home now, as much as Austria or Canada or the United States, and it was clear that Israel needed all the help it could get. But an artist is not a statesman or a soldier; his only means of defending his country, or at least of supporting it, is with his art.

The urge to go to Israel was strengthened when he heard that the Israel Philharmonic had been stranded without a conductor for concerts scheduled during that period.

Three American Jews—conductor Erich Leinsdorf, soprano Roberta Peters, and tenor Richard Tucker—had been billed as the attractions for concerts in Tel Aviv, Haifa, and Jerusalem. When the outbreak of war seemed imminent, foreign embassies advised their citizens, through the news media, to leave Israel. The next morning Leinsdorf's bags were packed. When the orchestra's driver appeared at the guest house, where the artists were lodged, the conductor asked to be driven not to the Mann Auditorium but to the airport. The singers and musicians were left without a conductor, at a rehearsal that would never begin. Hearing of this incident, Zubin fired off a telegram, offering his help to the orchestra.

Meanwhile the political tension was stretching the Middle East toward the breaking point. Arab leaders, certain this would be the finish of Israel, began speculating publicly as to how the spoils would be divided. The Palestinian Arab leader, Ahmad Asaad Shukairy, boasted in front of reporters and television cameras that all young Jewish males would be put to death and that he personally would take care of the women and children. Finally, Zubin made up his mind and called on another Casals Festival guest, Isaac Stern, knowing of Stern's close connections with the Israeli consulate in New York.

"Isaac," he said, "I can't help it—I've got to go there."

As Stern contacted his Israeli friends in New York to speed through a visa, Zubin cabled his European agent, Ruth Böttcher, to cancel his guest appearances in Budapest and Paris. It was the first time he had ever canceled a concert.

Aboard the TWA flight to Tel Aviv, Zubin's thoughts were of the Israel Philharmonic, with which he had fallen in love at first hearing. His schedule had not permitted him to return every year, as the musicians asked him to in 1961, but the encounters were coming ever more frequently.

Exactly one year earlier, in June of 1966, he had conducted the Israel Philharmonic in twenty-one concerts in twenty-four days, because a tour of the U.S.S.R. had been abruptly canceled by the Russians. They had shuttled from Tel Aviv to Haifa to Jerusalem with a busload of musicians, sharing with them the giddiness that comes from too much success and too little sleep. He bade them farewell only to be called for an emergency substitution. The Israel Philharmonic had been going on a tour of Australia, New Zealand, and Hong Kong with two conductors—Antal Dorati and Carlo Maria Giulini—but Giulini had suddenly canceled. Without putting up much of a fight, Zubin let himself be talked into going along. And what glorious music they made on that tour!

He especially loved the way the Israelis played Mahler. With their unique *Yiddishkeit*, they brought out the Jewish half of the composer's personality the way no other orchestra could, not even Vienna, not even Los Angeles. Sometimes he felt so moved when he conducted them that he hardly knew if his feet were touching the podium. Sometimes the players were so good it embarrassed him to tell them that the morning after a concert. He found himself stammering, lost for words, realizing in the end that they really had no idea how well they could play.

The special truth he kept to himself was that they really had no right to be that good. After thirty years they still had never worked under a permanent conductor. The endless hopping, from guest conductor to guest conductor, while it made them versatile as chameleons, left them without a true color of their own.

Sometimes he got so flustered with them he had to laugh, finding his rehearsals bogged down in thick debate over *the* definitive way to play a phrase. "So-and-so in Poland, who studied with the composer, told me it must be like so." "Ah, but so-and-so in Russia, who *taught* the composer, told my old professor it was meant to be this way." It was musical anarchy until he finally restored order, but he loved them for their feistiness and for wanting to be so involved.

And then there were the strings. He felt especially proud of the way they had blossomed and come together under his guidance, and he cherished the warm relationship he had developed with hard-working manager Abe Cohen.

Zubin's work in Israel was not only with the musicians. Gradually, he was nudging the Israeli audiences toward more than just the classics, which had been all they ever wanted to hear. With Daniel Barenboim, he had performed the Bartók First Concerto in 1966. The same season he prodded and coddled the brass and woodwinds until they actually enjoyed Webern's Six Pieces, something that would have been inconceivable when he first came to them. . . .

Somewhere over the Mediterranean Zubin's thoughts were broken by the droning, mechanical voice of the pilot. At the same time, he felt the huge plane turning back toward the west. As calmly as though he were reciting weather conditions in Cleveland, the pilot announced: "Uh, ladies and gentlemen, uh, we have just been told that war has broken out and we will be unable to land in Tel Aviv. Uh, we have been diverted instead to Rome."

Arriving at Rome Airport can be an agonizing experience even under normal conditions. By the time Zubin fought his way through customs, obtained a visa, registered at a hotel, it was already noon. Immediately he telephoned the Israeli Embassy in Rome to seek help in getting into Israel. Despite Zubin's pleas for urgency, the best he could get was an invitation to dinner at the ambassador's house.

"There's really nothing I can do." The ambassador smiled. "My office is filled with students who want to get home so they can fight, but the Ministry says no. The airports are shut down except for military planes. They're afraid any commercial planes would be forced down by the MiGs—or worse. So you see, it's really quite impossible."

But Zubin insisted. He remained until long after dinner, badgering the ambassador until he got at least a promise that he would try and "see whether something can be arranged."

Since that seemed to be the best he could do, Zubin left. Anyway it was almost midnight Monday, and he had not slept decently since Saturday night in Puerto Rico.

Tuesday morning Zubin was awakened by a call from the Israeli ambassador.

"You still want to go?"

"Of course I want to go. You have a way?"

"Be at the airport at five o'clock. There will be one El Al flight leaving. But for God's sake don't tell anybody. If these students find out I let a musician go and wouldn't let them go to fight, they're liable to burn down the embassy."

"Don't worry," Zubin assured him. "I won't tell a soul."

"Good," said the ambassador. "*L'hitraot.* And by the way, don't expect the flight to be comfortable. No hors d'oeuvres will be served."

The ambassador's statement on comfort was a masterpiece of understatement. The plane's seats had been removed and the cabin filled with crates and boxes, all unmarked. Zubin found himself seated on a box with three other passengers. One was a member of the Israeli Parliament, one was the Rome bureau chief of *Newsweek*, Curtis Bill Pepper, and the other was an Israeli named Horowitz, the governor of the Bank of Israel.

Sometime after the plane was in the air, the banker turned to Zubin and asked, in Yiddish, *"Du vayst goornisht vos is in die Schacteln?"* ("Do you know what's in these boxes?") Zubin shrugged and shook his head.

"What's that?" asked the reporter.

"Zug nit!" warned Horowitz.

He did not want Pepper to know what the others knew, that they were sitting on crates filled with weapons and ammunition.

It was supposed to be top-secret information that the United States had "laundered" some secret emergency military aid to Israel through several foreign countries. The Israeli Army was hoping El Al airliners would have a better chance of getting past Arab antiaircraft missiles than would a military transport plane.

Zubin was enjoying the excitement too much at the moment to wonder whether all this risk was really worth taking in order to conduct an orchestra in concerts that might never be played.

Tel Aviv was under total blackout, and the runway lights at Tel Aviv Airport were flashed off when the El Al plane touch down. As they disembarked, they heard the distant thud of artillery. Thirteen miles to the northeast, Israeli soldiers were crossing the Jordanian border into the West Bank.

The four passengers were sped by military car into town, where Zubin was met by an excited fellow in his pajamas. Zvi Haftel, head of the orchestra committee, had been awakened by a call from the Foreign Ministry to say it was flying in a conductor. Haftel told him he was not the first to arrive.

"Jackie and Danny beat you here."

"Fantastic! How long ago?"

"Eight days. Danny canceled a *Cosi Fan Tutte* he was supposed to conduct and he and Jackie have been playing recitals at the *kibbutzim*. They're planning to get married soon. Richard and Roberta [Tucker and Peters] are here, too."

"I know. Are they in the city?"

"No, they're somewhere out in the front lines. Golan, I think. Singing arias and duets to keep the spirits up. Other armies have bugle boys; we get Metropolitan Opera stars!"

At the Orchestra House, the guest house for visiting artists, Zubin was reunited with Jacqueline du Pré, Daniel Barenboim and his parents, and Sergiu Comissiona, the Rumanian-born conductor and former director of the Haifa Symphony Orchestra. They, along with Mrs. Comissiona, were all camping out in the Orchestra House basement, a sort of temporary air-raid shelter. However, nobody was really expecting an air raid, since the entire Egyptian Air Force had been destroyed in the first Israeli attack. But light and movement in the city were restricted, so they kept themselves entertained with conversation and jokes.

"We had one whale of a time that night," Zubin recalls fondly. "After everything I'd been through to get there, we stayed up all night laughing and kidding around.

"We didn't get any sleep, I remember. We kept playing jokes on Comissiona. He went out to get a glass of water and I climbed onto the mattress with his wife. When he came back, the room was all dark and he found somebody there with her. *Kinderspiel,* you know, but with the war going on all around us we thought we'd better keep our sense of humor."

Exuding confidence, they planned a "victory concert." Zubin would conduct, Daniel would play the *Emperor* Concerto of Beethoven, and Jackie would play the Schumann Cello Concerto, with Beethoven's Symphony no. 5 as a rousing show closer. One of the principal Israeli objectives of the war was to reunify the divided city of Jerusalem, so they decided that would be the appropriate place for the concert. The only hitch, of course, was that no one could be absolutely sure when the victory concert would be held. But there was no doubt it would happen.

Wednesday morning the orchestra members were called in to rehearse, and again it was like a family reunion. The musicians attacked the Beethoven Fifth with the fervor of Israeli soldiers on the front lines. For many of them this would be their only chance to participate in what would surely be a glorious moment for Israel.

After rehearsal, Zubin talked his friend Memi Shalit, head of the Israel Tourist Office, into lending him a car to drive to Jerusalem ahead of the orchestra and make preparations for the concert. Shalit also handed him a map marked with a little-known, circuitous route through the mountains.

Driving over the rough back roads, Zubin came upon a squad of Israeli infantrymen coming from the Syrian front. He stopped to pick them up. What news, they asked, did he have of the fighting in the South? He laughed at the irony of soldiers seeking military information from a musician.

A *musician*? What was his name? They assumed from his complexion and curly black hair that he was a sabra, a native-born Israeli. When Zubin told them who he was, one of the soldiers exclaimed, "This is the fellow we've been hearing about on the radio."

"On the radio?" Zubin was puzzled.

"Sure. They keep telling how Zubin Mehta flew across enemy lines to make a dramatic appearance and how you'll be conducting a victory concert when this *Streitfall* is over. You're a hero."

The exhausted soldiers soon dropped off to sleep, leaving Zubin to negotiate his way to Jerusalem in silence. It was nearly dusk when he spotted the skyline, still dominated by the massive old King David Hotel, which was his destination.

Suddenly he found his car surrounded by tanks, jeeps, and artillery pieces. Every one of them was piled with soldiers, singing and cheering. One of the men in the car woke up and shouted to a lieutenant in a passing jeep.

"What's happened?"

"We've taken the Old City," the lieutenant called back. "Jerusalem is reunited!"

Sandwiched between two Israeli tanks, Zubin entered the city like a commanding general. The streets were filled with shouting, flag-waving people who seemed hardly able to believe that the Holy City was once again united, that it belonged once again to the Children of Israel. Zubin sat on his automobile horn like a New York taxi driver, so caught up was he in the orgy of joy. "Well," he shouted to the soldiers above the din, "I guess I'm going to get some work to do after all."

Dropping off his passengers, he went to the office of Teddy Kollek, mayor of New Jerusalem—now mayor of *all* Jerusalem. He was welcomed heartily by the mayor and by his guest, David Ben-Gurion.

The old man did not rise from his chair, only lifted his gnarled hand in greeting as Zubin entered the office. The tufts of hair billowed like white flames from the huge dome of his head. Zubin was astonished to find himself conversing with this amazing patriarch, actually being thanked for coming here by this figure out of history books, who had carved a Jewish state out of Arab desert.

As they spoke, word came that the Egyptians were retreating from the Sinai Peninsula, abandoning their tanks and artillery in a smoldering heap at the Mitla Pass. It was reported that the Egyptian Army had literally left its boots behind as soldiers leaped into the Suez Canal in a frantic effort to escape the advancing Israelis.

Ben-Gurion laughed. "Well, what do you know! It seems we have captured the Sinai. *Ach!* We'll have to give it back, I suppose. What do we need with more desert, anyway? But now we also have the Wailing Wall. And this we shall never give back. Never!"

Zubin was the only guest Wednesday night in the blacked-out King David Hotel. Sometime after midnight he was startled awake by what sounded like a gunshot close by. He knew there must be sporadic fighting still going on, with a few Jordanian Army stragglers left in the city. Paying little heed to the shot, he dropped off to sleep again.

Next morning he awoke and noticed that the painting above his head was hanging at a crazy angle. Straightening it, he saw a splintered hole in the frame and a bullet lodged in the wall behind it.

Memi Shalit arrived shortly after six A.M. to find Zubin washed and dressed. Together they walked through the New City, which seemed still drowsy from a night of war and celebration, and came to the wall that surrounded Old Jerusalem. Stepping over the rubble and spent ammunition cases, they reached the Mandelbaum Gate, symbol of the Holy City's division. Since 1948 no Jew had been permitted to live on the other side of that gate, but now there was no one to stop them from walking through, into Old Jerusalem.

"You know, you're the first ones." The voice of a young soldier leaning against the "Arab side" of the wall startled them.

"What do you mean?" Shalit asked.

"You're the first civilians," he said, "to come through the Mandelbaum Gate."

Walking rather aimlessly, the two men came to the Ambassador Hotel, which the "occupying" forces of General Chaim Herzog had turned into a command post. Pleased to see them, the general invited them in to breakfast, then rounded up a car for them.

"Now," said Memi, "I am going to show you something." They drove to the outskirts of the city and turned north into the hills. He stopped the car at the foot of Mount Scopus.

The few Israeli soldiers nearby were surprised to see civilians. The shooting here had ended only a short time before, they said.

Memi led Zubin up the hill to an amphitheater built as part of the old Jerusalem University. Long neglected, it was overgrown with grass and weeds. Nearly twenty seven hundred feet above sea level, the amphitheater commanded a sweeping view of the surrounding hills and the Dead Sea in the distance.

"What do you think?" Memi asked proudly.

Zubin grinned, "It's no Hollywood Bowl, you know. It needs a little work."

Unabashed, the publicity-minded tourist chief put his hands on his hips and gazed down at the Holy City. "As soon as the shooting stops, you're going to give your victory concert right here."

Zubin laughed. "But this is Jordan."

"It used to be Jordan. Now it's Israel."

On Friday it was clear that the war would not go on much longer. There was still fighting on the Golan Heights, but most of King Hussein's army had retreated across the Jordan River and the Egyptians were treating their wounded on the other side of the Suez Canal. Israeli military intelligence indicated it would all be over by some time Saturday, so the victory concert was scheduled for Saturday night.

Orchestra and soloists were summoned from Tel Aviv, and Memi Shalit got a gang of boys and girls to help get the amphitheater into shape. It was going to be one of those rare working *Shabbaths* in Israel, when everyone assumed the Lord would understand.

On Saturday morning, however, Zubin and Memi arrived at Mount Scopus with their cleanup crew to find the area cordoned off by soldiers. An officer walked up to their car.

"Sorry, gentlemen," the officer said. "We can't allow you up there."

"And why not?" asked the tourist chief, ready for a fight.

"Because we've just discovered this whole area was mined by the Arabs before they pulled out."

"But we were up there two days ago," Zubin protested.

"Then you are damned lucky you didn't get blown up."

As the soldier walked away, Zubin said to his friend, "You know, we probably would have had one hell of a time getting people to come all the way up here just for a concert anyway."

The gala victory concert was held at Binyanei Ha'ooma Convention Center, with about half the audience wearing khaki. It was not the best music the Israel Philharmonic ever made, but it was perhaps the most emotional.

In the flood of tears and congratulations after the concert, Zubin's most vivid recollection is of David Ben-Gurion's warm embrace. And then, as though from another time, the voice of Ben-Gurion's wife, Paula, who in her usually single-minded manner questioned the appropriateness of a concert.

"Why?" she asked, shaking her head at the ground. "Why are you playing all this music when my boys are dying on the front?"

The old man looked at Zubin as though he were going to say something, then he simply turned his wife and led her away.

The following morning, Sunday, Zubin went with Memi and some other Israeli officials, including Foreign Minister Abba Eban, to see the Western Wall. He had been told the significance of this "wailing wall" (as Westerners know it), that it was believed to be the actual western wall surrounding King Solomon's temple, that it was one of the most sacred shrines of Judaism.

But Zubin was not a Jew. What he saw was an ancient stone wall surrounded by the carcasses of shacks, Arab slums that had grown up around the wall in the nineteen years of Jordanian control, flimsy as the *chawls* of Bombay. Soldiers were knocking down the hovels and carting away rubble, trying to clear a path to the holy wall. In the other men's faces he read strange emotions: joy mixed with deep sadness that it should ever have come to this. In the eyes of men who had been killing and facing death, he saw quiet tears.

A journalist came up and began to question Abba Eban about the aftermath of the war, the prospects for a lasting peace.

"By the way," said the reporter, "what are we going to call this war, anyway?"

Eban smiled and then, after thinking for a moment, answered, "I guess we'll have to call it the Six-Day War, won't we?"

Somehow, in the midst of war and confusion, Daniel and Jackie had set their wedding date for the following Wednesday. Jackie had gone to great lengths to prepare herself for conversion to Judaism and an Orthodox wedding, even to the point of requesting the ritual *mikvah,* or purifying bath.

"Since I was the only one driving, in my borrowed car, I had to take everyone everywhere," Zubin recalls. "We went to pick up this old rabbi and then drove him and Jackie to the *mikvah.*

"We were sitting outside in the waiting room, and all of a sudden Daniel spots these other rabbis peeking into the room where Jackie was undressed. He starts screaming at them. 'Hey, that's not allowed! You're not supposed to do that.'

"After that I drove them to the place that is now the Mishkenot Sha'ananim, the Jerusalem Music Center. That was just on the edge of the no man's land that used to divide the city. We went there to the home of another rabbi, who married them outside, just below the big windmill.

"Daniel said only Orthodox Jews can be witnesses, but I was determined to be a part of it, even though in those days I didn't know a word of Hebrew. So Daniel told the rabbi I was a Persian Jew who had just immigrated. My name was Moshe Cohen. They let me in the wedding, and I held one of the poles of the *chupah.*"

Jackie du Pré Barenboim remembers passing under the *chupah,* the wedding canopy, and seeing the joy of her dear friend, whose shoulders had once carried the man she was marrying. "I looked at Zubin," she says, "and there was his face streaming with tears. I shall never forget that."

After the ceremony, the newlywed Barenboims, Daniel's parents and "Moshe Cohen" had lunch together in the restaurant of the King David. Seated at the table next to them, discussing the future of the newly expanded state of Israel, were David Ben-Gurion, Mayor Teddy Kollek, and Defense Minister Moshe Dayan.

The wedding party's talk was perhaps less momentous, but nevertheless important. The Israel Philharmonic was throwing together a goodwill tour to the United States and Canada, a fund-raising effort to help replenish the nation's depleted treasury. They wanted Zubin, Jackie, and Danny to kick off the tour in New York with a repeat performance of the victory concert. Meanwhile, calls were going out all over the world to other conductors and soloists who might volunteer their services.

Zubin was called from the table to take an overseas telephone call.

When he returned, he was shaking his head.

"You won't believe who that was," he said. "The manager of the Orchestre National in Paris. He says they have been waiting for me since ten o'clock. My soloist Nathan Milstein is there, everybody is waiting for Maestro Mehta to begin rehearsals, so when am I coming? I said, 'Well, I'm not coming, didn't you know that?' And he says, 'But, *monsieur,* we have already printed the program with your picture in it.' So I said, 'Then perhaps you can find someone who looks a little bit like me to conduct, because I won't be able to make it.'"

From Israel, Zubin, Danny, and Jackie flew to New York for the first stop of the benefit tour. They were just settling into the Essex House when Daniel received a call from a Pittsburgh newspaper reporter who had been sent to do an advance article on the Israel Philharmonic to publicize the orchestra's date in that city. Since Daniel was scheduled to be with the orchestra in Pittsburgh, the reporter was requesting an interview.

"I thought we might use your suite for the interview," said Daniel to Zubin. "We're a bit crowded down here."

"Fine. Just tell the reporter to come up to my room."

Some time later, Zubin received the reporter, who began to speak without giving Zubin time to introduce himself. The young man was positively effulgent at being in the same room with so eminent a musician as Mr. Barenboim.

Zubin listened to the man prattle, amused at being mistaken for Daniel and thinking what a fine joke it would be on the reporter when finally he discovered his mistake. He wondered how long the joke could be drawn out. He certainly knew Danny's biography and current concert schedule well enough to answer the fellow's questions.

"No, no. I wasn't born in Israel, I was born in Argentina. My parents brought me to Israel when I was nine."

The door opened and Jackie appeared. She was about to apologize for Daniel's being late when Zubin preempted her.

"Ah, there you are, darling." He rose to meet her. "Come in and meet the gentleman from Pittsburgh." Then, lowering his voice so that only she could hear him, "He thinks I'm Danny. Don't spoil the fun."

Jackie stepped right into the role, holding Zubin's hand as they spoke of their recent marriage and their musical life together. When Daniel appeared, it only took him a moment to realize what was going on, and he went right along with the joke.

"Now," said Zubin, "that's enough about me. You must talk to Mr. Mehta here, my very good friend. I expect to see his name very prominent in your article."

"No, no," Daniel demurred. "This gentleman is here to interview you,

Danny. He doesn't want to hear about Zubin Mehta."

"But you know I'd be nowhere without you, Zubin."

So it went, the reporter dutifully taking down the pithy remarks of these two famous musicians, each so gracious in his deference to the other. He went back to Pittsburgh and wrote his article, the joke lasting right until the moment the man he knew as "Zubin Mehta" walked out on the stage in Pittsburgh as Daniel Barenboim.

The orchestra went on to play sixteen cities in the United States and Canada, with a galaxy of soloists and conductors donating their time and talent to the Israel Emergency Fund. Among them were Claudio Arrau, Van Cliburn, Leon Fleisher, Jascha Heifetz, Eliahu Inbal, Yehudi Menuhin, Robert Merrill, Eugene Ormandy, Rudolf Serkin, William Steinberg, Richard Tucker, and André Watts. In all likelihood, there never would have been a tour had Barenboim, du Pré, and Mehta not been there in Israel to help get it started.

Zubin returned to Los Angeles for a series of Hollywood Bowl concerts that were trial runs for concerts the orchestra would be doing on an upcoming international tour. Beginning in mid-September, the tour would take the Los Angeles Philharmonic to Belgium, Luxembourg, Germany, Austria, Yugoslavia, Rumania, Turkey, Greece, Cyprus, Italy, and France, concluding with concerts in Iran—the homeland of Zubin's ancestors—and India—the land of his birth.

Between the Hollywood Bowl and the tour, Zubin had ten days to himself, so he decided to accept the invitation of some Los Angeles friends, Ted and Jarma Bensinger, to accompany them on a shooting safari to Kenya. Perhaps there is something of the hunter in Zubin's blood, for he recalls vividly his visits to the homes of relatives on his mother's side in Bombay, Poona, and Hubli, where he saw stuffed tigers and leopards promenading through the rooms and sambar heads mounted on the walls. At any rate, in Kenya he fired the first four shots of his life and brought down four running animals: a zebra, a Grant's gazelle, a small antelope, and an impala. Since these animals were to be used as bait for the big game, he returned with no trophies. He couldn't stay around for a shot at the lions, since he was scheduled to play a concert in Belgium.

Zubin joined the Los Angeles Philharmonic in Antwerp for the start of the whirlwind tour, which was to include forty-two concerts in nine weeks. The programs consisted of Samuel Barber's *Medea's Meditation and Dance of Vengeance,* Beethoven's *Eroica* Symphony, Bruckner's Seventh Symphony, Dvorak's Eighth Symphony, William Kraft's Concerto for Percussion, Mahler's First Symphony, Moussorgsky's *Pictures at an Exhibition,* and Richard Strauss's *Ein Heldenleben.* André Watts was to be soloist in piano concertos by Brahms, Liszt, and MacDowell. Those were the scheduled, musical events; of nonscheduled, nonmusical events there were many.

In Belgrade, a television crew set up lights and cameras in the theater for a nationwide broadcast of the concert—without bothering to consult with anyone from the orchestra. Zubin was furious when he saw the glaring lights, and he refused to go out on stage. The concert was delayed twenty minutes before he gave in and allowed the televising. He and the orchestra were rewarded with applause so long and loud that they were required to play four encores.

The reception in Bucharest was just as feverish. The Moscow Philharmonic, with Kiril Kondrashin conducting, was also in town, but, because the Russians were so disliked by the Rumanians, they were forced to "paper the house" in order not to be embarrassed. Free tickets were handed out to the California musicians, who heartily enjoyed the Muscovites' interpretation of Shostakovich's Eighth Symphony. The following evening, Kondrashin and several Soviet dignitaries were in the theater to see a lavish display of affection for the American orchestra, with Rumanians rushing to the stage to hug and kiss Zubin and the musicians at the end of their concert.

At the concert in Istanbul, the President of Turkey demonstrated his overworked condition and boredom with Western music by falling asleep in the first row. "It was during *Pictures at an Exhibition,*" Zubin recalls. "If that piece can't keep you awake you must be a very sleepy person." The President woke up for the end of the concert, in time to present Zubin with a Golden Palm award.

In Athens, where young King Constantine's monarchy had only recently been overthrown by a bloodless military coup, Zubin was treated to marvelous curries prepared by the Queen Mother, a devoted Indophile. At a reception after the concert, he was congratulated by one of the ruling generals, who bragged of his daughter's accomplished piano skills.

"That's wonderful," Zubin replied. "Do you also play?"

Constantine, who was standing nearby, interjected icily. "He plays only with tanks and guns."

In the middle of the tour, the president of the board dismissed the Los Angeles Philharmonic's new general manager. The burden fell on Jaye Rubanoff, Zubin's right-hand man ever since George Kuyper had left in 1964, and Rubanoff became the manager in name as well as function.

From Cyprus, Zubin had to leave the tour himself, in order to attend a Paris meeting with actor-director Jean-Louis Barrault. The Frenchman wanted to go over his concepts for a new production of *Carmen* that he would be staging and Zubin would be conducting at the Metropolitan Opera the following season.

After two rather unproductive days in Paris, Zubin flew to Rome, where he was scheduled to meet a United States Information Agency film crew from California. The USIA was putting together a film on Zubin for international distribution, and it wanted footage of him with the orchestra in Teheran and Bombay, the final stops on the tour.

Zubin had forgotten one important matter: the visa for the orchestra tour was a *joint* visa; his permission to travel to Iran was voided by his separation from the orchestra, and Pan-American Airlines officials would not let him on the flight from Rome to Teheran. Just as the plane was about to depart, and just as it appeared that Zubin would miss his opportunity to conduct in Persia, the Pan-Am officials gave in to the arguments of the film crew, whose visas were correct and whose equipment was already in Teheran.

They reached Teheran in the middle of Coronation Week. The streets of the capital city were lighted in a dazzling array of colors that made the place, in Zubin's words, "a fairyland." Each street had its own color of lights, enabling the musicians to find their way around at night in the otherwise indecipherable maze of thoroughfares and Arabic-lettered street signs.

The Los Angeles Philharmonic concerts turned out to be the grand opening of the newly built opera house, and Zubin decided to mark the occasion by playing a Persian composition. It was a dance named after a percussion instrument, something like a tambourine minus the cymbals, which was featured throughout the short work. However, when Zubin announced the piece at the opening concert, his well-intentioned mispronunciation of the Persian made it sound like "Dance of the Diarrhea," which gave the audience a good laugh.

Yet the music was well received, and from the sound of the applause Zubin anticipated another evening of multiple encores. After only one encore, however, the Shah and his Queen stood up and left their box.

Iranian protocol demanding that when the Shah leaves everybody leaves, the rest of the audience rose and, still applauding, started to file out. Then they saw the Queen return to her seat, so they all took their seats again. Zubin played a second encore; the Queen got up to leave, the audience got up to leave, then the Shah came back in. Zubin played another encore and the confusion started all over again. After the fourth encore, Zubin saw the royal couple leave their box once more—so he left as well.

At last came Bombay, the first time Zubin had seen the city since 1954. When their plane landed in Vienna he had told the musicians, "Welcome to my home." Now he told them, "Welcome to my *real* home."

He was received as a hero in Bombay. The orchestra was greeted at the airport by girls in saris who placed garlands of flowers around the musicians' necks. Air India had plastered the city with billboards and placards reading, "Welcome to Bombay, Zubin Mehta and the Los Angeles Philharmonic." People had waited outside the convention hall all night to purchase tickets.

Somehow the airline had managed to lose Zubin's luggage, so he was forced to wear the casual shirt and slacks he had worn on the plane to a meeting with Indira Gandhi and other Indian notables, who welcomed him home with more enthusiasm than they ever could have felt for his music. "Suddenly—" and Zubin smiles—"everyone in Bombay became my closest relative."

Many of his real relatives were there, of course, including his mother, who had flown from the United States a few days earlier. Together they visited the fire temple, placed incense and sandalwood on the sacred fire, and said the prayers they would never forget, in the ancient and dead language of the Avesta.

"It was a soul-stirring moment for me," Zubin says. "As soon as I stepped off the plane, it was as though I had never left Bombay. I knew it would always remain my true home."

Zubin returned to Los Angeles in the fall of 1967 to find his board members wearing long faces and worried expressions. Was it true, they asked, that New York had offered him the job as Leonard Bernstein's successor? That he had accepted the offer? What could they do to change his mind?

It was clear that he had become a central character in a journalistic speculation play, though he had not even been approached by the New York Philharmonic. He was definitely not interested, but the queries from reporters were coming at him thicker than the anxious questions from his board of directors.

In the journalistic imagination, "Zubi baby," colorful and dynamic, seemed the ideal replacement for Lenny. A playboy Parsee—that would be gratifying grist for their entertainment page mills. They assumed that naturally any conductor would leap at the chance to emigrate from California anonymity to the where-it's-at of New York City.

But to the excited reporter from the *New York Times*, Zubin was direct and firm, allowing for no misinterpretation: "My orchestra is better than the New York Philharmonic. We play better than they do. Artistically, it would not be a step up for me. I don't want the job. I'm very happy here."

The article published December 12 went on to quote Zubin as saying that only Philadelphia and Cleveland, out of all the orchestras in the United States, could be considered superior to the Los Angeles Philharmonic. "The New York orchestra is perhaps more prestigious," he admitted, "but since I don't place much value in prestige, I'm not interested."

In true *Times* provincial-snobbery fashion, often imitated but rarely equaled, the writer one-upped Zubin by giving him "credit" for bringing his orchestra in Los Angeles, "in only seven years [actually, he had been music director for five years] from nowhere to at least a second level of prominence." No reader had to be told that the New York Philharmonic most certainly resided in the upper reaches of that valhallic region known as the First Level of Prominence.

That should have been that. Score 1–0 or 0–1, depending on which coast you were reading from. Unfortunately, the more reporters kept calling, the angrier Zubin got at their insistence that there must be something to the rumor. As several of his close friends have ruefully noted, "Sometimes Zubin shoots his mouth off." This time it was loaded, and he shot it off in the wrong direction. The broad side of the barn he hit was the December 18 issue of *Newsweek* Magazine.

> An American should lead the [New York] Philharmonic. And he should be able to deal both with the orchestra—they step over conductors—and with New York. A lot of us think, why not send our worst enemy to the New York Philharmonic and finish him off for once and for all.

In 1854 Thoreau wrote, "You do not get a man's most effective criticism until you provoke him. Severe truth is expressed with some bitterness." Zubin had been provoked into this severe truth, and not only by the badgering of newspeople.

Far greater provocation was his friend Lukas Foss's experience with the New York Philharmonic only a few months before, an experience that seemed to justify Zubin's observation that the New York musicians "step over conductors."

While few people would argue that Foss, particularly in 1967, was among the world's leading conductors, certainly his achievements as a composer, conductor, and teacher had placed him in the inner circle of American music and had earned him the respect of most American musicians. Not, however, the respect of the New York Philharmonic.

Foss conducted the orchestra a number of times in the mid to late sixties, including his directorship of a Stravinsky festival in 1966; there never seemed to be a strong bond between conductor and musicians. The critical incident occurred during a rehearsal of Wagner excerpts.

According to someone present in Philharmonic Hall, the orchestra was demonstrating no more respect for the soprano soloist than for the conductor. At one point, a player in the cello section drew an ill-concealed chuckle by giving a nasal, mocking imitation of the singer.

That was too much for the conductor, who slammed his score down on the podium and shouted, "My four-year-old son would not have done that!"

Contending that Foss had uttered this and other disparaging remarks about them, the musicians' reaction was swift and indignant. They demanded an apology. Foss refused. From that day on the stage was the battleground in an undeclared war. Even Wagner barely survived the concerts. Relations between Foss and the Philharmonic were left to fester like an open wound which might never heal.

Lukas Foss meant a great deal to Zubin, as a musician and as a human being. By his unselfish intercession with Siegfried Hearst, Foss had become one of the key elements in Zubin's early success. Now Zubin saw New York as a graveyard where his friend's conducting career lay buried; that may have been in his mind when he blurted out his remarks to *Newsweek*.

As luck would have it, Zubin was in New York rehearsing the Met's new production of *Carmen* when the *Newsweek* article hit the stands. He longed to escape to California, but he was stuck with *Carmen* through the first two weeks of January. There was no getting away from Local 802 of the American Federation of Musicians.

Some of the Philharmonic's musicians had played in the orchestra since the 1920s, as far back as the Willem Mengelberg regime. Nearly all of them, excepting a few newcomers, had played at one time or another under virtually every major living conductor, and when the Philharmonic players considered a conductor unworthy to lead them they were quite capable of taking the matter into their own hands. Management generally looked the other way.

This time, however, Philharmonic manager Carlos Moseley could ill afford to ignore the situation. He had Zubin Mehta scheduled as one of the orchestra's guest conductors for the 1968–69 season, and, if he did not take some action now, those concerts were likely to turn into musical bloodbaths.

The situation was not improved by the ill-timed airing of the *Bell Telephone Hour*'s "profile" of Zubin. Nothing more than "an hour of adulation," sniffed the *New York Times* television critic. Out west, of course, the show created quite a different impression.

New York's music columnists did their best to keep the pot boiling through the Christmas-New Year holidays. Zubin and the Philharmonic management remained incommunicado, but the *Times*'s Harold Schonberg got a member of the orchestra to speak "not for attribution."

The musicians were concerned, said the unnamed violinist, over an alarming "show-business trend in the thinking of management." Between the lines, the word "Hollywood" stood out in 10-point boldface print. "All they want are glamour-boy kids," said the violinist. "What orchestra can respect those?"

Schonberg had his own idea about the attitude of Local 802, however, and dug back in his files for a for-instance dusty enough to be inoffensive. He recalled the Lewisohn Stadium incident in 1953, wherein, playing under an inept conductor, the musicians "went through the motions, but the Girls' High School Orchestra could have done better."

"Any good orchestra has to be prodded," Schonberg concluded, "and the better the orchestra is, the sharper the prod has to be." He urged the musicians to accept the Mehta remarks for the truth they contained, not to stiffen their backs.

Behind the scenes, a meeting was arranged between Zubin and the musicians so that the matter might be settled out of press. On the afternoon of January 9, Zubin (or "the uninhibited young conductor of the Los Angeles Philharmonic," as the *Times* characterized him) appeared at a meeting of Local 802's executive board.

For ninety minutes they met behind closed doors, the union chiefs explaining that they only sought respect for their members, Zubin insisting that all he wanted was respect for his orchestra in Los Angeles, that he had been misquoted by *Newsweek* (whose editors stood behind every word of their story), and that his opinions of New York had been distorted out of all proportion. Nowhere is it recorded that anyone actually apologized to anyone else.

Zubin left the meeting, giving reporters no more than a smile. The telling of the tale was left to Max Arons, president of Local 802.

According to Arons, "Mr. Mehta said he was happy to come in and clear up the misunderstanding." The meeting had been "strict and stern, but friendly." At the end, the union was satisfied that Mr. Mehta did indeed respect its musicians and that his remarks were not intended to slur. Arons said he advised Zubin to "study what he says before he talks, like studying a score. It's like a bad note, you can't take it back once it's played."

The musicians also used the meeting to remind the conductor that he was not a member of their union and that whatever success he had in the United States could be attributed to the Federation's generosity.

"He is not a citizen and can't be a member," said Arons to reporters. "But we had to approve his coming in with the Immigration Department. He also understands that the musician's union could cause him trouble everywhere in the United States if it wanted to."

At the moment, the union seemed content with causing him trouble only in New York. Although Arons claimed he was "satisfied" with Zubin's appearance and would "make no suggestion to management," the handwriting on the wall was quite legible.

That same day the newspapers reported that Zubin's appearances with the Philharmonic were "postponed." As a matter of fact, it had been several weeks earlier, when the *Newsweek* issue hit the stands, that Carlos Moseley suggested to Zubin over the phone that, under the circumstances, it might be prudent to call off next season's appearances. Zubin had agreed immediately.

Several months later, the management put an end to speculation over Leonard Bernstein's successor. The speculators got out their various lists of candidates, now narrowed to two or three, hoping for a chance to say "I told you so." The Philharmonic's choice, however, was none of those who had figured in the speculation. Passed over were all the glamorous, hot-item possibilities for a relatively uncolorful Frenchman, Pierre Boulez.

Jean Martinon's post in Chicago went to Georg Solti, Leinsdorf's in Boston to William Steinberg. The rumors of Ormandy's leaving Philadelphia turned out to be false. Although he felt obliged to relinquish his Montreal directorship, Zubin Mehta stayed in Los Angeles. After all, he had the promise of the then board chairman, Joseph Koepfli, that, "We're going to be as flexible as we can to suit you, because whatever this orchestra is and does, it's yours."

11

~~~❦~~~

His Soul Mate

The almost unbelievable pace of 1967 is made even less believable by the fact that it is not atypical of all the Zubin Mehta years since 1961. His life and his work have been inseparable, almost indistinguishable. Brief spaces between concerts—usually no more than a few days at a time—have been filled with study, meetings, and marathon strategy sessions over long-distance telephone lines.

Zubin's friendships with Hollywood stars, such as Danny Kaye and the late Jack Benny, have been a natural outgrowth both of his own celebrity status and of those other celebrities' interest in Zubin's orchestras. The friendships did not come about, as a few of Zubin's more caustic critics have inferred, from any infatuation on his part with the "swinging" Hollywood life.

One critic in particular, the Los Angeles *Times*'s Martin Bernheimer, has played variations on the theme of "playboy conductor" for so long that reality has become inextricably entangled with myth in the media net. Whereas Zubin laughingly declares that "that kind of 'Rubinstein' book will never be written about me," he does admit to having had a "pretty busy life" as far as women are concerned.

"I suppose there must be a few broken hearts around, but I was always honest with them. I don't think I've had an ugly relationship, not with

167

any of the women I've been involved with. I never made false promises or gave delusions of love."

In the years that followed his divorce from Carmen, Zubin backslid naturally into bachelorhood. There were always parties after concerts, against which he continually protested but at which he nevertheless felt obligated to put in appearances. Friends were forever pairing him with eligible young women who offered little or no resistance to the combination of Mehta charm and musical deification.

"Look, we've all been through that," protests Zubin, referring to the built-in glamour of a performing artist's job. "The minute you walk on stage, whether you're tall, dark, and handsome or pale, fat, and ugly, you're creating an illusion in the minds of those people out there. It's the illusion they love, not the reality."

Obviously, in Zubin's case the illusion did not dissolve on the way from the podium to the bedroom. Everywhere he traveled, anytime he was photographed, it seemed he always had a pretty girl along. The playboy image grew and prospered in the press, especially in Los Angeles.

Dorothy Chandler saw the reputation coming and tried her best to head it off. Knowing of the Mehta family closeness, she sought a way to bring Mehli and Tehmina to the West Coast, where they might provide a stabilizing influence in her young conductor's life. In 1963, when Lukas Foss resigned his position as head of the orchestra department at the University of California at Los Angeles, Mrs. Chandler proposed Mehli as his successor. Mehli had acquired an excellent reputation as a trainer of musicians in Philadelphia, leading the student orchestras of both the New School of Music and the Philadelphia Music Academy. He was invited to conduct a Santa Monica, California, youth orchestra concert on Easter Sunday of 1963. Mrs. Chandler convinced several of her fellow U.C.L.A. Regents and members of the Music School faculty to attend the concert, which convinced them that Mehli Mehta was indeed their man.

He and Tehmina moved to Los Angeles in time for the 1963–64 season. Tehmina quickly became involved in women's fund-raising and social activities while Mehli buried himself in work—not only at U.C.L.A., but also as music director of a Los Angeles area musicians' training program which he eventually nurtured into the American Youth Symphony.

Somewhat to Dorothy Chandler's chagrin, however, neither Mother Mehta nor Father Mehta showed a great deal of concern over their son's uninhibited sowing of wild oats.

"After all," said Tehmina, "he's a bachelor now. And he works very hard. He needs to relax sometime."

So the "carefree" life continued. Carefree, that is, if one ignores the fact that he was burdened with the cares of building and operating orchestras in Montreal and Los Angeles, overseeing the growth of the Israel Philharmonic, tending to his own growth as a conductor of both symphonies and operas and managing his career. (After the death of Siegfried Hearst in 1963, Zubin never had a personal manager or even a secretary, except for Europe, where his affairs have been looked after by Ruth Böttcher, a friend since his earliest days in Vienna.)

Through it all, he never lost sight of his duties to his children. Nearly every week they received a letter or a phone call from him. He spent as much time as possible with them in Montreal, taking them on picnics, to amusement parks, or just to the top of Mount Royal for a look at the city below. As soon as Merwan and Zarina were old enough to travel, Carmen would let them join their father on tour for a glimpse of the exotic, faraway places which they might otherwise never have a chance to see.

There were, of course, problems for the children, probably inevitably so in a "broken home," and these were worsened by the regular appearances of "Zubi-gossip" in magazines and Montreal newspapers. Yet, at age nineteen, Zarina could look back on those years with a firm conviction of being loved and wanted.

"Anytime he was anywhere near us he would find time for a visit," says the young lady who has inherited her mother's warmth and her father's charm. "For instance, even if he was in New York, just for one day, for a rehearsal at the Met or between flights, he would manage to catch a plane up to Montreal, even if he could only spend 45 minutes with us before he had to fly back. Now that's what you call a real father."

In 1966, the home life of then six-year-old Merwan and seven-year-old Zarina was stabilized by the addition of a stepfather. Stabilized but in some ways confused, since their new stepfather was also their Uncle Zarin.

Zubin's younger brother moved to Montreal just as the marriage to Carmen was in the final stages of dissolution. Zarin had been considering emigrating from England to Canada, since the laws among Commonwealth nations were not prohibitive. It took him hardly any time to move into the commercial life of Montreal and Carmen was glad to introduce her brother-in-law to the social and cultural life.

Even though Carmen and Zubin stopped living together, there was never, as Zubin has pointed out, any hatred or bitterness about the parting. Carmen continued sitting in the company box at Montreal Symphony concerts, usually with Zarin as her escort. It seemed like a natural arrangement.

"Carmen certainly wasn't the only girl I went out with in those days," Zarin says, "but we did see a fair amount of each other. After a year, we realized we were growing closer together than we had been as brother and sister-in-law."

Paul Lasky, Carmen's father, had known right from the first that his daughter had ended up with the wrong Mehta. "Now there's the man she should have married," Lasky had confided to his wife after meeting Zarin in Liverpool.

No one else had spotted this affinity then, not Carmen or Zarin, and certainly not Zubin. As he watched the relationship between Zarin and Carmen dévelop, Zubin was uncertain what his own reaction should be.

"At first I was amused. I mean, it's not an everyday phenomenon. And then I saw it was sincere on their part.

"I have become very grateful that Carmen did not fall in love with and marry a stranger. And I will be grateful to the end of my days to my brother for bringing up my children the way that he has."

Carmen and Zarin were married in 1966. A year later they had their first child, Rohanna, a girl, followed a year later by a son, Rustom. Carmen has become one of Montreal's best-known voice instructors, on the faculties of McGill University and Concordia College. Zarin joined the prestigious international accounting firm of Coopers and Lybrand, quickly attaining the status of partner in the company. Meanwhile, he found a niche for himself in Montreal's musical life as treasurer and later vice-president of the Montreal Symphony board of directors.

For a time it seemed as though Zubin would never settle down. There were rumors of impending marriage to Teresa Stratas, but, as he put it, "We never found ourselves with the same day off in the same place at the same time. How could we get married? Besides, Teresa is a confirmed bachelor."

On the other hand, Zubin found himself yearning after the security and stability of married life. The relationship with Stratas had cooled and finally died a natural death; his brief encounters with jet-set ladies dropped from headline stories to one-line notes in the gossip columns. In Los Angeles, his suite at the Sheraton West (now the Sheraton Town House) was becoming less and less distinguishable from those in all the other first-class hotels he slept in, from Berlin to Florence to New York. He even put a down payment on a studio apartment in a condominium that was going up near the Music Center, hoping for at least a hint of permanence in his pied-à-terre. If not a wife to come home to, at least his own refrigerator and tea kettle. Then, in the fall of 1968, Zubin was invited to a dinner party given by Vincente Minnelli (father of Liza Minnelli) and his then wife, Denise.

The party was at an intimate, rather dimly lit restaurant in Beverly

Hills, the sort of place that promotes whispered conversations among small groups of people, even when they are seated at a rather large table. Had the light been better, Zubin certainly would have directed his attention to the stunningly beautiful blond actress seated across from him. But, in the dark, he could only make out the people on either side of him.

Someone mentioned the "Middle East" and "oil" and someone else cited the prosperity of Iran under the Shah.

"You know," Zubin interjected, "we were there during his coronation, and I must tell you, Teheran was absolutely a fairyland. So many lights . . ."

"You're absolutely right," chimed in a voice from across the table, a very firm yet very feminine voice. "Teheran *was* a fairyland at the coronation."

The voice belonged to the blond actress. Her name was Nancy Kovack.

The only thing artificial about Nancy Diane Kovack is the color of her hair; she was born a brunette in Flint, Michigan. Her professional name is the same as the one given to her by her Polish-born mother and her father, the son of Czech immigrants.

Michael Kovack was a practical, pragmatic man, a supervisor at the Chevrolet plant in Flint. Mrs. Kovack was a forceful woman of ideas and ideals, whose earlier exposure to the diverse cultural life of Boston and New York made her chafe at her daughter's lack of opportunity in the farmlands outside of Flint.

Some of Nancy's earliest memories are of the Saturday afternoons she spent hiding in the branches of apple trees as her mother called from the back door of the house, "Come quick, Nancy, the Met broadcast is coming on the radio."

Mrs. Kovack's pursuit of her daughter's education led her into a battle with the Michigan Board of Education as she argued that the child's grade level should be determined by aptitude and achievement rather than age. Pushing her forward steadily in school, she got Nancy admitted to the University of Michigan at Ann Arbor when she was only fifteen.

Mrs. Kovack's devotion to self-determination was boundless. Before long the entire family converted from Catholicism to Christian Science, to which Nancy has remained faithful.

Graduating in liberal arts in 1955 at the age of eighteen, Nancy traveled to New York City for a friend's wedding. Instantly, she understood what her mother meant by the "cultural deprivation" of Flint. There was no question in Nancy's mind of going back home, but how could she afford to stay?

She met another friend of the bride, a budding actress, who talked of nothing but the horrors of auditioning. To Nancy it seemed like fun, so, on a dare to herself, she bought a bathing suit and signed up for what was known as a "cattle call." Jackie Gleason was looking for a bevy of starlet types for his television variety show. Nancy found it odd that the auditions were being held not in a theater but in a gymnasium.

"I got there and they handed me a number," she recalls. "Just like one of those plastic numbers you take in a butcher shop. I'll never forget my number—it was four hundred twenty-seven."

Awed in the presence of so many beautiful girls, Number 427 waited and watched as one after another the would-be actresses swiveled onto a small stage, turning and posing as Gleason, June Taylor, and five other potentates looked at each other for a sign. After a few seconds, a woman Nancy came to think of as "the butcher" said either "Thank you," which meant no, thank you, or "Stay," which meant a girl had passed that round of inspection on the meat rack.

At last it was time for Number 427 to smile and pose and turn, but no sooner had she mounted the platform, it seemed, than the Butcher called out, "Thank you." It might have been the end of an acting career as a dejected young girl headed out the door and back to Flint, Michigan. But something, perhaps the voice of her mother's indomitability, stopped Nancy and turned her toward the ladies' room.

From her bag she pulled out a sweater, which she slipped over the bathing suit, and a length of ribbon, with which she did up her long hair, giving herself what she hoped was a new look. She slipped out a side entrance and walked back through the main door to take another number. This time it was 633.

Two hundred girls later, Nancy Kovack stepped onto the butcher block again, and this time she heard the magic word, "Stay."

"*Chutzpah?*" says Nancy today, and laughs. "Not at all. That was just logic. They hadn't even looked at me the first time around."

About two hundred "finalists" were selected and told to line up around the walls of the gym. This time the judges walked around, looking over one candidate at a time. Each girl received a tap on the shoulder from the butcher lady and a "Thank you" or a "Stay." For Nancy, it was "thank you" time again.

"I said to myself, 'Phooey. What the heck? So off came the sweater and ribbon, I sneaked back to the end of the line, and this time they said, 'Stay.' I think I reached some great conclusion about life then."

After that came a camera test, and ten "Glee Girls" were chosen, among them Nancy Kovack, an actress by perseverance.

It did not take her long to realize that the proper descriptive title of her job would be Decorative Sex Object. She deserted the Gleason Show for summer stock, which she found "dirty and unappetizing." Then came a string of leggy model-type jobs in quiz and game shows, such as *Beat the Clock*; a pleasant year as one of television's first "anchorwomen" on Dave Garroway's *Today Show,* and finally, at the insistence of her agent, a small role in a Broadway play called *The Disenchanted.* On Broadway she was spotted by a Columbia Pictures executive and signed to a five-year Hollywood contract.

As much as she loved New York, it was not painful for Nancy to leave the live theater. "Everybody thinks, Oh! the glamour of it. Backstage! Ugh. I hate the backstage atmosphere. Why don't they paint the walls or something? I'd love to decorate all the backstages of the world."

In Hollywood, she tried to take her acting seriously, studying technique and speech, reading anything she could find that might help her understand her roles, her art, or her own human nature. But it was a struggle.

When she was cast as Annie Oakley, she researched the character enough to know that Ms. Oakley had been a brunette with a hint of red in her hair. She showed up on the set with an auburn rinse only to hear the director bellow, "You're supposed to be a blonde, dammit."

"No," she insisted, "I looked it up and—"

"When Betty Hutton played Annie Oakley, she was a blonde. If you wanta play Annie Oakley, you've gotta be a blonde, too."

So Nancy became a blonde, and she stayed blond when she played Medea in *Jason and the Argonauts.* Location for the film was southern Italy, far from the luxurious appointments of Roman hotels.

Between shootings, there was nothing to do. No television, no movies, no night life. There were only stacks and stacks of old magazines lying about, due in part to the notable lack of American-style toilet paper in the region. It was in one of these journals that Nancy came upon a lengthy article on Iran and its upward mobility in terms of everything from automobiles to art galleries.

For a reason which at this date is buried in the mire of destiny and her own complex psyche, Nancy Kovack developed a fascination, almost a mania, for Iran and for anything faintly Persian. She read about Persia, dreamed about Persia, wrote letters to Persian dignitaries, all in the hope of somehow, someday, visiting Iran. Had she been convinced that there might be a way to earn a living there, she would have abandoned her career in Hollywood and moved to Iran.

At last, in 1965, there was a call from an Iranian motion picture company. Shooting was scheduled to begin in six weeks on a film called *Almosei Sei o Sei,* or *Diamond 33.* Would Miss Kovack be available for the leading role? They would pay her four thousand dollars for three weeks' shooting in Iran.

"Call my agent," said Nancy, wondering how she would learn to speak

Persian in six weeks. She found a teacher and learned quickly, even though the Iranians would have been quite happy to dub in a Persian voice track over Nancy's English.

The three weeks on *Diamond 33* stretched into more than a year, with the producers begging Nancy to do another film after that. Since she found the reality of Iran no less exciting than the fantasy she had concocted, Nancy agreed to stay. After all, how could she miss the festivities surrounding the Shah's coronation in 1967?

"You're absolutely right," Nancy said, breaking into a conversation across the table, "Teheran *was* a fairyland at the coronation."

Even as she spoke, her mind was marveling at the incongruity of a baritone voice in Los Angeles saying, with no trace of a double entendre, "a fairyland." There was a hint of an accent in the voice, which she placed as Indian. Who from India would be at a Vincente Minnelli party?

"You must be Zubin Mehta."

"That's right," answered the shadowy figure across the table. And Nancy could swear she heard Denise Minnelli snickering four seats away.

Denise knew Nancy had a "thing" about Zubin Mehta, a "thing," in fact, about all the Hollywood glamour-types with their fast cars and their faster talk that was always about themselves. She couldn't forget the *Time* Magazine article she read where Mehta was quoted about children being too much of a distraction for a musician as important as he was. How could a man feel that way about his own children?

For months Denise had been doing her best to pair her off with this sloe-eyed lady-killer, even though Denise knew very well that all Nancy wanted right now was to find the right man and get married. For keeps. None of the Hollywood-to-Reno revolving door business. "Zubi baby" topped her list of men-to-steer-clear-of. She heard him talking about Teheran again, about the lovely Muslim mosques with the ancient Kufic inscriptions that coiled around their domes like patterns impressed by the wind.

"The only trouble," Zubin was saying, "is that today nobody in Teheran can read those inscriptions."

"Sure they can." Nancy into the fray.

"What are you talking about? My people came from Persia two thousand years ago. I ought to know."

"I came from Persia two *months* ago [which wasn't true, but what the heck] so I ought to know better." In Iran, she pointed out, many old copies of the Koran contain the more angular, rigid Kufic letters.

"That's nonsense," Zubin declared, his voice rising in pitch as it does in heated conversation.

"Who the hell cares?" Somebody down the line asked, but Nancy knew she was right.

"Do you speak Persian?" she asked.

"No," answered Zubin. Then he added, rather smugly, Nancy thought, "But I do speak English, Gujerati, Hindi, German, French, Italian, Yiddish, some Hebrew, and a few other languages."

"How interesting," Nancy countered. "I *do* speak Persian. And if I can figure out those Kufic inscriptions, I should think there would be others in Teheran who could do the same."

The pointless argument continued well into the entrée. At last Zubin looked at his watch and cut Nancy off by pushing his chair away from the table.

"Sorry," he said, "but I'm afraid I have to go."

There were loud protestations, including one from Nancy, who wanted her point conceded. But Zubin rose and said, "I have a plane to catch."

"But Zubin," said Vincente Minnelli, "you already told us you have no performance or rehearsal tomorrow."

"Quite so," he answered. "I have the whole day off. So I'm flying to Montreal to be with my two children."

For three weeks Nancy fretted over the incongruities of this man who could be "distracted" by children yet fly four thousand miles just to see them on his day off, who could appear so sensible on one hand and so bullheaded on the other. Late one night she was awakened by a phone call from Europe. It was Zubin, wanting her to be his guest at his concert that Saturday in Los Angeles. Against her better judgment, Nancy accepted.

Her memories of that first "date" begin after the concert ended. "We went to his suite in the Sheraton West so he could change clothes. On the way up he asked a bellboy to bring some drinks, so I said I would have orange juice. The bellboy asked Zubin what he wanted, and he said he would have orange juice, too. I thought, Boy, what a schlump. Can't even think of anything to order on his own."

It was not until some time later that Nancy discovered orange juice was Zubin's favorite drink—he'd become addicted to it in California just as he developed an addiction to chocolate in Vienna. He never touched alcohol. Coincidentally, neither did Nancy, who has never had a drink in her life; orange juice just happened to be her favorite beverage, too.

Perhaps it was inevitable that two people who so loved orange juice should fall in love. Neither Zubin nor Nancy can offer any sounder explanation. Their "courtship" consisted mostly of long-distance telephone conversations, with Zubin conducting in Berlin and Vienna and Israel and Nancy filming television shows in Los Angeles or on location.

"I remember one time I was in Hawaii and he would call me regularly around three-thirty in the morning. I don't think it ever sank in that, even though it was afternoon in Europe, I only had two hours before I had to get up and start work. He would talk on and on.

"Later on he showed me tremendous telephone bills: five thousand or seven thousand dollars for one month. That would make me very upset, because in those days I didn't see that kind of money. His mother agreed with me, but she said, 'Nancy, let him talk. He might as well spend his money talking to you as to somebody else.' I figured she was right about that."

So the telephone calls continued. Usually their dates were built around Zubin's concerts in Los Angeles, putting in occasional appearances at cocktail parties, receptions, or dinners given by board members or friends of the Philharmonic. As for taking Nancy out to a restaurant or for a "night on the town," that was something outside the range of Zubin's social experience, ever since his student days in Vienna when meals were eaten in a crowd and always Dutch treat.

"That first date we had," Nancy recollects, "I was the one who suggested we get something to eat. It was never in his mind, because he never took girls to dinner. I bet there are a lot of girls who would document that.

"There was only one other time he took me to dinner, and that was to a little fast-food place, like a diner, called Tiny Naylor's on Wilshire Boulevard. He said he wanted to go there because they had terrific chocolate pudding. And Zubin's crazy about chocolate pudding."

Nearly ten years later, Zubin also recalls that unique dinner date. "But that's not why I took her there," he says with a wink. "If you must know, I think Tiny Naylor's has awful chocolate pudding. She was hungry and that was just the closest place I could think of to my hotel room!"

Zubin did ask Nancy on dates out of the country, but she refused, setting her sights on marriage or nothing. He'd been planning a trip to India for some time, to go on his second safari, and wanted to take Nancy along. Though she wanted desperately to see that part of the world, Nancy turned him down. She booked herself on a cruise to Antarctica instead.

"I knew he wanted to bag a tiger, but I have this protective attitude toward animals. I did my mental work to know that that animal could be protected, was in his right place, and could reflect the intelligence to sense Zubin's motives. I guess it worked, because the mighty hunter came back without his tiger skin."

Even today, Nancy carries her "protective attitude" to extremes, warning visitors to her home not to swat gnats because "they really aren't hurting anybody." Meanwhile, up in his study, Zubin swats away, waging a private war against the "damn bugs."

The winter of 1968–69, the period of Zubin and Nancy's intercontinental courtship, was a difficult time for Tehmina and Mehli Mehta.

Nearing the age at which most men retire, Mehli felt he was just hitting his stride as a musician. His reputation had grown enormously throughout southern California in five years, and he was respected as the area's chief educator of orchestral musicians. Frustrated for so much of his life at trying to make music and thereby bring pleasure to others, the energetic man was making up for lost time. Besides his growing number of violin students, Mehli now had no fewer than five orchestras under his command. These were the U.C.L.A. Orchestra, the U.C.L.A. Chamber Orchestra, the much-traveled American Youth Symphony, the Doctors' Symphony of Los Angeles, and the Whittier Symphony Orchestra. Five days a week he performed his duties on the Sunset Boulevard campus of U.C.L.A.; on Saturdays and Sundays he rehearsed his youth orchestra and the doctors; every night of the week was given over to rehearsals, performances, or teaching. Tehmina was proud of her husband, but also very worried. Her worst fears were realized when Mehli suffered two coronary attacks in quick succession.

"I am not proud of that," says Mehli. "In fact today I am ashamed of it. But you must understand that I was so ambitious, not to make money but to make *music*. I suppose you can say I was a little bit insane."

Laid up in the hospital for seven months, Mehli decided to give up all his duties except those with the U.C.L.A. Orchestra and the American Youth Symphony. It was a difficult decision, but one he has never regretted.

Zubin, of course, continued calling the hospital room at frequent intervals from various parts of the world, considerably increasing his monthly contribution to the telephone systems of the world. The phone call Mehli remembers best came in early April, just before his scheduled release from Mt. Sinai Hospital.

"My wife was with me in the room when the phone rang, and she answered. She said it was Zubin, calling from Florence, and he wanted to speak with me. Zubin said, 'Daddy, I want to tell you something very important.' I thought it was going to be something about his music, some performance he'd given or a new work he'd discovered, but he said, 'I would like to marry Nancy Kovack. Would you give me your permission?'"

Zubin was thirty-three years old and had no need of Mehli's permission to get married, but the closeness of the Mehta family and the strong bond that had always existed between father and son were not likely to be affected by Zubin's growing older. Mehli gave his permission and the wedding date was set for July 19, 1969, the next open weekend on Zubin's schedule. The wedding to Nancy turned out to be, if anything, even more complicated than the one to Carmen in 1958.

First, there was the matter of introducing Nancy to her new stepchildren. Zubin was tied up in Florence, directing the spring festival there, so it was decided that Merwan and Zarina would fly there, as soon as their current school term was finished, and Nancy would meet them in Italy.

At about the same time, Nancy remembered she had been nominated for an Emmy award as a result of a supporting dramatic role she had played in the *Mannix* television series. The awards were to be given out in Los Angeles on the night she was scheduled to leave for Italy.

Not really believing she could win, Nancy nevertheless put in an appearance at the awards ceremony, knowing she would have a difficult time making her flight. The evening dragged on, with its technical awards and music awards and writing awards and production awards, until at last they came to the category of Best Supporting Actress in a Regular Dramatic Series.

"I was on the edge of my seat waiting for them to announce the winner. When they opened the envelope and read the name, it wasn't mine, so I dashed out the door, picked up my bags, and made it to the airport just in time. I'll never forget changing from my gown to a pants suit in one of those tiny lavatories aboard the plane.

"The first thing Zubin asked when he met me at the airport in Rome was 'Did you win?' And I said, 'No.' He said, 'Well, who did win?' I hadn't the slightest idea. I just knew the name they read wasn't Nancy Kovack, so I got out of there as fast as I could. To this day I still don't know who won that Emmy."

In Rome, Nancy and the children took to each other from the start, and were close friends by the time they left together for Israel. For Nancy, it was a foretaste of what life as the wife of a famous conductor would be like. Wondering if perhaps she hadn't gotten in over her head, she struggled to keep a grip on the wedding plans as Zubin busied himself with the Israel Philharmonic. By telephone, Nancy worked out some of the details with a friend in Los Angeles, but she arrived home in late June to find that many of the critical details remained to be settled.

She wanted nothing so prosaic and unmemorable as a civil ceremony. It had to be a church wedding, with all the trimmings. After all, she intended it to be her *only* wedding. Unfortunately her church, the Church of Christ, Scientist, had no such thing as a wedding service. Suddenly it came to her attention that the Parsee priest who had married Tehmina and Mehli thirty-four years before happened to be on the faculty of U.C.L.A., teaching Eastern religions. However, the priest, Dr. Framroze Ardeshi Bode, had no legal right to perform weddings in the United States. If they wanted a Parsee wedding, it would have to be part of the "trimmings." At last Nancy found a Methodist minister, Dr. F.

Harold Essert, who agreed to marry them at his Westwood Community Church before the Zoroastrian ceremony. The Parsee wedding would be performed at the Bel Air Hotel, after which there would be a reception for about four hundred guests.

Two weeks before the wedding, Nancy had to change her plans when she was informed that according to the Parsee rites, the second ceremony would have to be performed in the afternoon, when the sun was at a certain position.

Carefully timing the required change of clothes and the drive from the church to the hotel, Nancy realized the church ceremony would have to be moved up two hours. When she found out there was another wedding scheduled at that time, she frantically got in touch with the other bride, hoping to strike a bargain. If the girl would switch wedding times, Nancy would have new wedding invitations printed up for her and sent out special delivery and would also leave all her expensive flowers, carpets, and candles at the church. It took every bit of her persuasive powers to talk the other bride into going along, but at last the bargain was sealed.

On July 19, 1969, as the world watched Neil Armstrong, Edwin Aldrin, and Michael Collins maneuver their Apollo XI spaceship into place for the next day's landing on the moon, Nancy Kovack held her father's arm and walked down the aisle of the Westwood Community Methodist Church toward the man with whom she intended to spend the rest of her life, Zubin Mehta. Daniel Barenboim had flown in to be best man.

"One thing about my wedding I will never forget," says Nancy, her malleable voice taking on a dark color. "When I walked down the aisle, all the faces turned toward me, all those faces of people Zubin had known and worked with for all those years. And they were not happy faces. Nobody smiled at me. I realized that, to them, Zubin was going away, that I was taking him away from them. For some of them, of course, that was true. But I kept on smiling. Nothing was going to spoil this day for me."

From the church the wedding party raced down Sunset Boulevard to the magnificent Bel Air Hotel, where the couple changed into traditional Indian wedding garb. Zubin wore a traditional Parsee turban, a long jacket of white muslin, and white trousers; Nancy donned a sari that had been specially made for her in Bombay, of white satin with sequins and stitching of real silver, presented to her by her new in-laws. Two days before the wedding she had discovered that part of the ceremony included a matched pair of chairs in which the bride and groom were to sit and which they would keep as symbols of their inseparability for life. She came up with two French provincial armchairs upholstered in bright yellow.

Tehmina had prepared the ritual coconut drink and symbolic condiments, which the couple ate as the priest chanted over them in the Avestan singsong, stopping every now and then to explain the ceremonies in English to the wedding guests.

Zubin cut off Dr. Bode's explanation. "Look here," he growled, "this is supposed to be a wedding, not one of your lectures. Get on with it." So the ceremony continued, Zubin and Nancy sprinkling incense over a sandalwood fire and having their hands bound together over the flame.

After what seemed like an interminable reception, they drove to Los Angeles International Airport. Originally they had planned a romantic, if brief, honeymoon in Tahiti, but, typically, Zubin had neglected to get a proper visa for Tahiti, so they wound up on a plane heading for Hawaii.

On July 20, 1969, as Neil Armstrong was taking his "giant step for mankind," Nancy and Zubin Mehta stepped off the airplane in Hawaii, receiving the traditional leis as greeting. Though it was not quite the honeymoon they'd intended, Nancy remembers the two days as being "*very* nice. Of course, Zubin brought his scores along to study."

12

⤜⤛⤜⤛

A Long Period of Mercury

The subscription audience in the Dorothy Chandler Pavilion sits in quiet amusement as members of their orchestra file on stage, each picking up a sheaf of music from a stool near the podium, then taking a seat, seemingly at random. The seating arrangement has percussionists, strings, woodwinds, and brasses jumbled together in groups of four. In fact, the ushers in their red silk *sherwanis* observe that the seating arrangement is quite different from what it was for the previous night's concert.

There is a certain amount of whispering as the piece begins, full of clatter and inconsequence, like the sounds of families fussing all at once in their separate apartments in a single building. The composer (who else but John Cage?) thinks that this is just what it *should* sound like. He has certainly heard worse interpretations of his difficult work, and worse receptions from an audience.

The Los Angeles audience, after fifteen years, has grown accustomed to Zubin Mehta's insistence on programming contemporary music. Some of them like it, most only humor him, listening to Searle and Subotnick for the sake of Beethoven and Brahms, much as children put up with spinach and string beans for the sake of hamburgers and ice cream.

181

He had told them of his intention from the start: "It is our duty to perform the works of contemporary composers. It is especially my duty as a young conductor. We cannot always know what will have lasting value, and, although some of the music may be hard to assimilate, we nevertheless should listen."

Zubin's attachment to contemporary music is a result of his early attachment to Hans Swarowsky, an intimate of Berg, Schönberg, and Webern. His interest in the second Vienna school has increased over the years and has helped establish him as a "modernist" in the minds of many Americans who are uncomfortable with anything, no matter how hoary, that smacks of atonality.

Even in supposedly sophisticated New York, when Zubin conducted the Schönberg Five Pieces with the Philadelphia Orchestra, there was a certain amount of disapproval. Despite what critic Alan Rich called a "splendid reading," the musicians were playing against a background of "coughing and rustling in the audience, over a piece that is now sixty-five years old."

Zubin has always faced a certain amount of resistance to twentieth-century music; he blames it not so much on the audiences as on the previous generation of conductors. In 1965 he told a symphony preview audience at the Music Center:

"If Toscanini and Bruno Walter, who were the greatest musicians at the turn of the century, had played enough of the music of their day we could have a better tradition today and a more progressive atmosphere. There were exceptions, of course. Both Otto Klemperer and Wilhelm Furtwängler did everything possible to play an enormous amount of modern music. But this was not done in America. And that is why today we are still struggling a bit with the appreciation of contemporary music."

There are critics, however, who maintain that "struggling" with contemporary music is a fault in a conductor. They accuse Zubin of putting up a show of modernity for the sake of appearances, of programming only those composers who are chic or trendy, of (to quote the Los Angeles *Times*'s Martin Bernheimer) playing "avant-garde music for people who don't like avant-garde music."

Bernheimer has been Zubin's loudest complainer on this point, as on others. During the 1975–76 season in Los Angeles, extensive and independent interviews with both conductor and critic produced what can be arranged into a dialogue on the subject of contemporary music.

> *Mehta:* I'm an advocate of the twentieth-century. In my first speech as music director I said I would introduce as much modern music as possible, even if we don't understand all of it. If, in twenty five years, we have discovered five new masterpieces, we will have succeeded.

Bernheimer: He says he has a definite moral feeling that one should play and hear the orchestra music of our time, but that doesn't mean he conducts it with a great understanding and sympathy. One applauds the initiative, but one isn't too happy about the sound.

Mehta: I have my likes and my dislikes. Luigi Nono and I don't get along politically, but he makes music and I admire him very much. I like Henze, George Crumb; I admire Elliott Carter, Bill Kraft, Morton Subotnick... I don't have to agree with everything they do. I love some of Lukas Foss, particularly *Time Cycle.* Lukas is sincere. I like Berio, a few of his things very much. And of course there are others. I wish I could find for myself the sort of relationship some conductors have had with composers. I could have that perhaps with Penderecki, but frankly I'm not pursuing it. I get tired, you know. In the Modigliani sense, it's the same thing all the time.

Bernheimer: Occasionally, very embarrassing things happen. This year we had the American premiere of the Penderecki First Symphony. The performance was originally scheduled to come after intermission and they had it printed that way in the program. That night, though, they did some diddly overture as an opener. Then Mehta came out and said, literally, "Ladies and gentlemen, we've given this some thought and decided that, if we did the Penderecki symphony after intermission as announced, none of you would be here"—ha, ha, ha, ha, ha, ha, ha—"so we're gonna play it instead right now." He didn't say, "We tricked you and now you're going to have to hear it," but that was the implication. And the audience tittered and giggled and thought it was all very funny.

Mehta: When we premiered Penderecki's First Symphony, I discussed with the composer beforehand what I thought the public's attitude would be. Every contemporary composer is used to the boos and catcalls of a certain segment of the audience, and he agreed with me when I suggested playing the symphony in the first half rather than in the second.

Bernheimer: Penderecki, who was sitting in the third row, well, he didn't have any reason to think this was so funny. Then he didn't like the way the orchestra played his symphony.

Mehta: Not only did Penderecki like this performance, he later dedicated one of his compositions to me. He says he wants me to do all his premieres.

Bernheimer: The orchestra is hostile, doesn't like to play the modern stuff. The tendency is to giggle at it, and I'm not sure that Mehta is the one to prevent that. He's no Boulez.

Mehta: In many modern works of music it is true that the orchestra and conductor do not immediately grasp the full meaning of the compositions.... When it's a new work I have to play, possibly because I commissioned it, I do my duty. I put my personal tastes aside and never let the composer feel I am against him.

Bernheimer: If it's a gutty piece, if it's a *Carmina Burana* sort of thing, watch out! But if it's a hard, thorny modern piece, if it's Elliott Carter, if it's Stockhausen [neither of whom, by the way, has Zubin ever performed in Los Angeles], if it's Penderecki, the implication is that this is bitter medicine, folks, but it's good for you, so listen.

Mehta: I only wonder, when we do these things, why don't some of them get into the general repertoire? I just wish conductors would stop being so vain. After the fashionable premiere of a work, nobody plays it again. And so much is written!

Bernheimer: But here in Los Angeles they do it, which is more than you can say for a lot of other major orchestras. They do it.

In recognition of which, the American Society of Composers, Authors and Publishers presented Zubin and the Los Angeles Philharmonic with one of its annual awards for "adventuresome programming of contemporary music, in 1975 and again in 1976.

A more consistent criticism of Zubin has been his limited repertoire. One finds frequent remarks in the press and in private conversations to the effect that he is an uneven interpreter of Bach, Haydn, and Mozart, generally of any music composed before the nineteenth century.

There is, to be sure, a reason for this criticism. Even one of his closest friends remarks that "Zubin has problems with the classical literature; it's not his métier, not one of the areas he feels most comfortable in. Still," adds the world-famous musician, "I'd rather hear him do it than a lot of other conductors. He makes things happen, he makes theater out of the music."

Checking a recent subscription season in Los Angeles, one finds that out of approximately sixty programmed works, eight fall into the pre-nineteenth-century category. Among these are such major works as Mozart's Symphonies no. 38 and 41 and Haydn's *Mass in Time of War,* all conducted by Zubin Mehta. Guest conductors also brought several classical works to the Los Angeles audience. There are no baroque works listed, yet a dearth of baroque music is hardly uncommon in any American symphony season.

Occasionally the criticism has been worded to suggest that what Zubin actually eschews is the small-orchestra sound of most Bach-through-Mozart composers. This is truest of his appearances on tour with the Los Angeles Philharmonic, the Israel Philharmonic, and, earlier, the Montreal Symphony. The explanation for this phenomenon is both simple and twofold. First, the out-of-town audiences expect the "big sound" from a Mehta orchestra, and a great deal of money and planning has gone into bringing that to them. Second, the expense of traveling with one hundred-plus musicians can hardly be justified unless most of them are kept busy.

Conducting his own orchestra at home, however, Zubin does not hesitate to decimate it for the sake of playing smaller-ensemble music, whether baroque or contemporary. A recent audience at the Music Center Pavilion was surprised and delighted by the Los Angeles Philharmonic—cut down to almost chamber orchestra proportions—

giving a spirited and thoroughly natural performance of six rarely heard German Dances, written by Mozart in 1791. At the conclusion of the final dance, "The Sleigh Ride" (or, as it is more mellifluously named in German, *Die Schlittenfahrt*) the audience applauded warmly, the smiles on their faces matching those of the orchestra.

If some of Zubin's latter-day critics would consult the files of the Los Angeles Philharmonic in pre-Mehta years, they would discover that both the orchestra and the audience were poorly disposed toward this sort of music. Season subscribers wanted Beethoven, Schubert, Mendelssohn, and Brahms, and that was what they got, almost exclusively. It was not until the 1963–64 season that Zubin slipped Bach, Handel, Mozart, and Weber into the programs, hoping his subscribers would be sufficiently dazzled by the opening of their new Music Center not to notice.

Albert Goldberg, then the Los Angeles *Times*'s chief critic, spotted the move and praised Zubin highly for "breaking down the resistance of the audience" to the less bombastic literature. Goldberg pointed out that even the Bach Brandenburg Concerto no. 4, while a familiar commodity to audiences in most cities, was almost a stranger to Los Angeles. The Philharmonic had played the Fourth Brandenburg only twice prior to its performance in April 1964, the last occasion having been in 1947.

Nevertheless, that unquenchable Mehta critic, Martin Bernheimer, finds Zubin's conducting of Haydn, Weber, Mozart, even Beethoven, "muscular and heavy and often brutal. We won't talk about the baroque!" Yet even Bernheimer is forced to observe, with a trace of bewilderment in his voice, that "they love him in Salzburg," which is, of course, the Mozart capital of the world.

Zubin's repertoire does in fact extend from almost the earliest orchestral music to the very latest, with the works he loves best, and perhaps conducts best, lying in the great ocean of music that separates those not really dissimilar extremes. Within that sea of expansive, expressive, and impressive music, it is generally agreed that Zubin is tremendously impressive. His orchestras are together, their sound is one of lush beauty; his interpretations are suited to the composer's intent.

What else have critics to talk about in their assessments of a conductor's work? Perhaps the one element that remains is that which most immediately impresses an audience in watching a man or woman on the podium, the element of style.

Describing in words the movements of a conductor is an unrewarding task, not unlike trying to make a still photograph of a ballet dancer that will say something meaningful about the experience of being there. Conducting, like the dance, is a thing of flux. Any effort to dissect it tends to be destructive. To analyze any part in isolation is, in some degree, to deny the relation of that part to the whole.

Yet, over the years in the life of a conductor, there are inevitable attempts at that sort of analysis. The remarkable thing about such descriptions in Zubin's case is that nearly all of them are complimentary. A lengthy rummaging through the Mehta clipping file in the Lincoln Center Library of the Performing Arts turns up only one truly disparaging remark, and that from unnamed "European critics." From other critics and from distinguished musicians who have played under him for years, the observations on his conducting style are uniformly ecstatic.

To violinist Itzhak Perlman, the first impression of Zubin was one of astonishment. "It was just unbelievable. He was like a dynamo. I had never played Tchaikovsky like that before. It was my first experience with someone inspiring me as a conductor. I came off the stage and said, 'Listen, I just did something unbelievable!'"

"It's simply a natural ability," echoes another violinist, Pinchas Zukerman. "I have not seen anyone in my career with such unique body English and phenomenal hands, so expressive that they always do the right thing at the right time."

When he recently recorded the Bartók Second Violin Concerto with Mehta and the Los Angeles Philharmonic, Zukerman asked the concertmaster to play the solo part in rehearsals so that he could sit in the back of the violin section and play in the orchestra, just to get a better feel for Zubin's conducting.

"It was very interesting," he says, "to be watching very carefully from all the way in the back. What he did was so convincing and so right. You look up and you know exactly where you are. You may disagree with it, but at that moment there is no question what kind of sound you have to make and where and how it should be done."

Zukerman observed what others have observed from both sides of the podium, that Zubin conducts not with a baton, nor with his hands, but with every part of his body.

"Some conductors do it just with the hands, others just with the face, others only with the body, but Zubin can do all of it. You can tell from the moment he lifts his arms to begin; his back muscles and his arms are so tense that if I tried to move him with all my force I couldn't do it."

From the audience, however, one often becomes entranced by the arms alone, by the numberless variety of their motions and positions. A *Time* Magazine observer in 1964 found himself comparing the podium to a pitcher's mound as he watched Zubin "winding his arm behind his head for broad, sweeping gestures, like a pitcher unfurling a fastball, while his spidery left hand deftly drew out the secondary voices."

One of the most detailed descriptions came from the typewriter of the New York *Herald Tribune*'s Alan Rich in 1965 after he returned to his desk from Zubin's first appearance in Philharmonic Hall with the Philadelphia Orchestra:

Mr. Mehta's beat is one of his interesting aspects. It consists of a lot of armwork along with what appears to be a totally independent repertory of wrist motions. Thus, there are strange moments when he brings his arms down hard and nothing happens. That's because you have to wait for the wrist, which is not so easy to see. A little disconcerting for the audience, perhaps, but the orchestra had no trouble at all.

Yet for all the easily observed, often poetically described armwork, there are those who say the most important parts of Zubin's body are his eyes. This became extraordinarily apparent to those who watched the telecast of *Die Fledermaus* from Covent Garden on New Year's Eve of 1978 and saw Isaac Stern's eyes glued to those of the conductor as they blended flawlessly in the unrehearsed last movement of the Mendelssohn E-minor Violin Concerto. For Stern, the experience was unique—being in position, albeit forty feet away, to look into a conductor's eyes rather than standing next to the podium, stealing over-the-shoulder glances. But to Zubin, bridging the distance with his eyes is nothing new.

"Half our trade is in the eyes," he told an interviewer in 1970. "There is a certain split second when the conductor gives with his eyes the indication of what and how the orchestra should play. It is a highly personal relationship. There is an implicit trust and understanding between conductor and musician that cannot be imparted with the hands alone. And you cannot have a conversation on stage."

If there has been any disagreement over the Mehta conducting style, it has had to do with the matter of showmanship. Sometimes called theatricality, sometimes flamboyance, Zubin's tendency toward the dramatic in his personal life and musical taste has carried over to his podium style. It was on this issue that the one maligning description focused.

Time, in its 1964 article "The Next Toscanini?" cited unspecified "European critics [who] carped that 'his visually arresting style is designed to conduct the audience.'"

Many who have sat through boring concerts, uninvolved with the music, might wonder whether this is actually a slur. Zubin's audiences in Los Angeles have delighted in being so conducted. Trying to describe his style in 1970, one concertgoer, in a marvelous confusion of metaphors, said, "He always reminds me of Mussolini. That chin stuck out, that hypnotic glare in his eyes, that strut. One feels he's going to turn his hand into a claw and rip up the furniture, to show how powerful he is, and shout, '*Ecco il leone!*' But he never does. He's just a lamb in a lion's skin."

Zubin himself has admitted to "conducting the audience" on occasion. "It all depends on what you are playing, who is playing it, and to whom you are playing. I know, for instance, how to direct the attention of the public to the soloist. Or I can appear heroic myself, with *Ein Heldenleben*."

To the Los Angeles *Times* in 1961, Zubin's conducting style was "seldom flamboyant; normally it is graceful and coaxing rather than agitated and histrionic." To *Musical America* three years later he was "not a 'showy' conductor, but a supremely theatrical one, in the best sense. Every movement has to do with the score." Still, on the matter of theatricality Zubin has grown somewhat defensive.

"Sometimes I exaggerate to draw out the players, but showmanship has to be natural. I don't think theatricality can be calculated and still be effective. If you're going to be sincere and logical you have to have the capacity to let yourself go either way, that is, the power to be controlled and introverted *or* to be controlled and exuberant."

His point is that any dramatics must flow naturally from the music and from oneself as well. Eugene Husaruk, who watched Zubin in Vienna and played under him in Montreal, feels that this is essential to an understanding of the man and of his work.

"With him, it was always what the orchestra needed. At first, perhaps he tried to baby-feed the orchestra with too many gestures, but after a while he was self-analytical enough to learn that certain movements were not necessary, so he became a bit more restricted. Then, when he needed some climax, the gestures were enormous and had a fantastic effect. But always he had to make movements that corresponded to his personality. It was an extrovert personality, so obviously his movements were extrovert."

And, to give Zubin the final word on the matter, "Intellectual snobs forget that showmanship is a great asset to the profession. We have to bring certain things over to the public magnetically, and that requires acting."

Those who have observed Zubin conducting solo performers, whether in concert or opera, have remarked on the rare electricity that seems to flow between him and instrumental soloist or singer. Ebb and flow of emotion, give and take within a tempo marking, fluctuations in solo-ensemble balance—these are things that are discussed in rehearsal, yet performed with enormous spontaneity.

As Itzhak Perlman puts it, "Zubin never disagrees with the soloist's conception, as long as it's reasonable. You know, if you want to take a rubato here or an accelerando there, that you are not bound by the limitations of the conductor. Zubin will always be with you. Always, we are creating something at the moment."

Baritone Sherrill Milnes observes that, even though the Mehta execution may be quite physical, the approach to music is metaphysical. "It's not just that Zubin understands what makes musicians tick. He knows what makes human beings tick."

Spontaneity often plays an important role in a Mehta program, be it symphony, concerto, or opera. Sometimes even the orchestra is surprised.

At his opening concert as music director he took the Los Angeles Philharmonic completely unaware with his interpretation of the Dvorak D-minor Symphony. The performance was radically different from its preparation. Zubin had found both himself and the orchestra taking the music a bit for granted, and he wanted to give them all something to think about. The notes, the tempo markings, the dynamics were all the same ones they had played in rehearsal, the same ones Dvorak had written down, yet the music came out sounding *different*. And therein lies the secret of the conductor's art, simple, yet—to many—unfathomable.

Zubin smiles. "Music, you see, is more than black notes on a white page. The important thing is what lies between the notes."

There is one thing no one has been able to teach Zubin about conducting—the proper way to stand. Hans Swarowsky told him in 1955: "*Mehta, die Füssen!*" Charles Munch yelled at him in 1958: "Put your feet together!" Twenty years later he still stands with his feet spread apart, but nobody argues about it any more.

Over the years, both critics and fellow musicians have commented on Zubin's close relationships with his orchestras. As Isaac Stern puts it, "His knowledge of all the instruments, of their every facet, makes him aware of every potential problem in a piece of music before it happens. The musicians know that, they know he's not just up there waving a stick at them. I think that's one of the big reasons he gains the respect, in some cases the adulation, of the orchestra men and women around him."

With two notable exceptions—the Royal Liverpool Philharmonic in 1958 and the New York Philharmonic in 1967—Zubin has had nothing but good relations with the orchestras of the world. One reason he is respected by his players is that he respects them. Where once he had a reputation for getting irritated when musicians failed to live up to his expectations in performance, he has learned that a momentary show of displeasure can be a destructive force to the music.

"It's the little things that bother me. For instance, I might tell the orchestra at rehearsal that I want a slight *Luftpause* [a barely perceptible break] between a certain two chords. And I will rehearse it that way and I think everybody's got it. The next evening we play it in performance and one of the violinists forgets and comes in just a fraction too soon. I know that he didn't write it down and this makes me furious. For a moment I'll lose my concentration and think the performance is falling apart; fortunately that doesn't happen, and we go on.

"That kind of mistake bothers me much more than something like a horn player cracking a note; the poor fellow can't help that, it's just a human error. But the lack of attention in a man's playing, the lack of involvement, the just plain boredom: that is what so aggravates me.

"Nothing is sadder to me than an *uninvolved* musician. There is no orchestra completely without them, the type who does just as much work, but somehow fails to fulfill that original promise or commitment that every musician makes to himself at the outset of his life, that commitment which makes the artist so special in this basically materialistic world. Uninvolved musicians might just as well spend their lives at a sewing machine, stitching on buttons."

Thus a Mehta performance can seldom justly be criticized as perfunctory. If he is conducting a piece he loves, the love always shines through; if the piece is not quite top drawer, Zubin generally finds some way to present it to his audience in the best possible light. An illustration of the latter instance occurred when he decided to program a work that is virtually unknown in America and only rarely heard in its native England, Elgar's *In the South.*

Exposed to the tone-poemlike overture through a recent recording by his friend Daniel Barenboim, Zubin's first examination of the score took place during the first week of January 1978. On February 2, he walked onto the stage of the Dorothy Chandler Pavilion in Los Angeles to conduct it from memory! In the wrong hands, *In the South* can and does come across like a feeble schmaltzy piece of post-romantic eclecticism. Under Zubin's direction it sounded powerful, noble, and sincere in its purpose. The Los Angeles audience—99.9 percent of whom had never heard it before—applauded it as though it had been Beethoven's Ninth Symphony.

How does Zubin account for this?

"Well, with pieces like this Elgar, sometimes a conductor must give it a little extra effort to find its best points and hold those up to the light for the audience. Another work, such as the Brahms *Tragic Overture* or the *Leonore* Overture no. 3, you don't have to help so much. A weak performance of the *Leonore* no. 3 still can show you some of the piece's merits and the audience will applaud. A weak performance of *In the South,* I think, would be murder."

Another example of Zubin's ability to give meaning and import to what some would call "weak" music is a concert that made headlines around the world, the "Music from Outer Space" concert of November 22, 1977.

Leading the Los Angeles Philharmonic in music from the films *Star Wars* and *Close Encounters of the Third Kind,* Zubin produced sonic pyrotechnics to equal a dazzling display of laser lights and fireworks that lit up the night sky in the Hollywood Bowl. At the conclusion of the concert, the sellout audience of nearly eighteen thousand erupted in uncontrolled, screaming frenzy. As the orchestra's executive director, Ernest Fleischmann, reports, "I didn't think they were going to let Zubin off the stage. They went wild, absolutely wild. The audience went out of their minds!"

Doubtless some will lay this to the effect of laser lights and gimmickry. However, it must be noted that the same thing was tried in New York, with a different orchestra under a different conductor, laser show and all, and it was a dismal flop. When Decca/London saw the popularity of outer space films as an opportunity to pull the company out of a sales slump, Zubin Mehta and the Los Angeles Philharmonic were called on to make a crash recording of the *Star Wars* and *Close Encounters* suites that quickly climbed to the top of the charts.

The recording industry, the public, even most of the world's music critics have come to expect above-average performances by Mehta-led orchestras. They know that, except in very rare instances, what he demands of an orchestra in rehearsal will be produced in performance, that his analysis and his balancing, the ensemble togetherness and intonation of the instruments, will not fail to do justice to a composer's intent. And on rare occasions, without warning, a performance will go beyond the limits of the good and the exact, transporting musicians and audience alike to another plane of awareness. This happened in early 1978 during a performance of Mahler's Third Symphony by the Los Angeles Philharmonic.

It was not a new work for the orchestra nor for Zubin. They had taken it on tour the year before and were scheduled to record it for Decca/London a few weeks later. The performance had been programmed as a "refresher" before the recording sessions, but the concert turned into something much more than a play-through.

"Often you feel a performance is good," Zubin says, "but there are different levels of good, and at the top is the level at which you feel that you are no longer on a podium but standing on air, the sort of thing that people who take drugs talk about. But you don't need drugs, only the music. You don't work at it. All of a sudden it's there.

"It started in the first movement. I could see Pan dancing before me, and, in the background, the dark mountain landscape outside Salzburg becoming an incredible *cosmic* landscape."

Out in the audience, Mehli and Tehmina felt it, too.

"It was as though lightning had struck him and the orchestra," says Mehli, his voice a tremulous whisper. "It was magic."

When the symphony was over, Zubin dropped his head like a medium breaking a trance. The musicians breathed with him as though they had scarcely drawn breath for the length of the symphony. His face was dripping and his jacket soaked with perspiration as he at last turned to face the cheering audience. One expected to see his knees buckle as he stepped down from the podium, shook hands with concertmaster Sidney Harth and somehow made his way to the wings.

Tehmina had not seen such a dazed, frightened look on her son's face since the time he lay in the grip of meningitis. To her it was the face of a man in contact with infinity. She leaned over to Mehli and whispered, "Look at him. He's still talking to Mahler!"

Weeks later, there was still a trace of that mystical expression on Zubin's face as he talked of the experience.

"It was not something I was responsible for. That night I was in extreme danger of losing control. But every single member of the orchestra was so tuned in that somehow it never fell apart. Those moments are very rare; they can't be rehearsed. And even as it is happening you can never afford to forget that, yes, it is a cosmic language—but it is also a trombone solo."

13

‿◦‿◦‿

His Own World of Art

"Playing a concert with Zubin is . . ." Jacqueline du Pré pauses, searching for just the right words, "is like riding on a magic carpet."

It seems to be that way for every soloist, renowned or not, who performs under the Mehta baton. No less an experienced musician than Artur Rubinstein, who has worked with the greatest conductors of the century, confides that "some of my most joyous and inspired performances have been in collaboration with Zubin Mehta."

In the twenty-plus years since his student days in Vienna, Zubin has won a cheering section of some of the most familiar names in the music world: Vladimir Ashkenazy, Alfred Brendel, Jacqueline du Pré, Placido Domingo, Shirley Verrett, Beverly Sills, Isaac Stern, Itzhak Perlman, Pinchas Zukerman, and of course Daniel Barenboim. Those are a few who have worked with him often. Many of them are also his closest friends, and that can make for rare moments in music.

When Birgit Nilsson canceled a scheduled "guest" appearance in Zubin's London *Die Fledermaus* on New Year's Eve, 1978, he had but to call around to see which of his friends was free; Barenboim and Stern dropped everything to be there. In 1969, again in London, someone suggested making a film of Schubert's *Trout* Quintet. The producers ended up with a virtuoso assemblage of Barenboim playing piano; Perlman, violin; Zukerman, viola; du Pré, cello—and Zubin Mehta playing a borrowed bass.

Another of those rare moments, also preserved on film, came after a rehearsal in Israel. Artur Rubinstein was there to play a Brahms concerto with the Israel Philharmonic. At the end of the scheduled rehearsal time, Zubin asked the pianist if there was anything more he'd like to work on before the orchestra was dismissed. Giving the matter only a moment's thought, the white-haired Rubinstein looked up from the piano and said, "You know, all my life I have wanted to conduct a Brahms symphony."

Taking the hint, Zubin asked the musicians if they would mind staying a few minutes late to grant Rubinstein's wish. Not one of the players made a move to rise. Handing the old man his baton, Zubin stepped back and took the role of interested observer. He was amused to see Rubinstein start the Brahms Third Symphony at an even slower tempo than the one he had used for the Schubert Fifth in the Liverpool competition. Apparently unaware that it was his own ponderous beat the musicians were following, Rubinstein urged them on. "Gentlemen, gentlemen, can't you play a little faster?" The "few minutes" turned into two hours as the Israeli musicians willingly plodded through the entire symphony.

"As far as I know," recalls Zubin, laughing, "it was the first and last time Mr. Rubinstein ever conducted. But I tell you, it was a treasured experience for all of us who were there."

Zubin's musical friends have become integral elements of his life, what his daughter Zarina refers to as "our second family." It must be noted, however, that not everyone involved feels quite that way.

Nancy Mehta sighs when she hears the question, "How do you feel about your husband's circle of friends?" Perhaps because that circle was already largely established—though certainly not closed—when Nancy stepped into it, neither she nor they seem to feel quite comfortable with the situation.

"I love Zubin's friends," says Nancy. "I really love them. I just wish they would love other things as much as their music. It's all they ever talk about, even though when I'm around I try to steer the conversation into other areas. I can't help thinking that a group of bricklayers or orthodontists or football players would have something else in common that they could talk about besides their work."

Many of those friends profess that, even though they have spent a fair amount of time in her presence since the marriage, they really don't know Nancy. As Pinchas Zukerman puts it, "She came into the picture with all of us being so friendly and it must be very difficult for her." Yet Zukerman, like nearly every one of Zubin's friends, credits Nancy with "changing Zubin's life." In Itzhak Perlman's words, "Nancy has brought out wonderful things in him."

The only one willing to identify those mysterious "changes" that Zubin has undergone is Nancy herself, though she is quick not to take credit for them. Rather, she feels somewhat grateful that Zubin has chosen to reflect some of the qualities that she considers positive aspects of her own personality.

"When we first got married, he would ask me, 'Why do you go around smiling all the time? Does everybody from Flint, Michigan, have to smile twenty-four hours a day?' I just said, 'Leave me alone about smiling.' On the other hand, he would always frown a whole lot. He used to walk on stage frowning, as though that was the only way people would think of him as a serious musician. I called it his 'Beethoven scowl.' Now he comes on smiling and I get letters thanking *me* for that. Maybe some of my smile rubbed off.

"But some of the changes were conscious, things we talked about. I saw that he didn't stop to think of others when I first met him. He just said what he wanted to say and did what he wanted to do and sometimes, even though it was right to say those things or do those things, he would injure other people in the process. It was a very hurtful thing for him to be different, but he really tried. He applied himself and now he is infinitely more considerate."

As for which one of Zubin's qualities Nancy would most like to see "rub off" onto her, "that's simple. If I'm envious of anything in my husband it's that he laughs so easily. He laughs his heart out. When I was a child I used to laugh like that, as though my whole stomach was about to come out. I don't laugh at anything like that any more."

Indeed it has become increasingly difficult for Nancy Kovack Mehta to laugh. In many ways her life has become a jumble of duties and uncertainties. Longing for personal fulfillment, she occasionally goes back to acting, then turns away from it in disgust, perhaps because the woman she is asked to portray is never herself. Determined to make the marriage work, she is nevertheless a bit resentful of the demands it makes on her as a person.

"If there were anything I could wish for this marriage," she says, "it would be that I could be married to Zubin and that he could be as happy as he is now, without having to be what he is. The fame and the glamour and the money, that I could do without. That's not what I married."

She does not enjoy the role of glamorous wife, no more than she enjoyed the role of sexy "Glee Girl" in her early television days. "Sometimes I tell people my job in life is to show up. That's terribly debilitating."

Tears come to her eyes and she considers saying no more, then decides to go on. "At one point I thought I was going to fall apart, maybe even commit suicide." A pause. "Then I realized that was no way out. I said to myself, You know, lady, you're in deep trouble, because any girl in the world would love to step into your shoes right now."

Still, she is quick to point out that she would never change places with any of those other women, not for a minute. She sits in the back of the Music Center in Los Angeles, sees the stage lights glinting off Zubin's wedding band and realizes that she did exactly what she set out to do, she married "someone of substance."

At such moments, the tears in her eyes are tears of joy as she feels what her husband can accomplish with his music. "I see little girls in the audience, white girls or black girls or Chinese girls, and in every one of them I see myself, that little girl in the orchard tree in Flint, Michigan, with so much to learn about life, and I weep over them."

If she dreams of anything, it is of someday having more time alone with Zubin. When he is working, they have so little time to themselves that after a concert they will usually drive straight home. Pretending that midnight dinners are not out of the ordinary, Nancy cooks a full meal, they eat, perhaps a game of backgammon, and when they go to bed it is nearly two. "It's the only time we have," says Nancy, "where there's really a sense of family. That time is really very precious because so much of our life is in constant suspension.

"Sometimes he looks at me and says, 'You're not really in love with me, you're in love with the marriage.' And I say, 'Right,' because I am tremendously in love with the concept of marriage, not in the romantic sense, but in the very real, pragmatic sense. And, for reasons I'd rather not go into, I believe this marriage was divinely authorized."

Even before the marriage, Nancy wasted no time talking Zubin out of his would-be apartment near the Music Center. She found a small house in Bel Air and they made their home there, in a "charming little cottage," as she refers to it, for four years. The year 1973 ended their cottage days for good, however. They bought a house built by the well-known California architect Cliff May and most recently owned by actor Steve McQueen. It sits atop a mountain in an area known as Brentwood, just west of Beverly Hills.

To reach the Mehta aerie by automobile (walking would be unthinkable), one turns off fabled Sunset Boulevard and drives past million-dollar estates, onto a winding strip of asphalt that seems to slant up a mountainside at something close to a ninety-degree angle. Along the way, there are intimidating signs that warn of "Vicious Attack Dogs," "High-Voltage Electrified Fence," and "24-Hour Electronic Surveillance," along with "Children at Play."

At last, amid a jungle of misleading street numbers, there is a high stone wall, a hairpin turn, and an immense wooden gate, complete with studding spikes, that looks as though it had been lifted from the set of *Camelot*. At this point, one stretches an arm out the automobile window and presses the button of a formidable device shaped something like a minesweeper.

Inside the house, pressing that button has caused a dozen electronic finches to warble, a noise Nancy selected over a normal doorbell. Identification is asked for and given. The great oaken gates swing open and the car is allowed to pass through unharmed—unless, as frequently happens, something has gone askew in its copper-wire nerve cells and only half of the gate swings open, making the grounds tantalizingly inaccessible. The driveway turns, and finally you arrive at a beautiful French villa of the sort one encounters on the Côte d'Azur, arched around a plaza, as though to embrace the welcome guest.

The roof is tiled, of course. Of course Zubin's car is a Rolls-Royce sedan, not a new one, but comfortably old, a 1957 model bought for only four thousand dollars in London. Of course there are great orange butterflies fluttering everywhere. One is not even surprised to find an old man crouched beside the Rolls-Royce, applying a coat of white paint to an antique wicker commode—commodes around toilets being one of Nancy's favorite affectations and a great nuisance to male visitors.

From the front of the house, which is actually the rear, one walks around to the back yard, which is really the front yard, and is enchanted by a gracious terraced lawn, cascading with its obligatory fountain down to a swimming pool, set among orange, lemon, and tangerine trees, which in turn are boxed in by capacious magnolias and truly towering pines.

Inside, the house is filled with plants and with antiques that seem out of place in modern Los Angeles, but which are perfectly at home here in their own company; many of them are from India and the Middle East: a ceremonial mask, a bronze elephant cart, a carved backgammon table with ivory inlays. The furniture is personable, comfortable, all in exquisite taste—with the possible exception of those gaudy yellow French provincial armchairs that were purchased for the Parsee wedding.

Visitors are led by the houseman, Ronald Gettings, back outside, to a narrow, almost capillary spiral staircase that leads to a planked veranda skirting the second story. Walking toward the corner of the veranda, one comes suddenly upon the magnificent view. Just below are the Hollywood Hills, beyond, the San Fernando Mountains, capped with snow, and to the other side the awesome Pacific Ocean. Always in the foreground are orange butterflies.

A sliding glass door opens and Zubin Mehta welcomes you into his studio, his sanctum sanctorum. It is somewhat cluttered, one imagines permanently so. A wood-paneled closet is half open, a trove of stereo equipment nestled under a large-screen color television set. The stereo represents work, the television relaxation. Zubin has been known to sit for hours on Sunday with a tuner in hand, switching from football to golf to basketball. Of course he always keeps a score in his lap so that one part of his mind brushes up on Bruckner while another part chuckles at reruns of *The Honeymooners.*

Across the little room are two chairs and a sofa, huddled around a coffee table, which is really only a glass slab laid across a wobbly woven basket. This affair threatens to overturn at the slightest disturbance, scattering unbound pages of *Il Trovatore* all over the Oriental carpet. The walls of the room, the couch, the chairs are all covered in the same red print fabric.

"Nancy did it for me one week when I was away," Zubin explains. "It was a surprise."

"It's very nice, really."

"Only if you happen to be very fond of red."

As he talks with his guests, Zubin occupies the sofa, drawing his legs up under his body in the "lotus" position, kicking off his thong sandals. Ronald arrives with a silver pot of Darjeeling tea and china cups, each with its own stick of cinnamon bark to give the tea a remarkable flavor. There may even be a sampling of chocolate mousse, made with real Viennese chocolate, which Zubin orders regularly from an old Jewish lady in the valley.

"I've worked very hard for this house," Zubin reflects. "I've lived in hotels so much of my life . . . and I so *hate* hotels."

But the mountain villa is not the only California house he has worked for, and Zubin is careful to point that out. There is also the house that Dorothy Chandler built. For sixteen seasons he has been music director of the Los Angeles Philharmonic, longer than any man before him. If Mrs. Chandler built the house, it is certainly Zubin Mehta who built the orchestra.

"A lot of people forget that," he muses. "So much is written about my work on the podium that they forget all the work that goes on behind the scenes. The problem of identifying an orchestra's defects and repairing them, building a solid repertoire, a good music library. Instruments! Do you realize that this orchestra now has a million-dollar collection of rare instruments?"

The million-dollar instrument collection, along with many other improvements Zubin has been able to make in the orchestra, is due in large part to the generosity of the Michael J. Connell Foundation.

The Connell family has played an important role throughout the life of the Los Angeles Philharmonic. It was Mrs. Michael J. Connell, a leader in Catholic Charities, who organized the city's business, financial, and social leaders behind William Andrews Clark's orchestra in 1919. The foundation she set up and named after her husband went on giving to the cause of music in Los Angeles long after her death.

In 1963 the foundation's trustees—John Connell and his two cousins—met with Zubin to ask what he felt the orchestra needed that money could buy.

After barely a moment's hesitation, Zubin started to enumerate his priorities. "What I would like very much," he said, "is money to pay some important people in the orchestra more than they're getting now."

Zubin had sat in the rear ranks of an orchestra; he had watched his father struggle on a violinist's salary; he knew, just as William Andrews Clark had known in 1919, that musicians couldn't make good music if they were constantly worried about paying rent and getting food on the table.

"The second thing he asked us for," John Connell recalls, "was sectional rehearsal time. He said he was distressed by the fact that there was no money to allow the different sections to work by themselves, only full orchestra rehearsals, and he said the orchestra badly needed those sectional rehearsals. We said all right to both his requests.

"Then he said, 'I would also like to have a revolving fund from which musicians could buy instruments without having to pay interest and then be able to pay back their loan in little pieces. So many musicians have such miserable instruments that it's hard to judge their skills.' So we did that, too. It came to about one hundred eighty thousand dollars."

"Thanks to the Connell Foundation," says Zubin, "we were able to begin a collection of fine string instruments which now includes four Stradivarius violins, two Gasparo da Salò cellos, a Pressenda violin, a Brescian viola, and many others. Many of the players have their own fine instruments as well."

Zubin's listing of the rare instruments reminds him of an incident that occurred during the first season at the Music Center. Nathan Milstein was the guest soloist, playing his own priceless Stradivarius in an impassioned performance of the Brahms Concerto. Suddenly, as Milstein geared for the difficult cadenza near the end of the first movement, one of his strings snapped.

Signaling with his eyes and a movement of his head, Zubin alerted then-concertmaster David Frisina, who quickly handed Milstein the 1710 Tate Stradivarius he played. The soloist rejoined the orchestra after a hiatus of only three measures, coming in just in time for the cadenza.

As Milstein played the solo part, there was a frantic passing back and forth in the section until Frisina had an instrument to play and a back-chair fiddler stepped offstage to restring the crippled Strad. At the end of the first movement there was more swapping, so that each player got his own instrument back before they went on with the rest of the concerto.

Most of the audience remained in the dark as to the cause of the frantic exchange, and the only note of regret was sounded by critic Albert Goldberg in the next morning's *Times*. Goldberg lamented the rapid repair to Milstein's violin, since he thought Brahms sounded warmer and mellower on Frisina's instrument. "One wished he had continued with it."

Making the best instrument available to his musicians has been one of Zubin's constant preoccupations, in Israel and Montreal as well as in Los Angeles. A less pleasurable but no less important duty has been seeing to it that the best musicians were hired to play those instruments. The unpleasantness lies in the necessity of emptying orchestra seats before one can fill them.

"It's something Lenny Bernstein and I discussed in Salzburg not long ago. He and I are both big softies when it comes to letting players go. But neither of us has discovered an easy way to do it. I think firing musicians has taken years out of my life. In all my years of experience, only one person has accepted it gracefully and said, 'You're right, my time has come.'"

In Los Angeles alone, Zubin engaged more than seventy musicians in sixteen seasons, while actually dismissing only about ten. Others were retired on a pension plan Zubin helped introduce during the first years of his tenure.

"In Los Angeles, the contract demands that if I find incompetence in a player, I have a meeting with him and give him a probationary period for improvement. After the given period of time, if I feel that he has not met the requirements, he has a choice of auditioning before the orchestra committee and myself, after which we vote on whether he stays or goes. Since that system was instituted, I don't think I've taken advantage of it. So far only three musicians have been fired."

That system has eased the pressure on the music director considerably. Prior to its institution, the business of calling a man or woman into the office, for a notice of dismissal or lowering of rank, brought Zubin to the verge of resigning. The most difficult case was that of concertmaster David Frisina.

Zubin considered Frisina not only a great concertmaster, but a valued friend whose advice he had relied on considerably in his early years with the Philharmonic. Frisina had been with the orchestra since 1937, only a year after Zubin was born; he'd served as concertmaster since 1942.

When he took over the orchestra, Zubin had been more than content with Frisina leading the strings. By 1972, however, Zubin decided it was time for the concertmaster to step down.

"That decision was one of the most difficult of my life. I hope I never again have to suffer the anguish I went through over David."

The problem of Frisina was not unique. The orchestra was improving at a rate that left some of its musicians behind. Zubin had to act, yielding at last to the wishes of the board and to his own better judgment. Eight key players were either replaced or their position strengthened by the addition of co-first-chair players. David Frisina was moved from the first chair to the fourth. Acknowledging the benefit to the orchestra, the violinist accepted the change.

"It was an awful time for Zubin," John Connell recalls. "He fought over every one of those musicians. He's a highly sensitive man and he hated every moment of it. At one point, when it was all over, he said, 'I've had it. I'm quitting.'"

Zubin did not quit, however. The furor died down and the musicians made it clear that they wanted very much to be the world-class orchestra he was trying to build. He never could have achieved what he did in Los Angeles without help from them and from others.

"On the management side," he says, "I was blessed from the start with George Kuyper as my general manager, the sort of man who could be invaluable to a young conductor. After Kuyper retired I had Jaye Ruban-off to help me run the orchestra, and then I received a godsend in the person of Ernest Fleischmann."

With a knowledgeable man like Fleischmann, who came to Los Angeles from CBS Records, Zubin for the first time had someone with whom he could discuss considerations of guest artists and repertoire. Among his many achievements, Fleischmann took over direction of the Hollywood Bowl season and used his long-established relationships with great artists to turn the Bowl concerts into profit-making events for the Symphony Association.

Artistically, another great contribution to the Philharmonic's development, aside from Zubin's own, has been that of Sidney Harth, the affable violinist-conductor who succeeded David Frisina in 1973 and became the first musician in the orchestra's history to hold simultaneously the positions of concertmaster and associate conductor. Harth's wide experience with bow and baton includes four years as the Chicago Symphony's concertmaster under Fritz Reiner and a period as head of Carnegie-Mellon University's Department of Music.

A principal ingredient in Zubin's Los Angeles success story has been a notable lack of interference from boards of directors and patrons. The attitude of Dorothy Chandler has been a particularly delightful surprise to the music director.

"I was warned shortly after I first came here that Mrs. Chandler was a lady who insisted on having her way and who always got it. She's the godmother of the symphony, after all, the one who always comes up with the money, so I suppose she would have the right to at least express her preferences. But I can honestly say that since my first season I have not had one word from her that one could interpret as domination."

The sole instance of the Los Angeles Board members wanting their own way with Zubin Mehta is in the area of exclusivity. They wanted him all to themselves.

The Montreal Symphony, with its short season and small budget, was never considered a serious threat to Los Angeles. It was inevitable that Zubin's own burgeoning career would carry him away from Montreal, as indeed it did in 1967. The Expo 67 concerts, at which the combined forces of Los Angeles and Montreal performed the *Symphonie Fantastique*, were Zubin's final appearances as Montreal's music director.

He has conducted there in every subsequent season, however, often going to great lengths to clear his calendar for the sake of special events in Montreal. In addition, his presence behind the scenes has been highly praised by MSO executives, his advice sought on everything from contract bargaining to the hiring of conductors.

"I do a lot of Kissinger work there," he jokes. "Shuttle diplomacy, you know. I love that orchestra and I love that city. I still consider it one of my homes."

The Los Angeles Philharmonic directors never voiced any objection to Zubin's activities in Montreal. After all, he was there first. They grumbled considerably, however, when they saw his increasing involvement with the Israel Philharmonic Orchestra. John Connell considered it a mistake from the start.

"I never was in favor of letting Mehta take on the Israeli orchestra," he said in 1975. "I'm sorry I didn't make a bigger issue of it, and I'm sorry I wasn't successful in my opposition. I just don't think it's good for *him*. He's built a wonderful orchestra here and now he's trying to build a wonderful orchestra there, but he doesn't have our kind of financial support in Israel.

"I think we should have full possession of him. I suppose the unselfish thing would be to say, 'Go ahead and help them in Israel,' but frankly I'd rather see him go to some place like Berlin and work with a first-rate orchestra instead of wearing himself out trying to build two orchestras simultaneously."

But Zubin had felt an affinity for the Israel Philharmonic since that first cryptic cable from the "Palphilorc" in 1961. At that time he and the orchestra were both twenty-five years old, and the self-governing Israeli musicians decided then and there that Zubin Mehta would be invited back to conduct them in each subsequent year until their mutual fiftieth birthday.

The men most responsible for founding the Palestine Symphony Orchestra, as it was then called, were Bronislaw Huberman and William Steinberg. Huberman was one of many immigrants to the Jewish land in the wilderness who, as he wrote, "simply could not abandon the cultural standard of life in their native countries."

The first conductor to lead Huberman's new orchestra, in December of 1936, was Arturo Toscanini, declaring it his duty to "fight for the cause of artists persecuted by the Nazis." There were sixty-one musicians in the orchestra then, Jews from Germany, Poland, Austria, Hungary, and Holland. Successful concerts in Tel Aviv, Haifa, and Jerusalem were followed by a Toscanini-led tour to neighboring Egypt.

After Toscanini, the orchestra hung together during the war years under the direction of several local conductors, notably Michael Taube and George Singer. Frequently, it would appear "conducting itself." In 1947 guest conductors began to arrive, first Bernardino Molinari, then Charles Munch, then Leonard Bernstein. In 1951 came the first North American tour, under Serge Koussevitzky and Bernstein, then a "round-the-world" tour in 1960 with Carlo Maria Giulini and Josef Krips.

The orchestra—which became the Israel Philharmonic at the proclamation of the State of Israel in 1948—kept its own counsel all those years. The musicians accepted advice and friendship from many famous conductors, but officially tied itself to none. Zubin's name was added to that illustrious list of friends and advisers shortly after his first meeting with the orchestra.

The friendship grew through the early and mid-sixties, but it was not until the Six-Day War of 1967 that the musicians of the IPO realized just how good a friend Zubin Mehta was. The following year the musicians voted themselves a music director, for the first time in the orchestra's history. They offered the job to Zubin Mehta.

Officially, Zubin could not accept. His Los Angeles contract ruled out his taking another music director post. After a great deal of arguing, the Los Angeles board overruled John Connell and allowed Zubin to accept the job of "music adviser" to the Israel Philharmonic.

The job with the Israel Philharmonic has been somewhat different from the job in Los Angeles. As John Connell so succinctly points out, financial support is a problem in a small, defense-minded nation, especially since the Habimah Theater Company, the Batsheva Dancers, and the Jerusalem Symphony—among others—all exercise legitimate claims for financial support as well.

Much of Zubin's effort has gone toward putting the IPO on the map, making people aware of its existence and of its standards of performance. In the words of Lukas Foss, one-time director of the rival

Jerusalem Symphony, "Zubin has a real knack for getting the headlines."

The political situation being what it is in the Middle East, those head-lines have centered around the orchestra's activities—first, as a cultural bridge or peacemaker, and, second, as a morale booster in times of strife. No more radiant example could be found of music as an instrument of peace than the Bethlehem concert of July 21, 1968.

The orchestra assembled on a makeshift stage in Manger Square, revered by Christians as the birthplace of Jesus. The streets were filled with countless thousands of listeners, and near the stage there were seats for several hundred Arab notables, Christian religious leaders, and the military and civilian officials of Israel.

They listened to Giuseppe Verdi's Requiem Mass, sung by Martina Arroyo, Shirley Verrett, Richard Tucker, and Bonaldo Giaiotti—three Americans and an Italian, the conductor a Bombay Parsee. It was a night unique in the annals of music

More typical of the headline-making events were the IPO's concerts during the Yom Kippur War of October 1973.

When the war broke out, Zubin was already in Israel, so there was no need for a repetition of the 1967 odyssey. With friends Isaac Stern and Daniel Barenboim, he took the orchestra to military outposts on both fronts. At an Israeli Air Force base in the Sinai Peninsula, they played what one newspaper called "a concerto for orchestra, Phantoms and Skyhawks." An unexpected guest appearance was put in by entertainer Danny Kaye, an old friend of Zubin's, as well as of his orchestras in Israel and Los Angeles. To further aid the Israeli war effort, Zubin led the orchestra in a number of additional afternoon concerts, asking the audi-ence to contribute whatever it could.

For Zubin and Daniel, friends for seventeen years, the experience was reminiscent of those exuberant days after the Six-Day War, with the Victory Concert and the wedding and "Moshe Cohen" holding the chupah. The biggest difference was that this time Jacqueline du Pré was not with them in Israel, forced to remain in London because of an illness.

When, telephoning from Zubin's room, Daniel tried to speak with his wife, he was told she had been taken to a hospital. The illness was diagnosed as multiple sclerosis.

"Neither of us knew exactly what this sickness meant, so I phoned a doctor friend of mine in Tel Aviv to ask him. I wanted to keep what he was telling me to myself, but Daniel sat on the bed next to me and put his head against mine so that he could hear.

"It was over the telephone, from a doctor he didn't even know, that my friend learned that his wife was crippled with a deadly nerve disease. We cried there together."

In the summer of 1977, when Lebanon's internal difficulties had served to ease relations between that nation's government and its Israeli neighbors, Zubin took the orchestra to the Good Fence, at the Israel-Lebanon border. There he conducted a concert for an audience of one thousand Christian Arabs and Jews, some in uniform, others in mufti.

A Lebanese Army captain was assigned to escort the orchestra, and a fast friendship grew between him and the conductor. When Zubin called on "Captain George" to translate his remarks to the Lebanese, Israeli journalists saw an example of international brotherhood at work. The captain's picture turned up on the front pages of newspapers on both sides of the Good Fence.

Some weeks later, Zubin and the IPO were giving concerts aboard a Greek luxury liner when they received word that the young Lebanese captain had been shot and killed. The Palestine Liberation Organization claimed responsibility for the assassination, branding the officer a "traitor" and a "collaborator with the Zionists."

Zubin's close musical friends, many of whom are Jewish, have tried to account for his affinity with Israel and the Israelis. To Isaac Stern he is simply "more Jewish than a lot of Jews I know"; moreover, Stern finds in Zubin a number of traits that have also been used to describe the "Jewish personality."

"His grasp of the human condition, his mixture of seeing into the heart of a problem and at the same time seeing its humor. His certain manner of self-deprecation, a mocking attitude that covers up a strong mind and a clear will. His way of being a strict disciplinarian, of demanding close attention to what he is saying, yet always mellowing his words with a gentle touch and a smile. This is Zubin Mehta to me."

Zubin admits to a special feeling for Israel, not only for the professional musicians there, but for the man on the street, who "is as big a fan of his orchestra as are Brazilians of their favorite soccer teams. If the first horn player comes down with a cold, everybody knows about it."

The IPO musicians have defined their dedication to music as "the same spirit the Israeli Army fights with," and Zubin confirms that comparison. "They pour their hearts out when they play," he says, "and that makes my whole life worth living."

Summing up his contributions as a builder of the Israel Philharmonic, Zubin cites three principal improvements in personnel.

"The major change, I would say, is the percussion section. When I first came, there was only one timpanist and two little assistants; now it is a real section with first-class instruments. We have tightened up the brass considerably. Also, at one time the lower strings were not so good, but the string sections are uniformly excellent now—and many of the players are students of Ivan Galamian, my father's old teacher in

America. Among the woodwinds we have soloists who could sit in any of the world's great orchestras."

In terms of repertoire, the greatest need was for contemporary music. The cause-and-effect relationship was the familiar circle: the orchestra didn't play modern music because the audience didn't like it, because the orchestra didn't play it.

Zubin's solution was to establish a series of instructional programs, the Musica Viva series, outside the regular season. The programs included Renaissance music as well as experimental contemporary pieces, to expose Israelis to the extremes of musical history, thereby making it possible for them to understand the need for what is called "contemporary" music and to recognize its place in the endless evolution of musical ideas.

For four years the Musica Viva series filled Fredric Mann Auditorium to capacity, its concerts becoming what Zubin describes as "the snob events of the cultural season." Contemporary music became so *au courant* in Israel that it was played by the Jerusalem Symphony on the radio, in museum concerts, at last finding its way into the Israel Philharmonic's subscription series.

"It became apparent that Musica Viva had achieved our goal. Everybody was playing and listening to contemporary music, and our series was no longer necessary, so we just let Musica Viva die a natural death."

Another "hole" in the musical life of Israel when Zubin took command of the Philharmonic was opera. Under Carlo Maria Giulini the orchestra did several small-scale works by Mozart and Rossini, but for nearly a decade opera had been missing from the repertoire.

Zubin's first steps were cautiously taken, with concert performances of *Carmen, Il Trovatore,* and *Aïda.* That they were successful can be illustrated by the remarks of one American critic, who wrote that "even though it was not staged, this was one of the greatest *Aïdas* of my experience . . . absolutely transcendent."

Then came staged productions. First there was *Samson et Dalila,* then *Otello,* and finally, at the 1977 Israel Festival, a *Fidelio* in which, for the first time in Israel, all the elements of music and theater came together, as they must to make really great opera.

The *Fidelio* cast was headed by Gundula Janowitz as Leonore and Jon Vickers as Florestan. The sets, designed by Munich's Günther Schneider-Siemssen, blended so perfectly with the rocks of the Roman amphitheater at Caesarea that the audience could never be quite certain where reality ended and fantasy began. "That *Fidelio,*" says Zubin, "was the crowning achievement of everything I had done in opera."

Had Zubin's commitments to Los Angeles and Israel not been so great, another "crowning achievement" might well have occurred in Vienna. In

1975 the Vienna Philharmonic, which had been taken over four years earlier by his old friend Claudio Abbado, extended to Zubin a rather unprecedented invitation. The orchestra wanted him as permanent conductor of its gala New Year's Eve concerts. It was, says Zubin, "a great and unexpected compliment" to be considered equal to that most Viennese of Viennese assignments.

Recalling the first time he had watched and listened to the revered Willi Boskovsky conduct the waltzes and polkas of Johann Strauss, Zubin longed to accept. But looking at his calendar, filled with New Year's engagements far into the future, he knew it would be impossible. He was forced to decline the invitation.

Nevertheless, Zubin's activities with the Vienna Philharmonic have steadily increased, with guest appearances in its symphony and opera seasons as well as numerous recording dates. His relations with the Viennese musicians are, if anything, even closer than those he has developed in other orchestras.

"Today when I stand in front of the Vienna Philharmonic," Zubin says with a smile, "I am conducting all my old colleagues. Eighty percent of those musicians were my schoolmates. I suppose that I am closer to them personally than even to my musicians in Los Angeles. After all, we studied under the same teachers and we went out with the same girls."

In 1977 several of the Vienna Philharmonic bass players told Zubin that his old bass professor, Otto Rühm, had been placed in an old-age home outside the city and was not getting along very well. They decided to drive out and see the old man.

"He recognized me immediately and started talking about how I had been a great bass student, because that was the only way he had ever thought of me. Then his eyes started to cloud up and I could tell he was trying to remember something. Finally he said to me, 'Mehta, I heard in the meantime you have done some conducting.'"

Some of Zubin's most impressive triumphs with the Vienna Philharmonic have come in its performances at the Staatsoper. His Viennese operatic debut came in February 1975, with a new production of Wagner's *Lohengrin*. According to *Die Presse*, he made the orchestra sound "the way it used to be in our very best days."

The critical acclaim was unanimous. Karl Löbl of the *Kurier* wrote that Zubin's conducting had "tension, beauty and balance. It never became exaggerated, nor was it academic. It was always vital, rich in nuances and always it followed the natural flow of the music."

The Vienna *Lohengrin* was, in some ways, the beginning of what Zubin calls "my dedication of the next ten years to Wagner." Since his first exposure to the music and spirit of Wagner, Zubin has kept the Wagnerian sound in his ear. In the 1980s the seed that was planted nearly twenty-five years earlier will come to fruition with complete cycles of *Der Ring des Nibelungen* in Vienna and Florence.

The two different *Rings* will begin in 1979 with *Das Rheingold* and end in 1981 with *Götterdämmerung.* "And then in June of 1982—" and here Zubin grins, rubbing his hands together like a child anticipating Christmas—"we'll do the whole *Ring* at once in Vienna, all four operas in sequence! That's what I'm waiting for."

There would have been even more opportunity to conduct Wagner had Zubin accepted the offer of musical directorship of the Berlin Opera. But that would have meant giving up Los Angeles, and at the time the offer was made Zubin was not ready to do that. However, Zubin has continued to build his reputation as an opera conductor, even without a permanent position at any opera house.

Many of the famous singers who have worked with Zubin over the years have commented on his exceptional ability to control the diverse elements of an opera while at the same time drawing out the most delicate nuances of the music. Says tenor Placido Domingo, who has sung under Zubin many, many times. "Aside from the power and drama he generates, it's also fun to work with Zubin. He has the ability to relax us just when the tension seems to be beyond endurance."

"He always conducts with love and feeling and care," comments baritone Sherrill Milnes. "On stage he gives me great confidence because I can look down and know exactly what he's doing. I don't have to study his movements for a couple of measures to figure him out."

Beverly Sills calls Zubin "the most exciting conductor I have ever worked with." Recalling a concert performance in Los Angeles of the final scene of Bellini's *Anna Bolena,* the soprano remarked to Zubin, "I had done that scene at least sixty times before and I was never driven in it the way you drove me. That was unquestionably my best performance ever of that final scene."

Perhaps the ultimate praise for an opera conductor came from Mehli Mehta when he asked Zubin to get him a front row–center seat at the Metropolitan.

"But, Daddy," Zubin protested, "nobody sits right behind the conductor—you won't be able to see the opera."

"I don't want to watch the opera," said his father. "I want to watch you."

It was a performance of Puccini's *Turandot,* but for Mehli it was also "a wonderful education. It was like he was doing a puppet show. Birgit Nilsson was there, Franco Corelli was there. Ping, Pong, Pang, the whole orchestra, the chorus—all at his fingertips. It was so marvelous the way he could control it. Then on television I saw him do the same thing with *Die Fledermaus.*"

Mehli's reference is to the historical performance of the Strauss comic opera on New Year's Eve, 1978, at Covent Garden. The performance was televised by the BBC over much of Europe and via satellite to Metromedia stations in the United States, the first transoceanic televising of an opera.

For Americans, the much-publicized broadcast was an all-too-rare opportunity to experience Zubin Mehta's abilities as an opera conductor. Although his reputation in the field has increased steadily in Europe and Great Britain, his opera work in the United States ended, for the most part, with his brief, five-season tenure as an intermittent guest conductor at the Metropolitan. His warmest recollections of the Met are of conversations in the Viennese dialect with Rudolf Bing, rather than of conducting achievements.

Zubin's operatic aspirations were almost completely frustrated in Los Angeles. After that first *Salome* in 1963, he had hoped to involve the Philharmonic in concert performances, then in fully staged operas, as he was able to do in Montreal and Israel. But, while there was money for nearly everything else he wanted for his orchestra, the funds for staging operas could not be found.

Critic Martin Bernheimer, rarely on Zubin's side of any issue, agrees that "the so-called musical establishment in Los Angeles has never defined opera as one of its priorities. If you back people against the wall, they'll say we don't really need it. The New York City Opera comes to town and it sells out, but the money people don't care. If the people who run the Music Center desperately wanted opera, we'd have opera."

That statement was made in December, 1975, and the situation has not changed since. His inability to create an audience for opera out of the devotees of symphonic music has been one of Zubin's few failures in Los Angeles, perhaps his only one. Indeed, as he approached the end of his thirteenth season as music director, it seemed his reign in Los Angeles would continue as Martin Bernheimer predicted, almost ad infinitum.

"He really has things on his terms here," the critic observed. "The power and, I'm sure, the pay are both enormous. This is a city that loves to worship heroes and it treats them accordingly." Zubin's hold on the Los Angeles Philharmonic and the Philharmonic's hold on him "will go on and on and on."

But almost as Bernheimer spoke those words, a meeting was in progress at the Mehta home in Brentwood, a meeting that would cancel all bets as to the length of Zubin's stay in the City of Angels.

14

❦

The Force of Destiny

One of the most famous orchestra-conductor relationships of all time was that of the New York Philharmonic and Arturo Toscanini. When Toscanini gave his farewell concert after nearly a decade as the Philharmonic's music director, fifty mounted policemen were called to subdue riotous crowds outside Carnegie Hall. No matter that most of New York's music lovers could not afford the two-hundred-dollar-top ticket prices—they had to be there to say good-by to the Maestro.

The date of that historic concert was April 29, 1936, the same day that Zubin Mehta was born.

There are any number of obscure connections that might be drawn between Arturo Toscanini and Zubin Mehta. The more obvious ones are their sharing of *Aïda* as Metropolitan Opera debuts and their attachment to the Israel Philharmonic, Toscanini having conducted that orchestra's first concerts, Zubin serving as its first music director. There are also those recurring references to Zubin, notably by Josef Krips and Charles Munch, as the heir to Toscanini's greatness.

Although Zubin never met the Maestro and never heard him except on recordings, he was to form friendships with Toscanini's daughters, Wally and Wanda, and with Wanda's husband, Vladimir Horowitz.

Wally and her own daughter, Emanuela, have been guests at the Mehta home, while in Italy Zubin has been granted the privilege of studying the Maestro's personal collection of scores, containing markings that unlock Toscanini's unique insights into their music. For his own music librarian in Los Angeles, Zubin hired the man who had served as Toscanini's librarian in New York, James Dolan. Zubin also developed close relationships with three of Toscanini's five successors to the New York podium, Sir John Barbirolli, Dimitri Mitropoulos, and, of course, Leonard Bernstein.

If there is any truth to the statements of the Hindu and Parsee astrologers who read Zubin's horoscope, there must have been something rare about the planetary configuration at his birth in India and at the parting of orchestra and conductor on the other side of the world.

With the New York Philharmonic itself, Zubin had had a rather tentative beginning at Lewisohn Stadium in 1960. His regular-season debut with the orchestra was to have come eight years later, but was postponed for yet another six years by his imprudent "place-to-bury-one's-worst-enemy" remark. When, in May of 1974, Zubin finally faced the orchestra in Philharmonic Hall, he decided it was time to apologize.

"Ladies and gentlemen," he said, "a few years ago I did something very immature, and I'm the one who has paid for it."

There was only scattered applause among the instrumentalists, but by the end of the week, they settled back to make beautiful music, in a curious sort of concert that critic Harold Schonberg called "an unusually noisy evening."

It was a program Zubin had chosen for dramatic effect, beginning not with one overture but with three, all from rarely performed Weber operas. Then came Olivier Messiaen's huge tone poem, *Et Exspecto Resurrectionem Mortuorum*, followed by the almost-as-huge *Organ* Symphony of Saint-Saëns. The concert got the attention of the audience and of the critics as well.

"Mr. Mehta is a conductor of temperament and of no mean technical skill," wrote Schonberg. "He is a man of virtuoso flair and makes the most of it."

In the New York *Post*, Speight Jenkins used the better part of a tabloid page to describe an evening in which Zubin strove for and achieved "the big effect: big sounds, dramatic crescendoes, overwhelming sonority . . . a very successful debut by a major conductor."

Not long after that concert, it became common knowledge that Pierre Boulez would not renew his contract with the New York Philharmonic, having agreed to take over the new Institute for Musical Research in Paris. The music critics, who had engaged in a great deal of speculation after Leonard Bernstein's announced retirement, only to be caught off guard by the choice of Boulez, kept their guessing at a much lower key this time around. No one claimed to know which conductor it would be.

The outgoing music director, though he would not discuss it with the press, gave the matter his careful consideration. "In terms of a successor," says Boulez, "I thought it should be someone from the younger generation. Yet it should also be someone of proven leadership, ability, and experience. Considerable experience. In my mind, those criteria narrowed the field to two men, and Mehta was one of them."

The Philharmonic board of directors came to the same conclusion eventually; everyone agreed that the choice had to be Mehta. But how to lure him away from Los Angeles, where he was unquestionably happy and apparently content to stay?

In an interview with the *New York Times,* Zubin said, "I'm thirty-nine years old now, and I've developed three orchestras. Today I have a real Rolls-Royce in Los Angeles. Why should I go somewhere else and start the same rigmarole? I'm an old man now."

Indeed, Zubin had two "Rolls-Royces" in Los Angeles, one in his garage, and the other on the stage of the Chandler Pavilion. In fourteen years he had become a wealthy man as he took a good second-class orchestra and molded it into a group of musicians capable of playing alongside any orchestra in the world. He had taken the Philharmonic on a dozen international tours. Together they had made more than forty recordings and given nearly thirteen hundred concerts in Los Angeles alone. He was married to a woman who loved Los Angeles; his parents had made themselves a permanent home there; his own home was all a man could want.

On the final day of 1975, Zubin showed a visitor the magnificent view of Catalina Island from his front yard and remarked, "I can never conceive of leaving this place." The next day he received another visitor, the president of the New York Philharmonic, Carlos Moseley,

They spent several hours in conversation before Zubin left to conduct a New Year's Night concert of light and happy music. The following morning, January 2, 1976, Moseley boarded an airplane at Los Angeles International Airport, where he was greeted by a surprised Martin Bookspan and his wife Janet, on their way back to New York, coincidentally on the same plane.

To the obvious question as to what he was doing in southern California, Moseley smiled innocently and said, "Oh, I just took a few days off to visit some old friends out here."

Later that evening, Mehli Mehta was in his living room, studying an orchestra score, when Zubin walked in and sat next to him on the sofa. Mehli noticed that look on his son's face that Nancy used to call his "Beethoven scowl." Clearly, there was something momentous on his mind.

"Daddy, I want to talk with you," he began. "I've just been offered the post in New York. What do you think?"

"Well, darling," said Mehli, using his favorite term of endearment, "you are a big man. Why are you coming to ask me about it? You can decide yourself."

"No, tell me," Zubin persisted. "What do you think? I want to know."

Mehli uncrossed his legs and leaned forward, clasping his hands together as though he were praying for guidance. There was a moment's pause before he spoke.

"You know, I hate to see you go so far away from us. There are lots of other people, too, who will hate to see you leave Los Angeles and this orchestra you've built up so far. But I think you should go. I think it's the most marvelous thing that could have happened to you."

"What makes you say that?"

"Well, you know, I have wonderful memories of the New York Philharmonic. That was the first orchestra I ever heard, outside of my own, and I listened to it night after night in Carnegie Hall, under the most famous conductors. That orchestra had a great sound in those days and it could have that sound again. Zubin, you could make them play that way again."

Zubin's face broke into a grin. "I had a feeling you would say that. I already told Carlos Moseley I would take the job."

It was not an easy decision, but Zubin knew his job in Los Angeles was over. He saw in New York the tradition of greatness his father described, a greatness that had reached its highest level in the Toscanini years, years that ended on the day he was born. To carry on that tradition of greatness was a challenge he longed to meet.

Seven weeks later, the morning of February 25, a brief story appeared in the *New York Times,* headlined, "Mehta May Get Boulez Place." The story was based on "unconfirmed reports," which orchestra management in Los Angeles and New York "would neither confirm nor deny."

Later that morning, Olive Behrendt went before her board of directors in Los Angeles to make the official announcement. "Zubin Mehta has decided not to renew his contract with the Los Angeles Philharmonic in order that he might accept the position as music director of the New York Philharmonic."

Mrs. Behrendt's official statement to the press read:

Zubin has contributed immeasurably toward making the Los Angeles Philharmonic one of the world's great orchestras. His superb artistry, wisdom and enthusiasm have given the people of Los Angeles and Southern California an exciting, thriving musical culture of the highest international standards. New York is lucky to get him, but we in Los Angeles have been immensely fortunate to have enjoyed his musical leadership for longer than most leading

American orchestras can call on the services of a world-famous music director.

From the board meeting, Zubin went straight to a rehearsal to break the news personally to his musicians.

"Ladies and gentlemen, this is not a happy speech," he began, then paused to look over the faces of his orchestra, of the men and women he'd conducted and cared for nearly all his adult life. "I might as well come to the point. I have decided to accept the musical directorship of the New York Philharmonic."

There was a long period of silence that can only be described as stunned. At last one of the women in the violin section whispered, "Oh, wow!"

Zubin looked up again and went on. "I need a change of atmosphere or whatever you want to call it. Whether I'm doing the right thing or not, only time will tell."

The press release from the Los Angeles Philharmonic office included a brief statement by the conductor, which read:

> For some time I have been torn with the feeling that perhaps both Los Angeles and Zubin Mehta needed a change. At first I thought that devoting more time to opera would satisfy my urge to meet new challenges. It was, however, only when I was confronted with a firm offer from the President of the New York Philharmonic that everything came into focus.

In the next morning's *New York Times,* Harold Schonberg speculated that the Philharmonic's final list of candidates had included Zubin, Daniel Barenboim, Lorin Maazel, Colin Davis, Seiji Ozawa, and Bernard Haitink. New York Philharmonic board president Moseley said there were "many reasons" for choosing Zubin out of that list of distinguished candidates.

"Mehta is a damn good conductor. He has shown that he can remain with an orchestra—he has been in L.A. for fourteen good years. The Los Angeles Philharmonic prospered well under him. He represents fine quality, a dramatic personality, leadership, and audience appeal.

"Another reason for the choice," Moseley continued, "was the amount of time Mehta is willing to give to New York. His three-year contract calls for a minimum of sixteen weeks each season with the Philharmonic and he may be active for as much as twenty-two weeks." That would be more time with a single conductor than the Philharmonic had enjoyed since the earliest years of Leonard Bernstein's tenure.

Later, Zubin spoke to reporters of his frustration at being virtually "the only show in town" in Los Angeles. He longed for a return to something like his student life in Vienna, when he could be stimulated night after night by the great performers and conductors of the world. The only times those people came to Los Angeles were when they were invited as guests with his orchestra, almost always when he was out of town. He saw New York as "really the place to be, the center of the world, the lion's den." In New York he could work with his own orchestra during the day and go out that evening to hear a visiting orchestra, a resident chamber group, an opera, or a solo recital. He felt an urgent need to hear someone else's music and to set new goals for himself. His job in Los Angeles was finished.

He had said only a few weeks before the announcement that he could not conceive of leaving his home in Los Angeles. He and Nancy agreed that their house on the mountain would not be sold. They would buy a brownstone in Manhattan and return to California whenever they could.

Since Zubin's contract with the Los Angeles Philharmonic did not expire until mid-1978, he would not be able to start work in New York until the 1978–79 season, more than two years away. But the time has flown more quickly than either Nancy or Zubin would have liked.

Watching the approach of her last California spring Nancy sighed. "I love New York, but the closer it comes to moving, the greener the leaves get, the more flowers appear. And the grass does seem so much thicker and the butterflies so much more abundant than they ever were before."

But something in her also yearns to be at the hub of activity, no matter how dearly she loves the tranquility of her home in Brentwood.

"Bloomingdale's! I *love* Bloomingdale's. I go there every time I'm in New York. Not to buy anything, just to look, to reinitiate myself into the world. I always start at the top floor, even though I don't give a hoot about unfinished furniture, and I work my way down through every inch to the basement. It's like a World's Fair.

"In fact, I've always felt that New York was one big store that belongs to me. Oh, yes, it does belong to me; I own every brick. It's just that all these other people have been keeping it for me till I return and then they'll give it back."

Zubin's children are also happy about the decision. Merwan, in particular, a student at Colgate University near Syracuse, expects to see a great deal more of his traveling father. Zarina, who has taken up residence with Zubin and Nancy in the last two years, thinks she will enjoy the proximity to other people when she travels home from her midwestern college; the isolation of the Brentwood mountain has been something of a nuisance to her.

As for Zubin's "other family," his close musical associates, they all look forward to his arrival in New York, no doubt feeling something akin to pride: the challenge is monumental, but they are certain he's up to it. Lukas Foss, who knows as well as anyone the size of that challenge, asserts that "if anyone can do what needs to be done with that orchestra, Zubin Mehta can."

"Zubin's principal problem," reflects Isaac Stern, "has to do with the incredible complexity of the New York organization. Zubin's abilities as an administrator make him superbly equipped to handle that. The rest of it is the musicians. They can play magnificently when they get all fired up. Zubin has to work with them until they play that way at almost every concert. He can do it. He's the right guy in the right place at the right time."

Pinchas Zukerman thinks that the Mehta personality will win the hard-boiled New York musicians' affection.

"I'm not saying Pierre [Boulez] was not a kind person, but Zubin has a different way of going about things, of getting to know and dealing with each person in the orchestra as an individual human being. A brother-to-brother relationship. The atmosphere just bubbles somehow when he's around; I have seen it in Los Angeles and in Israel."

And from Itzhak Perlman: "He's got that dynamic personality that New York needs. He's going to set a fire under the orchestra and take New York by storm."

This confidence in Zubin's ability to inspire the New York Philharmonic is made all the more noteworthy by his friends' certain knowledge of the difficulties he faces. Perhaps foremost among these is the adversary relationship that has existed in recent years between the orchestra and its management. It is a problem Zubin has not had in Los Angeles since Ernest Fleischmann's taking over as general manager.

"I have noticed an extremely frank relationship between the orchestra and its management in New York," says Zubin. "The new music director must be the bridge in that relationship. If a musician feels somebody is constantly looking down his throat and threatening to fire him, he's not going to play with his heart and soul. He's probably not even going to play well."

In many respects, Zubin has picked an especially good time to take over the New York Philharmonic. In terms of his own experience, and repertoire, as well as in terms of the orchestra's situation, the stage is set for what could be a dynamic relationship.

The Philharmonic's home in Lincoln Center, probably the most criticized hall in musical history, has recently been reconstructed and renamed Avery Fisher Hall, after the businessman and philanthropist who provided the bulk of the funds needed for the improvements. While the hall is still not acoustically perfect, the new sound was highly acclaimed after the hall had been extensively redesigned by acoustic engineer Cyril Harris. There were times in Philharmonic Hall when the musicians knew that, no matter how well they played, most of the audience would not appreciate their efforts.

In terms of repertoire, Zubin feels the orchestra is unusually well rounded. With the Philharmonic's long season, mid-September to mid-May, playing a new program every week, the orchestra covers virtually the entire musical spectrum in the course of three years. It is time, he feels, for a return to the heart of the central European repertory, what Zubin calls the "meat-and-potatoes music."

This ties in perfectly with the current needs of Columbia Records, which has the New York Philharmonic under contract. Columbia executives have told Zubin that the orchestra's recordings of such basic-library music are old and electronically outdated. The music the orchestra must record is essentially the same music Zubin wants to program in subscription concerts.

Zubin's own contract with Decca/London extends to 1980. Columbia and London have therefore agreed to share him and the New York Philharmonic until that time, thus presenting a rare opportunity to enhance the orchestra's image via recordings on two international labels in the new music director's first two seasons.

As for Zubin's ambitions, "I'm coming to New York to make music. I can only do it with one hundred percent involvement, and I expect the same in return. If I cannot make that happen, I will pick up my hat and let somebody else try."

In Zubin's mind, the challenge is a personal one, but in the minds of many New Yorkers who have observed their Philharmonic over recent seasons, there is also the challenge of making great individual musicians play like a great orchestra. That may well be the job Zubin cut out for himself when he accepted the job of directing the New York Philharmonic. Indeed, the orchestra that, a decade earlier, he had characterized as artistically inferior to his own offered the only challenge interesting enough to end his musical marriage in Los Angeles.

Despite his fervent desire to conduct more opera, Zubin has turned down offers from two of the world's great opera companies. Perhaps those offers will come again, but right now Zubin looks upon the New York Philharmonic as his last job.

"Who knows, maybe it won't work out. I'm taking it very realistically. I'm not going there as some sort of medicine, though, because if I don't enjoy it myself then I won't stay. You see, I love my work very much, probably more than anything else. And if I like my work in New York, and if everybody else likes it, then I'll stay in New York. That's all there is to that."

15

Epilogue: Dictates
of His Own Heart

Saith Darius the King: "By virtue of Ahura Mazda and me,
much else was done by me that is not written on this inscription. For this reason is it not written: lest, whoever shall
examine this inscription in the future, what has been done
by me shall seem to him too much, and it should not convince him, but he should deem it false."

—Rock inscription at Behistan,
Column IV, ca. 500 B.C.

In 1978, as this volume goes to press, Zubin Mehta is only forty-two
years old, about half the average lifespan of conductors, who are an
unusually long-lived breed. According to many reports, he is already at
the summit of his profession.

As for what lies ahead, perhaps the prophesy of Zubin's old teacher,
the late Hans Swarowsky, is worth consideration. It was in 1963 that
Swarowsky predicted his former pupil would be accounted "a great figure in the history of music."

218

History does seem to have shown more than a passing interest in Zubin Mehta already. Born on that curiously coincidental day in 1936, he entered a world about to be torn apart by the most calamitous events in human history. His father already had a place in Indian history as the man who organized Bombay's first orchestra.

As a child Zubin witnessed first hand the granting of Indian independence, then saw his country thrown into turmoil by the creation of Pakistan and the murder of Gandhi. His first public concert was given for the victims of another political turmoil, the Communist suppression in Hungary and the Revolution of 1956.

In Israel, Zubin has gone out of his way to involve himself and his orchestra with that nation's struggle for survival. During the anti-Vietnam war movement in America, he organized volunteer orchestras to play concerts for peace on California campuses.

His musical career has been a long series of "firsts." He was the youngest man to conduct the Vienna Philharmonic and the Berlin Philharmonic, the youngest to become music director of a major American orchestra, the first and, so far, the only music director of the Israel Philharmonic. His debut in London, on the night of Sir Thomas Beecham's death, was the first time any person from the former dominion of India had appeared with a major British orchestra.

The life of Zubin Mehta would seem to be a banner for those who believe in the force of destiny. Tehmina's *jotisi*, the astrologers, read greatness in his stars. Colleagues, professors, and eminent conductors of an older generation saw greatness in his earliest work. Zubin himself has come to feel the presence of unseen powers in his life.

"Always at the right time, the idea comes or the opportunity presents itself. Something guides me. I feel that very strongly, that protecting force over me.

"Even in my first steps toward a career, if my cousin's family had not been forced to leave Shanghai, if his teacher in Paris had not passed away, if he had not written me from Vienna, I would have probably gone instead to London. Then, who knows?"

The implication is that this "protective force" will determine Zubin's path into the future. Yet there is really very little of the fatalist in him. Already he has tried to get the ear of the Israeli government, hoping to take the Israel Philharmonic to Egypt, as Arturo Toscanini once did.

"I tell you this for a fact," he says, in that forceful whisper that brooks no doubt, "one concert by the IPO in Cairo would be worth a hundred military or diplomatic conferences."

And further east there is India, that teeming subcontinent still unrecovered from the shock of freedom, still very much the place Zubin left in 1954 and Mehli abandoned a year later, still a place unmoved by the music that is Zubin's life. He remains an Indian citizen, returns often to the land of his birth, to hunt tigers in Bengal or to climb in the remote Himalayas. But only once has he returned to make music there, in the place that will forever be his home.

A second visit, in March 1978, was aborted when India's newly elected Prime Minister, Morarji Desai, refused to grant landing rights to the Israel Philharmonic Orchestra, a refusal that Zubin says "has broken my heart. What a great pity that I cannot bring together the two nations I love so dearly. I can only hope that the political madness that obsesses the people of the Middle East will end one day and allow people to bring joy to each other.

"I have never really left India, you know. It is still today the only place my dreams take me to. Of course, in my dreams there are my wife, my children, my friends, but always they are in Bombay. Every morning of my life I wake up in Bombay."

Who can say whether, twenty years from now, that perverse, unreasonable music of the West will be heard again in Bombay? By the vendors selling in their hundred tongues, by the brown children who run behind the cars, by the blue-turbaned Sikhs, by the Muslim beggar women in their burkas, by the swamis in their saffron robes...

Index